THEOLOGY:
Expanding the Borders

María Pilar Aquino
Roberto S. Goizueta

editors

The Annual Publication
of the College Theology Society

Volume 43

XXIII

TWENTY-THIRD PUBLICATIONS
Mystic, CT 06355

Copublished by the College Theology Society and

Twenty-Third Publications
185 Willow Street
P.O. Box 180
Mystic, CT 06355
(860) 536-2611
800-321-0411

ISBN 0-89622-933-5
Library of Congress Catalog Card Number 98-60499
Printed in U.S.A.

Acknowledgments

The editors are very grateful to all those persons who have contributed to the preparation of this volume. We want to express our gratitude to the authors and readers of the essays included in this collection, as well as those scholars who submitted essays which we were unable to include. We would like to thank Dennis Doyle, Gary Macy, Sandra Yocum Mize, and William Portier for their support and encouragement. Special appreciation goes to Xavier Edmundo Cagigas for his generosity in providing editorial and technical support. Neil Kluepfel and Dan Connors at Twenty-Third Publications have been a pleasure to work with, while also keeping our noses to the grindstone. We are grateful to the College Theology Society for inviting us to participate in this exciting and, we believe, important project. We are especially grateful to our families for their forbearance during the always hectic and time-consuming editorial process.

CONTENTS

Part II
The Church and Borders

Part III
The Border Between Theology and Society

Introduction

As the great nineteenth century historian Frederick Jackson Turner argued, the character of the United States has been defined by the frontier. The growth and development of our nation has been fueled by the drive to extend the nation's boundaries and influence through the continual expansion of the frontier, a historical process legitimated by the "frontier myth."[1] Indeed, the symbol of the frontier is central to the modern notion of historical progress. At its best, the frontier has served as a catalyst for human ingenuity and creativity. At its worst, it has served as a context—and pretext—for violence.

Too often, human progress has been identified with expansion of "civilization" through the violent conquest of "uncivilized" territories and peoples; on this side, lies civilization; on the other side, lies its opposite—barbarism, chaos, the unknown.[2] If this myth has resulted in unparalleled advances in virtually every area of human life, it has also had horrific consequences, often unintended. The assumption that the boundaries that separate "us" from "them" are also the boundaries between civilization and barbarism, or good and evil, has been used to rationalize the conquest and destruction of millions of human beings, their cultures, and the natural environment. The victims continue to resist the expansion of the frontier—and they are increasingly being heard. What they are challenging is not only conquest and destruction but also the very notion that the boundaries that establish human differences can or should function to exclude what is "different."

While borders are necessary to protect and affirm human differences, they can also function, not as an instrument for exclusion, but as "meeting places" for engagement and interaction. Increasingly, theologians are daring to question modern, imperialistic assumptions about borders and, instead, developing creative interpretive paradigms for viewing borders in ways that affirm the need for such engagement and interaction.[3]

This collection of essays, most of which were presented at the 1997 Annual Convention of the College Theology Society, seeks to promote such engagement and interaction by exploring the different ways in which theologians are reconceptualizing the border, construed in its broadest sense as including the many kinds of borders that both demarcate identity and, too often, preclude dialogue and interaction. These include not only territorial or national borders but also epistemological, ethnic, racial, gender, disciplinary, ecclesial, and religious borders. The essays in this volume make an important contribution to the theological search for new ways of understanding borders in the present context of capitalist globalization.

We have divided the sixteen essays in this volume into three parts. The essays in Part I examine fundamental epistemological issues raised by borders. The essays in Part II probe the ecclesiological implications of different notions of the border. Part III explores the border between theology and society, which, in modernity, has often functioned to privatize theological questions and, conversely, immunize social structures from theological critique.

In the first essay, Anne E. Patrick analyzes the role of border as marker, barrier, and frontier. She suggests the possibility of understanding borders as both affirming difference and making authentic encounter of "others" possible. Virgilio P. Elizondo also addresses the ambiguous character of borders, emphasizing the significance of Christianity and, especially, the Galilean Jesus for a liberative understanding of borders. In his contribution to the volume, Ruy Suárez Rivero focuses on the reality of one particular geographical border, that between Tijuana and San Diego, and the challenge it represents for Christian theologians. Evelyn A. Kirkley traces the various ways in which epistemological, ideological, theological, and cultural barriers have made U.S. Latinos/as invisible in much U.S. religious historiography. She then offers recommendations for promoting a more accurate understanding and portrayal of the religious life and the important role of U.S. Latinos/as in the history of the United States. Matthew Ashley raises questions about the epistemological barrier that has traditionally separated religion from science. He suggests how spiritual traditions, the "new science," the history and philosophy of science, and theology can contribute to epistemological border-crossings that would, nevertheless, respect the integrity of each discipline. In the last essay of Part I, Francis J. Buckley advances suggestions for crossing disciplinary and epistemological borders through the practice of team-teaching.

In Part II of the volume, Zaida Maldonado Pérez details the visions recounted by early Christians and the role those visions played in helping Christians forge their identity over against dominating powers, both outside and inside the church. Keith J. Egan presents a study of the ecclesiology of Teresa of Avila and its significance for the church in the twenty-first century. Drawing from insights implicit in her writings and reading those insights in the light of Avery Dulles' models of the church, Egan argues that Teresa's ecclesiology has great relevance to contemporary ecclesial movements, especially those among women and the poor. Bradford E. Hinze outlines an ecclesiological model that would affirm racial and ethnic diversity while promoting a "trinitarian catholicity." He argues that such a trinitarian ecclesiology would make authentic diversity possible. By bringing the works of Hans Urs von Balthasar, Elizabeth Johnson, and Roberto Goizueta into dialogue with each other, Dennis M. Doyle proposes a communion ecclesiology that would also promote an authentic unity-in-diversity.

Jorge Luis Valdés addresses the increasingly important issue of ecumenism within the U.S. Latino/a community. Using a Johannine understanding of unity to interpret the border between U.S. Hispanic Protestants and U.S. Hispanic Catholics, he examines the issue of unity-in-diversity within the U.S. Hispanic community, arguing that the Johannine notion of unity can help address current religious divisions in that community. The issue of ecumenism is also taken up in Tom Poundstone's essay, which draws out the implications of the Second Vatican Council for Roman Catholic moral theology and the hierarchical magisterium. In this last essay of Part II, Poundstone calls for the development of an ecumenical ethics and sets forth its preconditions.

In the final section of the volume, Carmelo Alvarez focuses on the marginalized communities of the Caribbean and traces their historical struggle for liberation. In his analysis, he pays special attention to contemporary attempts to forge an ecumenical solidarity among the Christian churches. Taking as his starting point Gustavo Gutiérrez's acknowledgment of the importance of Maurice Blondel's work in helping pave the way for liberation theology, Peter Bernardi examines the dispute between Blondel and Pedro Descoqs and contemporary analogues involving liberation theology and its integralist critics. Jennifer Reed-Bouley presents an assessment of another attempt to bridge the border between theology and social structures, namely, the United Farm Workers movement. In her essay, she brings to light the complexities involved in attempts to implement theoretical principles (such as those enunciated in Roman Catholic social teaching) in concrete historical situations, where practical constraints might force one to choose between competing ethical demands; in the case of the United Farm Workers, the demand for labor rights and the demand for immigration rights. Finally, J. Milburn Thompson examines the equally complex question of the ethical justifiability of military intervention in defense of human rights. He argues that such intervention may, at times, be justified, so long as its aim is not simply "rescue" but also nation-building.

At a time when the very notion of the border is playing an increasingly central role in national and ecclesial discussions, the essays in this collection challenge us to appreciate the full significance of those discussions for our lives as individuals in community. They invite us to join those discussions in the political and ecclesial arenas, so that together we might come to a deeper understanding of both the destructive and the liberating potential of borders. Such an understanding will require that we draw on the rich resources of Christian tradition through a critical appropriation of that tradition, as we strive to respond in creative, imaginative, and prophetic ways to the ever-widening divisions in our nation and world. Ultimately, the border is not merely a conceptual or even an epistemological category, but a concrete, historical reality which, as *locus theologicus*, can reveal the presence of God in our midst, among those persons who have been marginalized or, indeed, completely excluded by the borders erected to "defend" power, wealth, and dominance. The editors thus hope that this volume will make a small contribution to the development of borders which, rather than divide and polarize, will instead promote a reconciliation grounded in the demands of justice.

Roberto S. Goizueta and María Pilar Aquino

Notes

1. See Frederick Jackson Turner, *Rereading Frederick Jackson Turner*, with commentary by John Mack Faragher (New York: Henry Holt and Co., 1994).

2. Ibid.

3. See, e.g., Virgilio Elizondo, *Galilean Journey: The Mexican American Promise* (Maryknoll, NY: Orbis Books, 1983), 49-88; Idem, *The Future is Mestizo: Life Where Cultures Meet* (Bloomington, IN: Meyer-Stone Books, 1988), 57-111; Justo L. González, *Santa Biblia: The Bible Through Hispanic Eyes* (Nashville: Abingdon Press, 1996), 86-87.

THEOLOGY:
Expanding the Borders

Part I
THE BORDER
AS EPISTEMOLOGY

Markers, Barriers, and Frontiers: Theology in the Borderlands

Anne E. Patrick
Professor of Religion
Carleton College

In *Borderlands/La Frontera: The New Mestiza*, the Chicana poet Gloria Anzaldúa provides powerful images of the borderland reality we confront as the College Theology Society, meeting in the beautiful but sundered metropolitan area of Tijuana/San Diego:

> I press my hand to the steel curtain–
> chainlink fence crowned with rolled barbed wire–
> rippling from the sea where Tijuana touches San Diego
> unrolling over mountains
> and plains
> and deserts,
> this "Tortilla Curtain" turning into *el río Grande*
> flowing down to the flatlands
> of the Magic Valley of South Texas
> its mouth emptying into the Gulf.
>
> 1,950 mile-long open wound
> dividing a *pueblo*, a culture,
> running down the length of my body,
> staking fence rods in my flesh,

> splits me   splits me
> *me raja   me raja*
> This is my home
> this thin edge of
>   barbwire.
>
> But the skin of the earth is seamless.
> The sea cannot be fenced,
> *el mar* does not stop at borders.[1]

The invitation to explore the theme, "Theology: Expanding the Borders," in the distinguished company of Carmelo Alvarez, Enrique Dussel, and Virgilio Elizondo, posed a question for me: What should I, a U.S. Anglo feminist theologian, add to this discussion? I whose cultural *mestizaje* is pale at best, invisible and imperialistic at worst, encompassing as it does, on my father's side, the complex ethnic and religious heritage of colonial Maryland and Virginia, and, on my mother's side, the Irish Catholicism of nineteenth-century immigrants to Minnesota. (The land these Irish immigrants came to in the 1870s had recently been confiscated by the U.S. government from the Dakota people, after an 1862 conflict the victors called "the Sioux uprising," although for the losers it was a desperate struggle against starvation.) I who further complicated this mix by joining the Sisters of the Holy Names, a religious community of women, originally known as *les Soeurs des Saints Noms de Jésus et Marie,* women who learned more than a century ago that in some United States settings it was necessary to obscure their French Canadian heritage in order to succeed as educators. This group was founded in 1844 in Quebec, the Province whose conflicted status within Canada could be the subject of a quite different convention about "Expanding the Borders." All of this background has given me much greater knowledge of issues, language, and culture, to the north than to the south of the borders of my native United States.

My first teaching assignment, as a music teacher at an

academy for girls in Tampa, Florida, was a broadening experience in many ways, although in 1960, at age 19, I was not well prepared for theological reflection on just why so many young Latinas from abroad had been sent to boarding school in Florida, especially from Cuba. There we took a memorable day off from classes in October 1962 to plant an olive tree for peace on the day the Second Vatican Council opened, and there we huddled, students and teachers together in the basement, preparing for Russian bombs to fall. All of this I understand better now that I have completed my various college and university degrees on the slow track that workers with adult responsibilities know so well, and especially now that I have been able to continue this education by reading feminist and liberation theology in recent years.

But I have been south of the U.S. border only twice, for a total of just four weeks: first in 1975, as a representative of Sisters Uniting, an umbrella group of U.S. nuns, at the first International Women's Year Tribune in Mexico City, and again in 1991, when a Center of Concern conference on Liberation Theology and Catholic Social Teaching in Petrópolis, Brazil, gave me the opportunity to learn some things firsthand in base communities of the Parish of the Martyrs in a São Paulo *favela*, and also in the colonial capital of Salvador (which figured so prominently in Brazil's 400-year history of slavery), in a visit to my missionary cousin in the mountains of Ecuador (whose pastoral training came from summer courses with Gustavo Gutiérrez), and of course in the Petrópolis meetings themselves, where I learned much from Central and South American theologians, women and men.

From the 1975 women's conference I returned with a poster of Sor Juana Inés de la Cruz, which intrigued me because the Mexican feminists seemed so anti-clerical and yet had a white-robed nun on their conference poster. And so I read her story and some of her writings, and since then her image has presided over my office at Carleton College. Sor

Juana was a seventeenth-century Mexican poet, who anticipated Mary Daly by three centuries in her willingness to critique dominant theology, and who predictably got into
trouble for her efforts. In 1689 she sent a critique of a sermon
by a contemporary Jesuit to her friend the bishop of Puebla.
The bishop's reply, signed "Sor Filotea de la Cruz," prompted Sor Juana to defend her efforts with a magnificent essay,
"*La Respuesta de la poetisa a la muy ilustre Sor Filotea de la
Cruz*," or "The Poet's Answer to the Most Illustrious Sor
Filotea of the Cross." In this famous "*Respuesta*," Sor Juana
justified her position brilliantly, but she had nevertheless felt
the sting of the bishop's accusation that for all their scholarly brilliance, her activities were worldly and unbefitting her
spiritual vocation. She eventually reacted to this accusation
(and to pressure from her confessor) by abandoning her literary and scholarly pursuits. She sold her library and musi-
cal and scientific instruments, and gave the proceeds to the
poor. She devoted the last two years of her life to asceticism
and died of an illness contracted while ministering to her sisters during an epidemic in 1695. It is, however, the image of
Sor Juana in good health and surrounded by her books,
which inspired the Mexican feminists of the 1970s and pre-
sides over my office today.[2]

From the 1991 visit to Brazil and Ecuador I returned with
many images of natural and cultural beauty, as well as of
poverty, injustice, and ecological devastation. As a result of
this experience, I developed and have continued to teach
courses for undergraduates on the ambiguities of five centuries of Christian influence in the Americas, as well as on
theologies of liberation. I have also begun to study the
Spanish language, a project I fervently wish were further
along than it is.

It is the mujerista theologian Ada María Isasi-Díaz who has
persuaded me to tell you these things about myself, for she
makes a good case that all theologians need "to be aware of
how our own social situation colors our analysis of the religion

of our communities and colors the way we say what we say in our theological writings."[3] The point of such self-disclosure, she argues, is to substitute for unreal claims of "objectivity" the more realistic position of "responsible subjectivity," which includes self-disclosure in the doing of theology precisely so that what is said becomes "understandable to others not only out of their own experience but insofar as they have the ability to go beyond the limits of their experience and see how my experience, because it is part of the processes of living, relates to and intersects with their experience, no matter how different both experiences are."[4] Others besides Isasi-Díaz have also set a precedent for including an element of self-disclosure in their theological writings, whether in whole chapters, the way Virgilio Elizondo has done in *Galilean Journey* and *The Future Is Mestizo*, and as Roberto Goizueta has done in *Caminemos con Jesus*, or else in brief asides or very fascinating footnotes, as Carmelo Alvarez and Enrique Dussel have tended to do.[5] I have been edified by their practice, which sets a good example for all theologians to expand our methodological borders across the artificial divide of supposed objectivity.

In what follows I shall first discuss some of the ambiguities latent in the metaphor that governs the theme, "Theology: Expanding the Borders." My purpose is to clarify certain aspects of the complex meaning of "borders." Then, in the final part of this chapter, I shall explore some of the borderlands where I judge theology will do well to deepen its commitment to the right sort of an expanded agenda, both by investing new energy in projects that are already underway and by venturing in new directions.

Markers, Barriers, and Frontiers

The idea of "expanding the borders" invites reflection on the several purposes that borders serve. Among the many dimensions of meaning the concept of "border" carries with it, there are three that warrant our attention: markers, barriers, and frontiers.

Markers

In the first place, borders serve the descriptive function of markers by establishing what is where, and what is whose. Although an excessive sense of personal or corporate ownership is problematic, the lack of any sense of boundaries on the part of an individual or a group is also problematic. It is true that what we usually think of as earth's boundaries are fictions; when the planet is viewed from space, what we see is not the mapmaker's patchwork of pink and green and yellow nations set against a background of blue seas, but rather a boundaryless blue-and-white marble with tan continents, fringed with green. Nevertheless, these cultural fictions of national boundaries, and other markers that distinguish individuals and groups, are important to us as historical beings. Indeed, the whole discussion of "difference" so crucial to various movements for social justice is premised on the fact that difference can and should be discerned, and it is borders in the sense of "markers" that enable us to recognize and respect the differences that make us who we are as individuals and societies. It would be a mistake, even a form of theological imperialism, for theologians, and especially for Anglo theologians from the United States, to aspire to "expand the borders" in the sense of denying the importance of difference or pushing toward all-inclusive control of what is presently "foreign" or beyond our reach. As Marquette University theologian M. Shawn Copeland observed in her 1994 address to this society, "Toward a Critical Christian Feminist Theology of Solidarity," the national temptations of this country have been twofold with respect to "difference": There is in the first place the racist pressure to absolutize one form of difference —skin color—and simultaneously obscure other differences; in the second place there is the temptation to "dissolve" difference, as she says, "to ignore it or to meet it with sly or shame-faced side-long glances," as when a white feminist speaks of oppression under patriarchy as if her experience encompassed what women of other groups have suffered.[6]

Copeland's incisive analysis of the tasks required for building solidarity among feminists is relevant to the wider community of U.S. theologians whose aspirations toward justice are expressed in terms of "expanding the borders." Her analysis suggests a note of caution, which is appropriate because the "border metaphor" of difference, if applied uncritically, can lend itself to promoting both of the problems she discusses: the tendency to absolutize one marker of difference while ignoring others, and the counter-temptation to dissolve or ignore difference altogether. That is to say, because on the one hand border imagery involves the idea of a line that divides two-dimensional space, there is the danger that it may reinforce a problematic tendency to think of groups reductively in terms of binary oppositions, as happens, for example, in discussions that get stuck at the border between "white" persons and "persons of color." As Copeland has shown, this way of thinking obscures other important differences beyond racial ones, such as differences of ethnicity, religion, class, geography, history, and personal experience, on both sides of the privileged category of division, and it thereby legitimates social injustice. The dominant group ignores its own diversity for the sake of one absolutized point of similarity and proceeds from there to control its borders against inroads from those who do not share this absolutized characteristic. As Copeland argues:

> [D]ifferently similar Celtic-, Anglo-, European-American men and women in the United States . . . are rendered the same. On the other hand, the *merely different* in skin color— African, Latino, Chicano, Korean, Japanese, Chinese, American Indian men and women—are absolutized as *the other* and ruled out of authentic human participation in the various dimensions of life in the United States social order.[7]

Furthermore, the pitfalls of insufficiently differentiated thinking also become evident when we consider the increasingly widespread phenomenon of bi-racial and multi-racial identities. This fact is of course rendering the category of *mestizaje*, which is such a central contribution of Elizondo's work, an increasingly important category for ethical and theological reflection. Texts that deserve much wider study include his volume from 1988, *The Future Is Mestizo*, as well as the more recent anthology edited by Arturo J. Bañuelas, *Mestizo Christianity*.[8] Its contributors do not need to be reminded, although their readers may, that the category of *mestizaje* is well utilized only when the distinct features of what is found in the various mixtures are recognized and respected. In employing this concept, European-Americans should, in other words, try to avoid the second temptation Copeland identifies, namely dissolving or ignoring difference. To put matters in the terminology of Enrique Dussel, instead of participating in the violent modern project of "eclipsing the other," the task for theology is to contribute to liberating projects that are welcoming of all "in their alterity, in the otherness which needs to be painstakingly guaranteed at every level."[9] What my discussion of "markers" is intended to do, in summary, is to argue that where the border as "marker" is concerned, theology's mandate should be less that of expansion and more that of complexification. However, the ideal of expansion does seem to apply well to theology's task regarding two other senses of "borders," namely its meanings as *barriers* and *frontiers*, and it is to these that I now turn.

Barriers

The lines that human beings draw to identify who they are and what is theirs have also served to keep those who are different from sharing in what is within the protected sphere controlled by groups in power. In reminding us that "The sea cannot be fenced,/*el mar* does not stop at borders," Anzaldúa is offering a means of respecting difference—borders as markers do exist—and also transcending it by an inclusivity of attention or consciousness. To put my own

position directly: If the consciences of Christians on the
north side of this barrier that divides San Diego from Tijuana
were really attuned to the life situation of those to our south,
the southern border of this nation would not be the "steel
curtain" that it has become.

How to engage these consciences in a new ethical agenda
is the task I undertook in my book on feminist moral theology, *Liberating Conscience*. There I argued that Christians are
now poised at a third great turning point in our history; having already negotiated the "turn to the Gentiles" in the first
century, and having survived the philosophical and scientific revolutions ushered in by the sixteenth-century
"Copernican turn," we are now challenged to make the
"turn to the oppressed."[10] This will require Christians, particularly those from wealthy and dominant groups in every
nation, to press more deeply than ever before for answers to
questions of human suffering and injustice, and, in light of
the answers that emerge, to undergo a conversion of life
much more radical than mere conformity to the bourgeois
standards associated with the waning patriarchal paradigm
of virtue.

Forces on all sides are inviting us to this conversion.
Powerful works of fiction—from Joseph Conrad's *Nostromo*
to Carlos Fuentes' *The Good Conscience* to Louise Erdrich's
Love Medicine—have helped European-American Christians
understand our ethical history and see the need to change
patterns of domination and exploitation. Also very important is the critical historical work conducted by Dussel and
others, which has uncovered the centuries of violence and
oppression beneath present political and economic arrangements.[11] Other forces calling us to conversion include the
witness of the many contemporary victims of violence, given
voice by survivors such as Rigoberta Menchú of Guatemala
and as well as by journalists and church workers.[12] The
steady flow of liberation theology and more recently of Latin
American and U.S. Latina feminist, mujerista, and ecofemi-

nist writings are also among these forces. The title of María Pilar Aquino's important work, *Our Cry for Life*, states clearly what is at stake in these movements, and her text describes well the conversion of morals that is required: "To take life as the primary ethical criterion," she asserts, "leads to many particular tasks devoted to the eradication of structures and realities that deny the poor and oppressed the means to life and exclude women from their right and duty to be active protagonists" [in history].[13]

Recently I have been struck by the way nature itself has added its voice to the invitations to conversion already extended by liberation theologians, ecofeminists, church leaders, and various others since the 1960s. (Please note that I refuse to personify nature as an angry female, as a "mother" abandoning her usual nurturing ways). The floods that have devastated western Minnesota, eastern North Dakota, and southern Manitoba this spring, have hammered home the lesson that the Red River of the North is no respecter of borders, although I did note that U.S. television seemed to lose interest in the story rather soon after the flood crest entered Canada. For weeks stretching into months, people from this ordinarily rich agricultural region experienced the nightmare of helplessness that is routine for so many human beings who live in the Caribbean islands and elsewhere south of our border with Mexico.

During the worst weeks of the flood, there was water on all sides, but none of it was safe for drinking, bathing, or doing the laundry. Surplus grain, stored in silos, absorbed this water, expanded and exploded through the roofs of these silos, and then scattered sodden and useless across miles of flooded fields. Thousands of families accustomed to comfortable homes and clean clothes were homeless and ill-clad for weeks on end, and found themselves exiled from the usual routines of work and school. Indeed, in April, before the leaves were even on the trees, entire school districts shut down for the year, and youngsters were told to go far from their homes if they wanted to attend classes in other districts. For Minnesotans, Dakotans, and Manitobans, a winter of eight major blizzards was followed by a spring of unprecedented disaster: flooding that happens only once in a century or five, something we turn to the federal government to remedy as fast as it can—the same government we feel should always be lowering our taxes without cutting our programs of privilege. But no clean drinking water, no school, no safe home, no jobs—this constitutes life as usual for millions of Haitians, Brazilians, Mexicans, and other neighbors to the south, who are also in many cases under regular threat of direct violence from the military, from the police, from criminals they cannot move to gated suburbs to escape, and from family members who turn their anger and despair against the bodies most easily within reach.

I have wondered this spring whether the flood experience may not have its salutary dimensions as well as its tragic ones. If we could learn two things from this disaster—first to probe the way *human choices driven by greed* may be related to the extreme weather patterns and to the unprecedented behavior of our rivers, and second, to *examine our own unusual deprivations in light of what life is ordinarily like for the world's poor*—if we could learn these things, then these floods will not have brought mere suffering, but suffering with redemptive possibilities for us and for those others who have reached much sooner than we the insight that Juan Luis Segundo identified as the starting point of liberation theology: "the world should not be the way it is."[14]

The barriers to opportunity for a life worthy of human dignity, which are symbolized in the steel "tortilla curtain" lamented by Anzaldúa, are blatant manifestations of what is wrong with the world. These barriers are what must be dismantled, what must be transcended, if the world is to become what God intended it to be. As Elizondo observes in his chapter "Beyond All Borders" from *Galilean Journey*, "True life and happiness is loving as God . . . loves, which means the rejection of any humanly made obstacles that limit our ability to love."[15]

It would be a mistake, of course, to limit our thoughts about borders as barriers too literally to the southern boundary of this country, however much this border has come to symbolize the violence and oppression we Christians of the United States are called to transcend. For the barriers to human dignity exist very much *within* and *beyond* the geographic limits of this country, and if the tortilla curtain were to become quite permeable tomorrow this would not by itself correct all the other injustices that are structured into our national life, and into our transnational economic systems and alliances of power. There are, for instance, the barbed wire fences of illiteracy and generally inadequate education, which defend privileged citizens from competition in the job market by members of groups our "economy" (the faceless and nameless abstraction that absolves its beneficiaries of responsibility for its effects on other persons here and abroad) prefers to destine for work in undesirable, minimum wage jobs. There are also the walls preventing access to health care, amazingly solid in view of their motley bricks being shaped from paper made of boiled down drafts of exclusionary legislation, recycled insurance forms, strands of bureaucratic red tape, and the clay of human greed. And among the forces defending the obstacles to lives of dignity are surely this country's national devotion to an absurd view of liberty where guns and money are concerned, an absolutizing of "free choice" the pro-life movement has yet to question in any serious way, although guns in particular are a great impediment to education and a terrible hazard to health.

These are some of the barriers to human dignity that urgently need to disappear, reflective as they are of the borders that interest groups construct and defend with the idolatrous forms of faith analyzed so incisively by H. Richard Niebuhr decades ago in *Radical Monotheism and Western*

Culture.[16] More recently, from Costa Rica, Mexican theologian Elsa Tamez has drawn on Latina experience and indigenous Mexican culture to add more concreteness and urgency to such analyses. In *Through Her Eyes: Women's Theology From Latin America*, Tamez sees the "god of the indigenous Mexican culture" as forming a "coalition with the God of the Bible . . ." and calling us to forsake the false gods, especially the god of riches and the god who requires human sacrifice, and turn instead to the One who is Life-giver and Liberator of us all.[17] It is this One who calls for the dismantling of whatever barriers stand in the way of justice and solidarity among peoples, and indeed for a rethinking of neighbor-love to include nature and the earth itself.

Frontiers

The balance needed to respect difference, and at the same time to dismantle the unjust barriers that human groups are always putting up against the "others"—which my discussion of the first two meanings of "borders" has been arguing we must achieve—seems well expressed on the cover of a Brazilian Catholic monthly published in São Paulo. This magazine is called *Sem Fronteiras*, and its subtitle adds the balancing nuance I find so important: *"A Igreja No Brasil Aberta ao Mundo."* The national marker of identity is retained, "the church of Brazil," but the posture is one of openness to the rest of the world. The Portuguese, *Sem Fronteiras*, which literally translates as "without borders," also connotes certain positive meanings that have long been associated with the word "frontier" in United States history, meanings which should not be forgotten entirely in our late-blooming repentance for the physical and cultural violence that characterized our national "expansion." I am suggesting here that the "myth of the frontier," for all the evil it has legitimated, may still be put to some good use. Insofar as the frontier has symbolized the as-yet-unattained ideal, and insofar as its rigors have called for some still-useful virtues,

I think we may well align a chastened form of frontier spirit with the ideal of "expanding the borders" proposed in this convention. What I have in mind here are such qualities as courage, hope for a better life, willingness to endure risk and hardship, and generosity among neighbors. All of these are qualities we can use today in the metaphorical borderlands that theology has reached on the cusp of a new millennium.

Theology in the Borderlands

In this concluding section I shall discuss briefly two border-lands where theologians find ourselves today, and where the frontier virtues of courage, hope for a better life, willingness to endure risk and hardship, and generosity among neighbors may stand us in good stead. (These virtues, I hasten to add, are not unique to the pioneers of U.S. history, but are precisely what help today's refugees and immigrants to brave dangers on land and sea in order to get to a place that holds promise of a better life). I approach this topic as a moral theologian, interested in praxis as well as in character, so I will share an example or two of practical action or implementation.

In the first place, we are always in the borderland between particular and general concerns, and I see no way around the need to camp here forever. The local church and the local school district demand our involvement, and so do the national and international dimensions of the issues we encounter in these local settings.[18] Consider the matter of health care. The United States has great problems in this area, but the full extent of the issue is a global one, and this fact must somehow become more present to our attention. As James Hug observed in a 1993 article on "Health Care: A Planetary Perspective," this country is home to less than five percent of the world's population, but it consumes 41 percent of the the world's health resources.[19] For moral theology especially, such issues of global distributive justice must come more to the foreground, but all theologians have citizenship in the universal human community, and all of us can be more creative in expanding the borders of interest beyond national discussions of such questions. There are many resources to support this creativity. One I am particularly pleased to report on here is the new International Network of Societies for Catholic Theology, which was set up at a gathering at Sherbrooke University in Quebec last summer, and which plans to use the Internet to foster sharing among Catholic theological societies worldwide. Among the groups represented at the founding meeting were societies from Brazil, Colombia, Chile, Argentina, Europe, the United States, and Canada, and also the Ecumenical Association of African Theologians.[20] The Catholic Theological Society of America is making its computer resources available for this international project, which hopes to foster solidarity that will also have ecumenical and interfaith possibilities as the plan goes forward.

Another promising resource for expanding the borders of awareness among Christians is a calendar developed by a Vincentian priest from India who has served small rural parishes in Minnesota while preparing several fine volumes of inclusive language prayerbooks. Father Joseph Arackal has also designed an International Worship and Freedom Appointment Calendar, which seeks to increase understanding among the world's peoples by providing for the daily entries information not only about the liturgical significance and biblical readings for the day, but also about the nations commemorating their independence on that day. Arackal's hope is that users may record significant world events and significant personal moments in the blank space, and pray for the "special needs and concerns of the people celebrating freedom each day."[21] A list providing thumbnail descriptions of all the world's nations is given at the end of the booklet, indicating size, population, location, languages, and political status, especially in terms of independence. What I find so creative and valuable about this booklet is the way it connects the personal life of prayer and scripture reading with global political awareness.

A second borderland we are destined to inhabit for a long time is the one between the church and the academy. There are important reasons for theologians to affirm the academy and the freedom it gives us to do research without fear of reprisals, and there are reasons to press for academic freedom within church-sponsored institutions. But the longer I think about issues of global justice, the more I find myself becoming concerned with the positive theological task of supporting the church community and its leaders, and indeed of bringing their best teachings about social justice more to the foreground of discussions, and thereby fostering the development of this teaching in light of new economic, cultural, political, and ecological situations. I confess to having been affected by some forceful words of Allan Figueroa Deck on these matters, particularly a 1995 article entitled "A Pox on Both Your Houses: A View of Catholic Conservative-Liberal Polarities from the Hispanic Margins."[22] I am not suggesting that progressive theologians can or should change our stripes, but rather that we may want to notice some cutting-edge issues where church leadership and theologians can be well occupied together. Concerns about racism, immigration, welfare, and education policy—these are not matters where theologians tend to dissent from the magisterium, but they are nevertheless extremely challenging intellectual problems, for the issue facing us is precisely how to win the informed consent of our Catholic population to some fine but unfortunately obscure documents of our bishops.

For people who are seeking to expand the borders, and for people who are camping in borderlands, the quality we need above all is hope. As this convention has been demonstrating so amply, theologians of the United States have much to learn about hope, as about other matters, from beyond our borders. I have been struck, for example, by the fact that women from the most ecologically devastated land on the American continent, El Salvador, could declare of their situation in 1990: "The ecological problem is not an unsolvable problem. In order to [remedy this problem] it is necessary to change the focus of development from an economic one focused on financial benefits to an ecological one focused on the survival of the country and the well-being of its inhabitants."[23] "Hope," our colleague María Pilar Aquino, reminds us, "is realized in actions, attitudes, in everyday language, even in the midst of great hardship and suffering. Neither women nor the poor of the earth can give it up."[24] Nor, I would add, can we theologians, who must continue to voice their claims for justice in the borderlands where we live and work.

Notes

1. Gloria Anzaldúa, *Borderlands/La Frontera: The New Mestiza* (San Francisco: Aunt Lute Books, 1987), 2-3.

2. This image, Miguel Cabrera's painting from 1750, *"Retrato de Sor Juana Inés de la Cruz,"* is also on the cover of a recent critical edition and translation of her works, Sor Juana Inés de la Cruz, *The Answer/La Respuesta, Including a Selection of Poems*, crit. ed. and trans. Electa Arenal and Amanda Powell (New York: The Feminist Press at the City University of New York, 1994). In their "Preface" to this critical edition, Arenal and Powell mention that Dorothy Schons, in a 1925 essay, "The First Feminist in the New World," was the first to characterize *La Respuesta* as "a declaration of the intellectual emancipation of women of the Americas," vii. For a contemporary theological interpretation of Sor Juana's contributions, see Pamela J. Kirk, *Sor Juana Inés de la Cruz: Religion, Art, and Feminism* (New York: Continuum, 1997).

3. Ada María Isasi-Díaz, *Mujerista Theology: A Theology for the Twenty-First Century* (Maryknoll, NY: Orbis Books, 1996), 76.

4. Ibid., 77.

5. See Virgilio Elizondo, *Galilean Journey: The Mexican American Promise* (Maryknoll, NY: Orbis Books, 1983) and *The Future is Mestizo: Life Where Cultures Meet* (1988; New York: Crossroad, 1992); Roberto S. Goizueta, *Caminemos con Jesús: Toward A Hispanic/Latino Theology of Accompaniment* (Maryknoll, NY: Orbis Books, 1995); Carmelo E. Alvarez, "Theology from the Margins: A Caribbean Response," pas-

sim, in this book; Enrique Dussel, *The Invention of the Americas: Eclipse of 'the Other' and the Myth of Modernity*, trans. Michael D. Barber (1992; New York: Continuum, 1995), 147, n.17.

6. M. Shawn Copeland, "Toward a Critical Christian Feminist Theology of Solidarity," in *Women and Theology.* The Annual Publication of the College Theology Society, vol. 40, eds. Mary Ann Hinsdale and Phyllis H. Kaminski (Maryknoll, NY: Orbis Books, 1995), 16.

7. Ibid.

8. Elizondo (cited in note 5); Arturo J. Bañuelas, ed., *Mestizo Christianity: Theology from the Latino Perspective* (Maryknoll, NY: Orbis Books, 1995). See also Roberto S. Goizueta, ed., *We Are a People!: Initiatives in Hispanic American Theology* (Minneapolis: Fortress Press, 1992).

9. Dussel, 132.

10. Anne E. Patrick, *Liberating Conscience: Feminist Explorations in Moral Theology* (New York: Continuum, 1996), 70.

11. Enrique Dussel, *History of the Church in Latin America: Colonialism to Liberation, 1492-1979*, trans. Alan Neely (Grand Rapids, MI: Eerdmans, 1981); see also Leonardo Boff and Virgil Elizondo, eds., *1492-1992: The Voice of the Victims (Concilium Special*; Philadelphia: Trinity Press International, 1990).

12. The experiences of Menchú, the 1992 Nobel Peace laureate, are described in her work *I, Rigoberta Menchú: An Indian Woman in Guatemala*, ed. Elisabeth Burgos-Debray, trans. Ann Wright (New York: Verso, 1984). See also Penny Lernoux, *Cry of the People* (1980; New York: Penguin Books, 1982); Sheila Cassidy, *Good Friday People* (Maryknoll, NY: Orbis Books, 1991); and Virgil Elizondo, ed., *Way of the Cross: The Passion of Christ in the Americas* (Maryknoll, NY: Orbis Books, 1992).

13. María Pilar Aquino, *Our Cry for Life: Feminist Theology from Latin America* (Maryknoll, NY: Orbis Books, 1993), 190.

14. Quoted in Robert McAfee Brown, *Gustavo Gutiérrez: An Introduction to Liberation Theology* (Maryknoll, NY: Orbis Books, 1990), 51.

15. Elizondo, *Galilean Journey*, 80.

16. H. Richard Niebuhr, *Radical Monotheism and Western Culture* (New York: Harper & Row, 1960).

17. Elsa Tamez, ed., "Introduction: The Power of the Naked," *Through Her Eyes: Women's Theology from Latin America* (Maryknoll, NY: Orbis Books, 1989), 13-14.

18. John Allen, for example, discusses the urgency of U.S. Catholics

giving more attention to educational needs beyond the parochial and private school contexts in "Inequity in Funding of Public Education Raises Justice Issues," *National Catholic Reporter*, May 2, 1997, 3-6.

19. James E. Hug, "Health Care: A Planetary View," *America* (December 11, 1993): 8-12.

20. The founding of the International Network of Societies for Catholic Theology took place in conjunction with the August 1996 meeting of the Conference of Catholic Theological Institutions at Sherbrooke University in Quebec. The International Network's headquarters are in Tübingen, Germany. The first elected president of the Network is Peter Hünermann (Tübingen); vice-presidents are Anne E. Patrick (Northfield, Minnesota) and Marcio Fabri dos Anjos (São Paulo, Brazil).

21. Joseph J. Arackal, V.C., *1993 International Worship and Freedom Appointment Calendar with Descriptions of the World's Nations* (Patmos Publications, P.O. Box 22, Vermillion, MN 55085-0022). A calendar for 1998 is forthcoming.

22. Allan Figueroa Deck, "A Pox on Both Your Houses: A View of Catholic Conservative-Liberal Polarities from the Hispanic Margin," in *Being Right: Conservative Catholics in America*, eds. Mary Jo Weaver and R. Scott Apple (Bloomington: Indiana University Press, 1995), 88-106.

23. Unidad Ecología Salvadoreña, quoted in Mercedes Cañas, "In Us Life Grows: An Ecofeminist Point of View," in *Women Healing Earth: Third World Women on Ecology, Feminism, and Religion*, ed. Rosemary Radford Ruether (Maryknoll, NY: Orbis Books, 1996), 24.

24. Aquino, *Our Cry for Life*, 108.

Transformation of Borders: Border Separation or New Identity

Virgilio P. Elizondo
Professor of Theology
Mexican American Cultural Center
University of the Incarnate Word, Pastoral Institute

Congratulations to the College Theology Society. You certainly chose one of the most important issues for the church, society, and the world at this moment of history and you could not have chosen a better place than San Diego/Tijuana to probe the question of borders. This is an area, like the entire border between the United States of America (U.S.A.) and Mexico, which both separates and keeps peoples apart while at the very same time providing the cradle for the growth and development of a new humanity which defies all previous borders of separation. I congratulate you on your prophetic and visionary choice, for at the very moment when the powerful nations of the world are tightening their borders to keep "undesirables" out, you dare to speak about expanding the borders—a courageous choice indeed.

A short time ago, we all rejoiced at the tearing down of the Berlin Wall, but today in the U.S.A., not only are we building an electronic wall to keep Mexicans and Latin Americans out of the U.S.A. we are even militarizing the border like that of a major war zone. We eagerly want Mexican trade and cheap

Mexican labor to produce U.S. goods in our assembly plants—*maquiladoras*—in Mexico but at no cost do we want poor, dark-skinned Mexicans and Latin Americans to enter our country. There is a similar attitude throughout the Western-Christian nations of the world: reinforce the borders so as to keep the poor and dark-skinned peoples of the world out.

We send our agents into the poor countries to open new markets for our products, thus exciting them about our "good life," we tease them about our "heavenly" existence of material abundance, we tell them through our products, movies, and publicity how good we have it in the U.S.A. While trying to sell our products and our way of life abroad, we are in effect inviting them to come join us, to come to the source of material bliss. Many of them will risk everything—including their lives—to come to this apparent earthly paradise, maybe not of milk and honey, but certainly of hamburgers and Cokes! But the reality is that we want their money or their cheap labor but not their bodies and their presence among us in our neighborhoods, parishes, and cities.

There is a growing fear seizing the Western world about the perceived invasion of the poor and dark-skinned peoples of the world, which results in a growing anti-immigrant phobia and attempts to seal the borders so that the unwanted do not get in. Furthermore, while many in the Western nations are into zero population growth, the immigrant poor see large families as a divine blessing. Hence their presence continues to grow. The media and the politicians make the immigrant poor and their children appear as the root cause of all the problems ailing our countries. Border patrols are increased and life is made most difficult for those who dare to penetrate the border-defenses. How quickly we forget that at one time, our founders were the unwanted poor of Europe. How quickly we forget that we are an immigrant country made great through the untiring efforts of those who dared to emigrate to a new country to carve out a new existence—a greatness which sometimes was the result of hard work and ingenuity, but quite often came about through the enslavement, exploitation, or elimination of others. When we look at the history of humanity, we quickly discover that throughout history there have been migrations, *mestizajes,* and new identities. As new groups forge their geographical-social identity, they tend to forget their ancient origins. Yet immigrations, *mestizajes,* and new identities are as old as the planet itself and as natural as life itself but they are feared worse than hell itself. They appear as a threat to one's defined existence and identity, thus borders of all kinds are set up and interiorized so as to protect the perceived "purity" of the group from foreign contamination. Any transgression of these borders (racial, national, religious, class, clan, even family and others) provokes disgust and even excommunication. The quest for national purity can easily and quickly become a death-bearing idol justifying such horrors as the holocaust and wars of ethnic cleansing. National pride and identity, which is certainly a cherished virtue, can easily turn others into despised enemies who are a threat to the national welfare existence.

Yet, as I look at our own experience of the Mexican Southwest of the U.S.A.—*La Frontera*—I dare to ask: Need the transgression of borders be feared? Could it not be welcomed as the natural way of producing a new humanity, a new pool of biological, cultural, and spiritual genes that will produce an even more human humanity? Is the transgression of borders destruction of life or the birth of new life?

My Personal Experience

My entire lifetime has been one of crossing borders! Sometimes it has been quite painful at the moment of crossing, but in the long run, each border-crossing has been most life giving. I was born and grew up in San Antonio, Texas[1] in the section of the city which might just as well have been

Mexico. Our language, our customs, our humor, our religious expression, our foods, our bodily language—everything was Mexico, U.S.A.!

My first border-crossing, and probably my most traumatic one, was when I crossed the street that was the sort of dividing line between Mexican San Antonio and Anglo San Antonio (this has long since disappeared) and went to an English-speaking school. It was my first encounter with "total otherness." I hated school—I didn't know the language, the customs were strange, and even the way of attending Mass was quite different (it was painful rather than joyful). I became very quiet and reserved. I kept to myself and was afraid to speak because I felt bad when people could not understand my English.

Later on, in yet another Anglo school, a nun took a special interest in me and made all the difference. All of a sudden, I started to like school and my grades improved immensely. The border-crossing started to be fun and exciting. I started to realize that I was not losing, I was gaining. I also, for the first time, started to enjoy, rather than be embarrassed by, this constant border-crossing which allowed me many options, including the ability to get along in two languages rather than just one. High school was even better. I was able to compete with all the other students as true equals regardless of our ethnic backgrounds.

College and early priesthood became times of great questioning: Was I "Mexican" or "U.S. American"? When visiting Mexico, no matter how Mexican I might try to be, someone would remind me that I was a *Pocho*, a U.S.A. Mexican; and in the U.S.A., no matter how "American" I tried to be, someone would remind me I was Mexican and of course Mexican in a quite derogatory sense. It seemed like the separation between the U.S.A. and Mexico reached to the very depths of our individual and collective soul. The separation seemed irreparable. It seemed that no matter where we were, Mexico or the U.S.A., we had to be constantly apologizing for who

we were—too "Gringo" for the Mexicans and too Mexican
for the "Americans." It became quite tiresome to be always
explaining, defending, clarifying: "No, I am not really fully
Mexican . . ., No, I am not really just U.S.A." We could easily say "No, I'm not . . ." but we could never simply say: I am!
All this produced a certain type of shame in being who we
were, for we had no place we could really call home, where
we could really be ourselves. The only being we knew was
our non-being and the only place we had was "in-between"
Mexico and the U.S.A.

In 1967, Father Francisco Aguilera, a Mexican mestizo
who was comfortable and proud of both his Spanish and
Amerindian ancestry, took me to visit the *Plaza de las Tres
Culturas* in Mexico City where the final battles between the
Aztecs and the Spaniards took place. In this sacred ground
where a colonial church sits upon the ruins of the old pyra-
mid-Temples and is surrounded by modern-day apartment
houses, there is an inscription which reads:

On this site
on the sad night of August 13, 1521
heroically taken by Cortéz
valiantly defended by Cuauhtemoc
it was neither a defeat nor a victory
but the painful birth of the Mestizo people
which is México today.

We then went on to visit Our Lady of Guadalupe. I had
been there before, but this was a totally new experience as
Father Aguilera explained to me how in and through her, the
Iberian soul had united with the ancient Mexican soul to
give rise to the Mestizo soul of Mexico. This was the ongoing miracle of Guadalupe, this is what truly made her the
Mother of the Americas, because she had given birth and
continues to give birth to the new people of the Americas.

This was the beginning of a real rebirth for me, a coming

to grips with the innermost reality of my being and that of my people. I immediately realized that what had appeared as "non-being" was in reality the beginning of new being. The carnal and spiritual borders of identity and belonging had been pierced, the geographical/historical being of "the other" had been penetrated, and, as through the violence of the conjugal act, a new being had been conceived and born who would be fully both and something new. I quickly re-read the Alamo story though the same categories—not of defeat or victory, but of birth—the birth of a people, the birth of a soul, the birth of a spirituality, the birth of a church, and the birth of a religion. I could be proud of my collective grandparents: Iberia and pre-Columbian Mexico, and I could equally be proud of my parents: WASPish U.S.A. and Mestizo Catholic Mexico.

In recent years, I have come to realize that my own quest for identity and belonging is not just limited to my people of the Mexican-U.S.A. *"Frontera"* but that it is the human quest of peoples throughout the world. Having traveled vastly around the world and experienced the quest of growing numbers of peoples like myself, I dare to say that in my very body and soul, I am today's great human quest. As Alex García Rivera would say, in the little story of one human being is the universal story of humanity. In the Mestizo peoples of the world, the new identity of the Third Millennium is beginning to emerge and proclaim its presence.

World Experience Today

It is evident to any casual observer that the old, established, geographical—biological—ethnic identities are fading away quickly. Just stay a few minutes in the center of any city or watch major events like the Olympics or the World Cup and you will see that you can no longer identify a country by the color of the skin or the ethnic and racial characteristics of its people.

Today, multiple and massive migrations are taking place

in every direction. The poor and formerly colonized peoples of the world are moving to the rich countries which are the homelands of their former colonizers. Their children have no desire to relocate in the "old" country or to continue the lives their parents fled from. Yet, they are still different from the native-born peoples in many ways no matter how much they might like to simply fade in. Intermarriage begins to take place and the children gradually become aware of their "otherness" in relation to the ethnicities of their parents.

The Western colonization of the former centuries prepared the way and opened the doors for today's immigration into the Western countries. Furthermore, as world business looks for new markets enticing poor peoples of the globe to buy into the "Good Life" of the Western world, the peoples take this as an invitation to come to the source of this "good life" and they will strive at all costs to come to these countries. The exportation of our products, our entertainment, our way of life, and even our religion is an invitation to come join us. We may not see it or intend it that way, but that is the way it functions. The West continues to project the image of "paradise on earth" to the poor peoples of the world and they will continue to sacrifice and risk whatever is necessary to get themselves and their families here. Many who die in the process are the modern-day martyrs of today's world.

Today's cities and towns are rapidly becoming world cities—the entire world is present in each major concentration of peoples. This is just as true of San Diego as it is of Los Angeles, Chicago, New York, London, Madrid, Paris, Rome, and even the small towns of any Western country. As evident as the mixture is, so are the growing racial, ethnic, and religious tensions around the world. So, we ask the crucial question: what humanity do we want for the Third Millennium? A homogeneous society where there will be no differences and everyone will the exactly the same? An ethnic/racial "cleansing" with all its violent consequences? A society of ghettos always living in tension with one another? A fragile coexistence that could easily erupt into violence? Or, do we dare to dream of something new and recognize what is happening right here in *La Frontera* as the beginning of that newness?

The Christian Contribution

At the very core of Christianity is the conviction that a universal human family beyond the blood and ethnic bonds which usually identify us and divide us is truly possible and desirable.

Initial border-crossing of Jesus Christ

From its very inception, Christianity is about crossing apparently impenetrable borders for the sake of a new unity, the unity of a new source of family belonging. The eternal Christ, the Word of God crossed the border between the eternal and the temporal, between the divine and the human to become Jesus of Nazareth. As the New Testament affirms, "Christ, though in the image of God, didn't deem equality with God something to be clung to—but instead became completely empty and took on the image of oppressed humankind: born into the human condition, found in the likeness of a human being" (Philippians 2:6–7). Even stronger, the eternal Word which was God became flesh and dwelt among us. And the very geographical-historical place where this took place was in Galilee, a crossroads of the peoples of the world, a place whose people were considered impure and inferior precisely because here the boundaries of identity and belonging were constantly crossed if for no other reason than for basic survival.

From this region of ongoing mixture, Jesus proclaimed the reign of God for everyone and lived it out in many ways, most especially through his joy of table fellowship with everyone and anyone. Isn't it amazing that what was most shocking and scandalous for all the pure-minded religious people of his time, breaking the barriers of acceptability in the context of a common meal, would become the most sacred and cherished activity of the followers of Jesus? What was contamination and scandalous to the ordinary good, religious, and saintly folks of his time becomes the most sanctifying, edifying, and purifying activity of the new movement of universal and universalizing love.

Out of this context, Jesus asks the crucial question of all his followers: who is my mother, my brothers and my sisters?" (Mark 3:33). It is definitely not those of my own race, ethnicity, nationality, clan or family, but those who do the will of God which is clearly expressed in the prayer of Jesus: that all may be one! Not that all might be uniformly the same, but that all might love universally. Jesus gave his body and blood for this so that through this, the curtains of sacralized division—be they prejudices, taboos, or national borders—might be destroyed, for nothing can hide the true sacredness of God which is the human person regardless of racial, ethnic, national, or familial identity: *"He opened for us a new way, a living way, through the curtain—that is, through his own body"* (Hebrews 10:26). The most sacred and cherished rite of the new group would be the festive family meal— sacred because it dared to exclude no one!

Early Christianity

From its earliest moments, those following the way of Jesus started to transgress the most sacred and absolute borders on behalf of the new way. Jews, Ethiopians, Samaritans soon became family members of the new way. Peter the staunch Galilean Jew went through defilement to enter the house of Cornelius the Roman while Cornelius equally risked derision in welcoming the militant rabblerouser into his home. In the context of their encounter, previous borders were relativized without either losing their original identity, yet both became more human in the process of entering into one another's world. When Paul confronted Peter on behalf of the Gentiles it was likewise a transgression for the sake of liberation—liberation from boundaries which keep us from appreciating the inner beauty and dignity of the other whom we have feared and even detested.

Without destroying anyone, the new way provided a new spirit through which people could break through whatever borders divided them and become a new race, which is precisely what the earliest Christians were called. Christianity introduced into the world the joy and excitement of the hyphenated existence: you continued being who you were, but now in a radically new way. It did not destroy peoples but it did destroy ghettoishness. It made people aware that precisely because we were all "foreigners" (1 Peter 2:11) in this world order, with "*no permanent country*" to claim for ourselves exclusively, absolutely, and permanently (Hebrews 13:14), our only lasting family and ultimate root of belonging will be in the love for one another which leads us to welcome all who come to us in need. For in the end all things will pass away and only love and hence the family of love will remain (1 Corinthians 13:8).

Christianity today

Although historical Christianity has often sinned and been a source of division and bloodshed, the original Christian spirit of welcoming rather than fearing others is the great contribution which Christianity can contribute to the making of the new human family of the next millennium. If in the past missionaries from the Western world went out to all the known corners of the earth to welcome peoples into the Christian family, today the mission of the church, at least of the Western World, is to receive the foreign poor into our own homeland, for in receiving the poor of the world, we are receiving God (Matthew 25:35).

Today's parishes have the marvelous opportunities of becoming the greenhouses wherein the new life of the next millennium will be cultivated and developed. By developing a spirituality of hospitality and welcome, rejoicing with each newcomer, and giving thanks to God for the gifts which each one brings for the betterment of the entire parish family, each parish can become a microscopic cell of the new humanity which will be inclusive of everyone. New friendships and marriages between the children of the old-timers and the newcomers will take place, and their children will enflesh the bodily, cultural, and particular characteristics of both parents, yet they will be something new. If in the worldly *mestizaje* of the past the mestizo children were usually ashamed of the "inferior" side of their heritage and tried to deny, hide, and forget it, in the Christian *mestizaje* of the new way, the children will be equally proud and grateful of all their ancestral traits, shades, and colors. Our Christian tradition, purified of its eurocentric absolutism, is in a privileged position to appreciate and foster the positive evolution of these new identities.

I recently baptized the child of a Nigerian father and an Irish mother born in the U.S.A. I challenged the parents and grandparents to make the child proud of both its African-Nigerian and European-Irish heritage while encouraging the child to develop its own synthesis in the context of the U.S. way of life. I also had an Anglo-Jewish-Mexican Catholic wedding where I challenged the Catholic to help her Jewish husband become a better Jew while challenging the Jew to help his Catholic wife become an even better Catholic and let their children grow up in a love and respect for both and through the grace of God (not the manipulation of pressure of either parent) develop its own new synthesis—faithful to both, yet creating something new! Look at Tiger Woods, the new golf champion who is an Asian, African North American. The mixture is happening with or without us but we have the graced opportunity of making it something really positive and exciting.

That it is happening, there is no doubt. Yet there is equally no doubt that the fear of others and especially otherness is becoming more and more violent. We want to make the foreign other the culprit for all our national woes. It is precisely here that you the theologians, the writers of great articles and books, have the greatest contribution to make. Why not write letters to the editors of your local papers, or Op Ed pieces giving a positive view of immigrants and *mestizaje?* Your professional writings are read by very few and in all honesty, probably influence even less. Yet your faith interpretation of reality communicated through the public media could easily influence and change the minds of millions! Humanity needs your voice. Someone like Cardinal Roger Mahoney of Los Angeles has been a heroic prophet in favor of the rights and dignity of immigrants. You could do likewise. Our Holy Father is constantly calling upon the church to be the voice of the voiceless and powerless in society. You could easily and very effectively be precisely that. The immigrant poor need you to give the wider society an alternate and positive view of immigrants, immigration, foreigners, and *mestizaje.* A prophetic article or letter in the public press in favor of the poor, the marginalized, and the "kept-out" could easily be much more valuable than the best of articles in professional journals or the most award-winning theological books of the theological academy. In the end, it will not be your academic peers who will judge the ultimate value of your work, but the poor of society who will testify on your behalf for having come to their assistance.

Transformation of Borders

Borders normally signify the limits of existence, identity, and belonging—beyond the border you are no longer in Mexico, France, the United States, etc. When you cross the border, you cross from belonging to being a foreigner, an alien, or a visitor—in any case, you become an outsider! But we are discovering a new meaning and function of borderlands as the frontiers of new existence. Just as they have served to separate and keep apart, they can equally be the privileged meeting places of persons and of cultures and thus the birthplace of truly new human beings—biologically and culturally— and the cradles of new cultures, that is of a new humanity. Borders will not disappear, differences will not fade away, but they need not divide and keep peoples apart. Rather than being the fences of separation they can well serve as reference points marking regional characteristics that are both appealing and humanizing. They guard against a dull, homogenized society without any differences. Borders should not disappear but neither should they divide and keep people apart. The very nature of our faith can lead us to a creative transformation in the meaning and function of borders. Rather than seeing them as the ultimate dividing line between you and me, between us and them, we can see borders as the privileged meeting places where different persons and peoples will come together to form a new and more inclusive humanity. Rather than viewing them as the ultimate chaos of mixture, impurity, and disorder, we can begin to see them for what they truly are: the cradles of the new humanity. Our sense of universal and universalizing love can transform these potential regions of ethnic and racial violence into the new civilization of love wherein differences will be brought together for the betterment and enrichment of the whole human family.

Every border-crossing relativizes human absolutes and challenges previously unquestioned taboos for the sake of the new family of unlimited love. The frontier people are often looked down upon as "impure" and despised in various ways by the "purists" of the great centers of identity and belonging—Boston, Paris, Jerusalem, Berlin, Mexico City, Buenos Aires . . . yet it is in the out of the way frontier places, in the Galilees of today, that a new humanity is in the process of being born. It is here that the boundaries of purity are pierced through and the previously "impure" become the ordinary stock of the new humanity which enfleshes the skin and blood of those who were previously irreconcilable! Jesus went through this when he touched lepers, dined with sinners, and conversed with the Samaritan woman. Peter went through this when he dined with Cornelius, Paul when he went to the Gentiles. This is the way of Christianity—a constant defiance and crossing of borders for the sake of the new human family, for the only one unquestioned absolute is the reign of God's love.

In this new humanity, no one person, culture, religion, or race will be accepted as universal, normative, and ideal for everyone else. Each one has its richness and its limitations, its expressions of grace and of sin, its vision and its blindness, its knowledge and its ignorance, its illumination and its darkness. Each has the need of the others to become more human. Every culture is good but no culture is perfect. Thus the difference is not a defect but a richness, for in the very particularity of each one, its richness and limitations will be revealed. Through every encounter with others, more and more will be revealed of oneself and of the others.

In the very encounters across defined borders, we become a source of revelation to one another for, in the comparison, we can all become more aware both of our own graces and sins as well as those of others and began to form a new identity, taking from the best of each and hopefully eliminating the bad of each. This is an intriguing and exciting process of both affirmation and purification, of pain and joy, of death and birth, of tears and celebration.

To appreciate this newness in a positive way, one must discover the positive and exciting value of diversity in a spirit of great humility, recognizing that no one person, culture, or region has an exclusive monopoly on the value, meaning, and destiny of human life. Each language has its ability to communicate as well as its limitations. When we are speaking of a variety of cultures, we are speaking about what will often appear as contradictions and ambiguities, for the ordinary and self-evident ways of one culture always appear as odd or even unnatural to the other culture. If one faces differences with the fear of contamination or even a threat to one's identity, these differences will never be understood or appreciated or enjoyed! Once one can make an inner conversion and begin to see differences as positive and exciting—new worlds to be discovered and enjoyed—the diversity, rather than threatening, becomes life-giving and enriching.

In spite of the positive potential for the renewal of humanity, every crossing is painful, for we have to let go of the absolute character of our ideas, customs, values, and taboos which were most sacred to us, yet that which appears as sacred can often be the ultimate barrier that keeps us from appreciating the godliness of others. As painful as this letting go is—for it is nothing less than a dying to one's self—it is equally liberating and joyful, for it is a resurrecting into a new and more human existence. This is the paschal mystery in the world today: in every death to my cultural-historical absolutes, I do not cease being who I am but I become much more of a human being for I become open to the beauty and treasures of the values, customs, traditions, and way of life of others.

The most painful border-crossing is that of *mestizaje,* which allows us to break through the most absolute of all borders at the deepest level of human existence: the body, the blood, and the human spirit! Through *mestizaje,* a new body, a new culture with its language, and even a new form of religious expression comes into existence. It does not destroy its own sources of life—the parent races and cultures—but it brings them together into a new form of human existence.

This which I am speaking about is not an academic theory about *mestizaje,* but an honest attempt to explore the great human adventure of the Americas, especially of the great border between Nordic (U.S.A.) American and Mestizo Latin America, between the WASP and the Catholic Mestizo, between the ancient religions, the Protestant, and the Catholic, as it is happening within my own self and within the millions of Mexican Americans who live in the great bor-

der between the U.S.A. and Latin America. All the barriers
are broken through and something truly new begins to
emerge.

For the emerging mestizo peoples of the world today, the
pressing issue is not so much that of multiculturalism or the
intercultural/interreligious dialogue which seems to pre-
suppose division and separation, but the searching and
probing word of truly intercultural human beings who seek
to conceptualize, articulate, and communicate the innermost
(spirit-soul) and outermost (body-culture) nature of their
new identity which defies even the most sacred barriers of
humanity for that which alone is sacred to God: the all inclusive human family. This is the great difference between the
intercultural (religious) dialogue and the intercultural
word—the former speaks out of separation, the latter speaks
out of unity! Between the two partners of an interracial (cultural or religious) marriage, there will be dialogue, while
their child will struggle to conceptualize and articulate its
own proper identity which is definitely some of each parent,
but equally something truly new.

This is happening right here in this city of San Diego
where we are meeting for this conference, in my own city of
San Antonio, and throughout *la Frontera* of Mexico/U.S.A.
Old animosities are evolving into new partnerships, and differences which had been feared are now being celebrated.
Where does this take place? It's taking place in many places
and in many ways, but most of all at the level of the gut and
the spirit! Mexican tacos are replacing the all-American hot
dogs at ball games while Mexican religious celebrations are
becoming the common religious-civic symbols of entire
cities.

For us today, the *mestizaje* is both a fact and a great challenge. That we are mestizo—the proud heirs of great races,
cultures, and religions—there is no doubt. What are we to do
with this? This is the great question and challenge. How can
we combine the most humanizing elements of our parent

races and cultures to help form an even more human one with more opportunities for all? This will not take place overnight or even in one generation, but we must begin the process, and indeed we have begun.

Closing Remarks

Today, on the threshold of the Third Millennium, we have before us the possibility of total human annihilation or the beginning of the ultimate human family. A few months ago, it was predicted in the *Journal of Foreign Affairs* that the ultimate and most devastating war would be a religious ethnic war between the civilizations of the planet which would bring humanity to an apocalyptic end. I do not agree. I dare to think that we can make the difference in helping to usher in the ultimate human family wherein no one will be excluded, no one will be shamed, no one will be marginalized; I dare to think that we can expand the table fellowship of Jesus to the universal banquet-fiesta where no one will be excluded from the table of abundance; I dare to think of a planet where people will move freely within the planetary human household; I dare to think of the day when we can all pray together to the god who is greater than our best expressions of God.

Idle dreams? Let me assure you we have begun, in a very small way, but we have begun. Every year on the feast of Thanksgiving, Moslems, Jews, Buddhists, Hindus, Native Americans, Orthodox, Catholics, Protestants, Fundamentalists of all races and backgrounds join at San Fernando Cathedral to celebrate a foretaste of what we all want to become: the human family united precisely as the very diversity which previously divided us and opposed us to one another and which still makes us enemies of each other in many parts of the world, but now, in the power of the spirit, we pray that in our very diversity, we might be a source of enrichment and encouragement to each other and united in harmony by the glory of God! If the second creation after the great flood could start through Noah's Ark, then why cannot the new humanity of the Third Millennium begin through the prayer of religions of San Fernando Cathedral—the oldest cathedral sanctuary of the United States?

Notes

1. For a more detailed presentation of my life-pilgrimage and my attempts to theologize out of my own faith journey, see my three books: *The Future is Mestizo: Life Where Cultures Meet* (1988; New York: Crossroad, 1992); *Galilean Journey: The Mexican American Promise* (Maryknoll, NY: Orbis Books, 1983); and *Guadalupe: Mother of the New Humanity* (Maryknoll, NY: Orbis Books, 1997).

Teología en la Frontera: Límite y Encuentro de Dos Mundos

Ruy G. Suárez Rivero
Professor of Systematic Theology
Universidad Iberoamericana - Noroeste

Todo punto de vista es la vista de un punto y, es a través de la vista de un punto preciso, la fenomenología socio-religiosa que presenta el área metropolitana conformada por dos ciudades fronterizas: Tijuana, Baja California (México) y San Diego, California (Estados Unidos de América), que me sitúo en el punto de vista a partir del cual desarrollo esta reflexión. Hablo de una reflexión tentativa y preliminar sobre algunos aspectos de la socialización de la experiencia popular de la fe del mexicano y del hispano/latino en y desde la hermanada realidad específica del catolicismo fronterizo. Realidad que, en el sentido fundamental de "locus theologicus," es decir, como lugar físico, espacial, geográfico de reflexión teológica,[1] presenta una pluriforme y compleja gama de vertientes y matices hasta hoy no suficientemente explorados en su especificidad.

Este modesto intento en el que expongo cuestiones meramente introductorias y contextualizadoras tanto en el campo sociológico como en el teológico, es parte integrante de un trabajo mayor todavía no concluido, y pretende sumarse a la ingente y trascendental tarea que, desde hace más de tres décadas, ha venido realizando un creciente grupo de destacados teólogos y teólogas estadounidenses de variado origen latino.

Aquí, teólogos y teólogas tratan de configurar un lenguaje propio para expresar la experiencia de fe de la comunidad que, en los Estados Unidos, es identificada con los debatidos términos de: "Hispana," "Latina" o "Hispanoamericana,"[2] sin que dicho lenguaje reemplace el propio de la comunidad. Este esfuerzo tiene el proposito de ayudar a penetrar y profundizar el entendimiento de esa experiencia de fe a través de un enriquecedor diálogo participativo enraizado en la vivencia y corazón mismo de la comunidad, tomando el universo de la religión popular como elemento epistemológico y hermenéutico esencial de su quehacer teológico.

Ese quehacer teológico se ha distinguido, muy señaladamente, por conceptualizar el catolicismo popular no únicamente como un mero fenómeno socio-cultural que debe ser analizado científicamente con el instrumental de las ciencias sociales, sino fundamentalmente como propia fuente de teología cristiana, desde donde se busca responder a una pregunta central: ¿cómo el catolicismo popular hispano/latino revela al Dios de Jesucristo? En este contexto, el catolicismo popular es el *"locus"* privilegiado de la revelación divina, toda vez que el carácter revelatorio del catolicismo popular es una afirmación cardinal de la tradición católica, muy particularmente cuando se tiene en cuenta hasta qué grado esa tradición concede un lugar privilegiado al *"sensus fidelium."*[3]

Así mismo, esa teología adquiere particular relevancia y novedad al incorporar con plenitud de derecho la voz y visión de las mujeres al discurso teológico, no como un simple cambio de lenguaje, sino como un verdadero cambio de horizonte epistemológico. María Pilar Aquino apunta:

> En los Estados Unidos, hasta recientemente, no había una teología capaz de expresar creíblemente las motivaciones, los valores y el significado de la existencia Latino/Latina y los imperativos que guiaron nuestras acciones para el cambio en el marco de un mundo socio-cultural diferente al androcéntrico, Euro-Americano. Nadie sabía cómo, hasta que comenzamos a hacerlo.[4]

Y en virtud de la calidad y profundidad de esas voces, cada día se reconoce con mayor amplitud que la entrada de la mujer en el campo de la reflexión teológica, como dice María Clara Bingemer, "trae consigo una nueva manera, un nuevo método para pensar y expresar la teología."[5] La comunidad Latina no es una comunidad homogénea— vista en su globalidad—sino profundamente diversa, no sólo por razón de sus raíces etnohistóricas, culturales y nacionales, sino también por sus diversos niveles de inculturación en la sociedad estadounidense. Esto hace que, como apunta Allan Figueroa Deck, S.J.,

cualquier conocimiento generalizado (de estas comunidades), debe ser complementado por un más detallado análisis del grupo particular con el cual uno está tratando. Los puntos sobresalientes en común entre este vasto y diverso grupo, son el lenguaje español y su particular tipo de catolicismo gestado en las Américas a comienzos del siglo XVI.[6]

Aunque el idioma español y el mayoritario origen católico se configuren como denominadores comunes de ese universo, habría que añadir como elemento de particular importancia el guadalupanismo y el mestizaje[7] que para los pueblos, las culturas y las personas de origen mexicano ha sido doble, toda vez que el primer mestizaje se dió en los albores del siglo XVI con la conquista española y el segundo con la anexión que Estados Unidos hizo de grandes extensiones de territorio mexicano a mediados del siglo XIX. Estos denominadores comunes, sin embargo, por la diversidad de origen étnico del universo en cuestión, no han eximido de la necesidad de implementar alguna clasificación que facilite la identificación y análisis de las particularidades de estos grupos. Figueroa Deck ha propuesto una quíntuple clasificación sobre una base histórico geográfica: "1). Aquellos cuyos orígenes se encuentran en mesoamérica, particularmente en México; 2). Centroamericanos; 3). Los provenientes del

Caribe (Cubanos, Portoriqueños y Dominicanos); y 5). Los fronterizos del suroeste americano y California."[8]

Hasta donde tengo conocimiento, no se ha hecho todavía una profundización de las particularidades de esas comunidades específicas asentadas en los Estados Unidos, agrupadas por su origen histórico/geográfico/cultural, desde la perspectiva del catolicismo popular, que sirva como base estructural para una ulterior profundización y sistematización.

Mi trabajo, como he mencionado con anterioridad, se centra en el espacio fronterizo que conforma el área metropolitana de Tijuana y San Diego. Esto implica concentrarse en un grupo específico y en una perspectiva situacional un tanto diferente a la tenida hasta el presente por los teólogos y teólogas estadounidenses de origen latino, toda vez que el abanico de análisis que sería necesario realizar, está abierto a realidades específicas que abarcan un espacio común compartido por dos ciudades pertenecientes a dos naciones diferentes.[9]

Las vertientes en las que se expresa la realidad binacional fronteriza Tijuana/San Diego no únicamente son de una extraordinaria amplitud y complejidad, sino que están inmersas en una dinámica de constante cambio como respuesta a las multiformes variantes del contexto mayor en el que se gestan. Por ello, limito mi exposición al breve abordaje de algunos elementos introductorios que considero de particular relevancia. Estoy plenamente consciente de que la tarea de analizar y articular los contenidos de una reflexión teológica *en* y *desde* la frontera, asumida como matriz que organiza y categoriza sus múltiples fuentes y niveles de interacción entre sí, no es labor de una sóla persona, sino un trabajo eminentemente colectivo que exige la intervención de otros especialistas en teología, sociología, antropología cultural, y otras disciplinas pertinentes.

Mi exposición la divido en dos partes. La primera, como necesario marco referencial, abarca perspectivas en las que se entremezclan elementos socioeconómicos, culturales, políticos, histórico-regionales y religiosos del área metropolitana binacional y otorgo particular atención a la problemática migratoria. La segunda, muy breve, comprende algunos apuntamientos teológicos y metodológicos para la elaboración de un análisis sobre la socialización popular de la fe en el contexto del marco referencial aportado.

Marco Referencial: El Espacio de Reflexión

Tijuana y San Diego constituyen un espacio fronterizo que es a la vez el límite y el encuentro de dos naciones con el sello de dos mundos: el tercero y el primero y de dos culturas: la latinoamericana y la anglosajona, cuya configuración presumiblemente forma un escenario de confrontación de dos maneras de ser muy distintas y, obviamente, de dos estratos divergentes desde donde se vive la socialización de la experiencia popular de la fe. Esta presunción, aun cuando sea correcta, sin embargo debe ser completada y matizada con la especificidad que aporta el mosaico formado por la religión, el lenguaje, la cultura y las raíces comunes que existen entre los residentes de Tijuana y los cerca de 600,000 Latinos radicados en San Diego, de origen mexicano la gran mayoría de ellos.

Sin duda, una buena parte de la compleja realidad étnica, religiosa, cultural, socioeconómica y política que se vive en este singular espacio fronterizo, es semejante a la que se vive en otras ciudades ubicadas a lo largo de la franja fronteriza entre México y los Estados Unidos. Sin embargo, la frontera Tijuana/San Diego presenta toda una serie de particularidades y características únicas entre las que sobresale, como factor indicativo de la mutua interdependencia y movilidad, el hecho de ser la zona con mayor número de cruces fronterizos en el mundo, superando con mucho la cifra de setenta millones al año.[10]

El 55.5% de los cruces fronterizos, corresponde a mexicanos que se internan a San Diego y el 44.5% a estadounidenses que ingresan a Tijuana. Del total de los más de setenta millones de cruces fronterizos al año, resalta el hecho de que un importante porcentaje de los mismos tiene por motivo la visita a familiares o amigos: un 40% es el correspondientes a residentes de San Diego que cruzan hacia Tijuana, mientras que sólo un 11% se relaciona con residentes de Tijuana que cruzan hacia San Diego. Los porcentajes se invierten notoriamente cuando el cruce fronterizo es por motivo de compras y/o diversión, puesto que el porcentaje de mexicanos que cruzan San Diego asciende al 42% mientras que el correspondiente a residentes de San Diego que cruzan a Tijuana, es únicamente el 9%.[11]

Este flujo y reflujo humano tiene sustantivas repercusiones económicas en ambos lados de la frontera: los residentes del área de Tijuana (incluyendo Tecate, B.C.) gastan anualmente cerca de 2,800 millones de dólares en San Diego, y los residentes del Condado de San Diego tienen un gasto anual en Tijuana de 2,600 millones de dólares. Es importante aclarar que, para el cómputo de estos datos estadísticos, fueron excluidas las operaciones que, individualmente, superaban los diez mil dólares.[12]

Obviamente, este impresionante gasto por parte de los residentes de San Diego es generado fundamentalmente no por la población Latina cuya mayoría es de muy escasos recursos económicos, sino por la mayoría anglosajona que disfruta de un poder adquisitivo substancialmente superior. A su vez, el gasto efectuado en San Diego por parte de los tijuanenses, podría dar la impresión—y de hecho la da hacia el interior de México—de que Tijuana es una ciudad donde el dinero fluye a manos llenas y se gana fácilmente. Sin embargo, la realidad es otra. Aunque el concepto de pobreza en esta frontera es bien distinto al de otras zonas de la República mexicana, el abismo entre pobres y ricos es igualmente dramático y lascerante, evidenciándose con mayor fuerza por el influjo económico producto del narcotráfico.

La experiencia de vivir en la frontera es diferente a la de

vivir en otras zonas de México o de los Estados Unidos. En nuestro caso particular, el habitante de Tijuana tiene fuertemente erosionado su sentido de mexicanidad por muy diversas razones, entre otras: por la lejanía en que vive de los centros históricos y culturales donde se gestaron los símbolos que han configurado la identidad de México como nación; por el atractivo e influencia del "american way of life;" por el hecho de que, mientras la población de la urbe está compuesta por gente proveniente de prácticamente todos los estados de la República, los nativos de la Ciudad son los menos; finalmente, por no tener localmente raíces históricas comunes que los aglutinen en un mutuo sentido de pertenencia.

Sin embargo se ha evidenciado, particularmente en la última década, una creciente conciencia sociopolítica en mayor grado que en otros estados de la República Mexicana. Este hecho ha llevado al Estado de Baja California y, muy señaladamente a Tijuana, a la ruptura histórica del monopartidismo político que había imperado en México por más de sesenta años, convirtiéndose así Baja California en el primer Estado de la República en tener un gobierno estatal nacido de la oposición.

Tijuana por otra parte, con una población asentada de manera estable que supera los dos millones de habitantes, ve incrementado de manera cuasi permanente su índice demográfico oficial con un flujo migratorio constituido en "población flotante," estimada en medio millón de personas. La mayor parte de esta población flotante se divide entre personas que pretenden ingresar a los Estados Unidos en busca de trabajo—siendo éstos la mayoría—y quienes arriban con la idea de residir temporalmente en la urbe con la ilusión de encontrar en ella lo que les fue negado en sus lugares de origen. Unos y otros, en mayor o menor grado, conservan la idea de que están de paso; piensan que regresarán a sus lugares de origen; no saben cuándo ni cómo, pero tienen la idea e intención de regresar. Esta firme idea genera en ellos un sentimiento de desarraigo y de falta de compromiso con la ciudad que los ha acogido.

Por su parte, aquellos de origen mexicano que residen en San Diego de manera permanente, "extranjeros en su propia casa," como atinadamente ha expresado Virgilio Elizondo,[13] son con mucha frecuencia tenidos por la sociedad dominante como advenedizos. Tal percepción es completamente injustificada dado el hecho de que sus ancestros no cruzaron la frontera para ir a los Estados Unidos, sino que Estados Unidos expandió sus fronteras y se encontraron así siendo parte de otra nación.

Esta población no se siente ni totalmente mexicana ni, por supuesto, totalmente "gringa," como muchos de ellos mismos expresan. Pero, al mismo tiempo, la inmediatez de la Ciudad de Tijuana y el sentir en lo más hondo de su ser que sus verdaderas raíces no corresponden al espacio sociocultural que habitan, les motiva muy poco a vivir la experiencia de ser "comunidad de mexicanos en el extranjero" como la viven, por ejemplo, los coreanos o filipinos, cuyos países de origen se encuentran a miles de kilómetros de distancia, o como la viven otros también de origen mexicano pero que habitan más al norte y, por tanto, más lejos de su "México lindo y querido."

La población Latina de San Diego ha estado conformada, de manera preponderante, por una clase de bajo nivel socioeconómico y escaso nivel educacional. Aparte del programa de "Amnistía" que incrementó en la ciudad el número de residentes legales de origen mexicano principalmente, una buena parte de ellos son producto de los flujos migratorios de trabajadores agrícolas cuyo arribo se remonta a los años de vigencia del programa "Bracero" implementado por los presidentes Roosvelt y Ávila Camacho en 1942 y que terminó en 1964 con una deportación masiva que nadie fue capaz de evitar.

Esta realidad de cientos de miles de personas de raíces mexicanas residentes en San Diego, unida al hecho de ser tenidos por la cultura dominante como inferiores, incivilizados y subdesarrollados, subyace a la fuerte problemática que enfrenta, entre otras, la pastoral "latina" de la Diócesis de San Diego y al raquítico compromiso apostólico del laicado que se encuentra inmerso en un espacio de notoria discriminación y desatención por parte de la iglesia anglosajona.

Mientras que la Diócesis de Tijuana cuenta con 205 sacerdotes, 650 religiosas y 68 movimientos apostólicos laicales,[14] la Diócesis de San Diego cuenta con 226 sacerdotes y 355 religiosas.[15] De esos 226 sacerdotes, increíblemente, sólo ocho se dedican enteramente al servicio y acompañamiento pastoral de la población "latina" católica—mayoritariamente de origen mexicano—que asciende a cerca de 500,000 personas. La falta de compromiso de la comunidad "latina" con la iglesia local, salta a la vista al considerar que únicamente existen seis movimientos de apostolado seglar organizado.[16] Estadísticamente, en lo que a la atención pastoral y compromiso laical se refiere, la iglesia de "Latinos" en San Diego, en palabras de un alumno mío de la Universidad Iberoamericana, "es una Iglesia de quinto mundo insertada geográficamente en el primer mundo."

El presbiterio de Tijuana mayoritariamente de corte conservador, pero con una nueva y prometedora generación de jóvenes sacerdotes más abiertos al compromiso del acompañamiento pastoral, se ha visto en serias dificultades para hacer frente al creciente influjo de las sectas que en número superior a 700 está mermando a pasos agigantados la feligresía católica. Por el lado de San Diego, se ha aportado abundante evidencia de que la discriminación y la falta de entendimiento de la cultura y formas de expresión de los "Latinos" en su catolicismo, ha provocado una falta de acompañamiento por parte de la iglesia anglosajona, con la consecuente deserción en las filas del catolicismo y el acelerado crecimiento de congregaciones evangélicas y fundamentalistas.

El pluriforme panorama de esta zona metropolitana binacional está, a su vez, marcado por una lascerante problemática migratoria con fuertes repercuciones que invariablemente inciden en las complicadas y no siempre venturosas relaciones políticas entre ambas naciones. Dicha problematica esta configurada como una permanente y dolorosa vertiente característica del complejo mosaico de realidades que singularizan la fisonomía de la socialización popular de la fe en esta frontera.

La Problemática Migratoria

Aunque no es este el momento para realizar un análisis exhaustivo de esta problemática, me enfocaré en los acontecimientos más recientes de la relación bilateral en materia de migración y me referiré sólamente a unos cuantos hechos que permitan apreciar su amplitud, complejidad y dramáticas consecuencias. En los ultimos años, tres han sido los aspectos centrales de la política migratoria estadounidense que han marcado un giro radical en las tradicionales relaciones entre ambos países:

1. La "Propuesta 187" de modificaciones a la ley del Estado de California, hecha por el gobernador Pete Wilson con motivo de su campaña de reelección y ganada a partir de esta iniciativa, estuvo dirigida básicamente a negar los servicios de salud y educación a los hijos de los inmigrantes indocumentados o "ilegales" como fueron llamados. Aunque esta ley se encuentra todavía suspendida por un tribunal federal, sin embargo representa la consolidación de una inaudita arremetida jurídica antiinmigrante como nunca antes se había visto en la historia de los Estados Unidos.

2. El inicio de la "Operación Guardián," en octubre de 1994, en la frontera Tijuana/San Diego con apoyo logístico del ejército. El operativo consiste en un incremento sustancial de las acciones de contención del flujo migratorio. Para dar una idea de su dimensión y alcances, baste citar unos

cuantos datos del Sistema de Inmigración y Naturalización de los Estados Unidos: antes de este operartivo, habían 980 agentes de la patrulla fronteriza, hoy en día esa cifra se ha elevado a 2,009; el número de inspectores de garita se ha incrementado en un 116.6%; los sensores sísmicos adaptados para la detección y captura de indocumentados eran 448, actualmente existen 1,045; los telescopios infrarrojos fueron incrementados en un 233.3%; el número de helicópteros se aumentó en un 50% y la cantidad de vehículos para el patrullaje fronterizo se elevó en un 71.4%; las computadoras utilizadas para los procesos de registro y deportaciones se incrementaron en un 600%.[17]

A través de la "Operación Guardián," se han atrapado en esta frontera grandes masas de trabajadores migratorios en medio de constantes violaciones a los derechos humanos y excesivo uso de la fuerza por parte de la "Migra." En 1996 hubo un promedio mensual de 51,800 repatriados.[18] Es usual el método de separar a las mujeres de sus maridos y deportarlas por fronteras lo más alejado posible del lugar de captura. Se han documentado casos de mujeres que, apresadas en unión de sus esposos en las cercanías de la garita de San Ysidro, son trasladadas al centro de detención de Las Vegas, de ahí, a Denver o Dallas, para ser deportadas finalmente por Nuevo Laredo o Matamoros. Por otro lado, tan sólo en 1996, en el área de San Diego hubieron 43 migrantes muertos y en enero de este año fueron 15 los que hallaron la muerte por hipotermia en las montañas tratando de evadir las acciones de la patrulla fronteriza.[19]

3. La implementación en septiembre de 1996, por parte de Congreso de los Estados Unidos, de nuevos ordenamientos legales, como el "Acta de Reforma de Inmigración Ilegal y Responsabilidad de Inmigrantes" (IIRAIRA, por sus siglas en inglés), la "Ley de Reforma de la Asistencia Pública" y el "Acta de Sentencia de Muerte Efectiva y Antiterrorismo." Estas leyes afectan, como nunca antes, a millones de inmi-

grantes de diversas nacionalidades, muy señaladamente a los de origen mexicano, por ser éstos la mayoría.

Con las medidas previstas en estos nuevos ordenamientos, varios de los cuales entraron en vigor el día primero de abril de 1997: se anulan los recursos legales de apelación y defensa en contra de la deportación; se reducen drásticamente los servicios de educación, salud y seguridad social para los indocumentados aún cuando sean menores de edad; los residentes legales se convertirán en criminales "removibles" cuando ayuden a cruzar sin documentos a sus cónyuges, hijos, padres, hermanos u otros parientes; se incrementan los requisitos para que un residente legal o un ciudadano estadounidense pueda solicitar la inmigración de un familiar, aunque sea su esposa o sus hijos. A partir del pasado primero de abril, un gran número de inmigrantes con residencia legal en los Estados Unidos, se han convertido en "ilegales" y, por tanto, han sido arrojados a vivir en la clandestinidad, toda vez que sus procesos de solicitud de amnistía fueron suspendidos por el Servicio de Inmigración y Naturalización. Con estas y otras muchas medidas no mencionadas, los Estados Unidos se prepara para expulsar de su territorio a cerca de tres millones de personas en los próximos cinco años.

Estas acciones emprendidas por el gobierno estadounidense, además de separar familias, de desplazar a los migrantes hacia las montañas y el desierto con el consecuente incremento de fatalidades, y de incrementar sensiblemente el número de "ilegales" al revertir la condición migratoria de quienes tenían residencia legal arrojándolos a la clandestinidad, provocará irremisiblemente el nacimiento de "generaciones perdidas" al impedir el acceso a cientos de miles de niños y niñas a los servicios públicos de educación, salud y seguridad social, sin importar si son nacidos o no en los Estados Unidos.

A su vez, estas acciones antiinmigrantes están comenzando a tener ya grave impacto en ciudades fronterizas, principalmente Tijuana, por ser esta ciudad la puerta que recibe el mayor número de deportaciones. Con ello, aumenta así su "población flotante" con las consiguientes repercusiones sociales y económicas que esto conlleva, toda vez que la infraestructura urbana no está capacitada para absorber tal flujo migratorio ni está preparada para brindarle ni siquiera una mínima asistencia social ¿Dónde van a vivir, en dónde y en qué van a trabajar? ¿Cómo, en definitiva, podrán subsistir esos miles y miles de recién deportados que arriban desmoralizados, con ilusiones rotas, familias desmembradas y bolsillos vacíos?

A estas preguntas añado otras de igual urgencia y relevancia: ¿Cómo la realidad de injusticia, angustia, opresión y miseria de estos millares de hombres y mujeres revela al Dios de amor y justicia? ¿Cómo estos miles de hombres y mujeres reciben, interpretan y viven la revelación de Dios en Jesucristo en su "aquí y ahora"? ¿Cómo y en qué grado, esta "nueva cotidianeidad" de la población "flotante" y de la perseguida en San Diego o deportada en Tijuana, pervade la percepción y vivencia de fe de la comunidad fronteriza binacional establecida de manera permanente?

Una reflexión teológica en y desde la frontera, no puede eximirse de reconocer, en toda su amplitud y profundidad, la relevancia que tienen los paradigmas, tradiciones y categorías que soportan la construcción social de la realidad que reside y opera en la vida diaria de la gente, en el "locus" de su cotidianeidad. De la cotidianeidad es donde surgen las transformaciones y tiene que ver con la totalidad de la vida. De las experiencias que configuran la cotidianeidad, es donde surge una lectura teológica de la vida diaria. Esta interpretación teológica está situada como una verdadera hermenéutica dogmática, pues ella intenta comprender la verdad de Dios precisamente en la densidad histórica de las personas en su aquí y ahora.[20] A este respecto, dice Clodovis Boff:

el postulado ontológico fundamental para que lo no teológico pueda ser capaz de volverse teológico, es su carácter teologal. Pues bien, si Dios es efectivamente (como es) el sentido del mundo y de la historia, entonces no existe en principio ningún objeto o acontecimiento que no pueda ser teologizado.[21]

La Tarea y el Reto

Es un hecho que el ser humano no vive sólo a base de conceptos e ideas, sino también y muy particularmente, de los símbolos e imágenes que han quedado profundamente grabados en su ser desde su más tierna niñez y juventud. Es un hecho también que la fe tampoco se mantiene viva a base sólo de dogmas, declaraciones y argumentos teológicos o filosóficos, sino de cada una de las grandes imágenes, símbolos y verdades que no sólo se dirigen al intelecto y al discurso crítico- racional, sino también a la imaginación y las emociones. La fe sería algo a medias si afectara únicamente al entendimiento y a la razón del ser humano y no a la persona completa, incluidos sus afectos, sueños, anhelos e ilusiones.

Así mismo, es un hecho que la fe y la reflexión sobre ella es vivida desde un aquí y un ahora. Como ha dicho María Pilar Aquino,

> Todo tipo de pensamiento humano mantiene una intrínseca relación con el contexto histórico en el que se origina y hacia el cual busca responder, sea para transformar o legitimar dicho contexto. La teología no está exenta de este principio, aun cuando se reconozca la estructura interna de la teología como disciplina que reflexiona sobre la experiencia de la fe a la luz de la revelación.[22]

Al ser esto así, definitivamente no puede separarse la teología *en* y *desde* la frontera, de la experiencia de la cotidianeidad, de la experiencia del "aquí y ahora" del hombre concreto y de la mujer concreta, de la experiencia nuclear de la comunidad fronteriza binacional en la especificidad de sus cambiantes contextos, en la permanencia de su densidad histórica como raíz de una identidad común y en la búsqueda consciente e inconsciente de "su" verdad, del sentido de su existencia a partir de su encuentro con Dios en esa cotidianeidad de una experiencia marcada por un "aquí y ahora" fronterizo. Aquino observa que, "En la vida cotidiana cristalizan los paradigmas actuantes, tradiciones y categorías subyacentes que operan en la conciencia y son objetivadas en la práctica real personal y colectiva de las gentes."[23]

Siendo la teología una disciplina que se dirige a la articulación del lenguaje de la fe en sus diversas manifestaciones y estando referida más a la experiencia enraizada en la vida que a la exposición de verdades abstractas,[24] se origina de manera primigenia en la experiencia de la cotidianeidad y reflexiona en acto segundo en la autocomunicación de Dios en la historia. Nos encontramos con Dios en nuestra vida cotidiana o no le encontramos en ninguna parte. De ahí la exigencia de incrementar nuestra capacidad de discernimiento, de un análisis de lo histórico-social, para buscar ahí los signos de la presencia de Dios en el mundo y las interpelaciones del Espíritu.

Ahora bien, esa autocomunicación de Dios en la historia, que está expresada como amor, como gracia, como poder liberador y esperanza entre los pobres y oprimidos de la tierra, en cuanto autodonacion de Dios por nosotros y que manifiesta aquello que es Dios, "no puede ser aprisionada, ni mucho menos manipulada, para impedir o resistir la intrínseca fuerza transformadora del Espíritu."[25] Esta autocomunicación divina sitúa la necesidad de realizar una seria reflexión para discernir críticamente el impulso del Espíritu en y desde la comunidad fronteriza binacional. Hablamos aquí de una comunidad que, en su gran mayoría, está marcada por la aguda y dolorosa experiencia de la continua lucha contra la pobreza, la opresión, la discriminación, el racismo y, en no pocas ocasiones para el indocumentado, lucha contra el hambre y la muerte que asecha vestida de uniforme verde.

Los desafíos y dificultades que presenta la reflexión y el análisis de esta realidad fronteriza desde la perspectiva teológica son, ciertamente, muchos y no fáciles de remontar. Por un lado, se presenta la compleja gama de vertientes, matices e influencias cambiantes que configuran el intricado contexto en el que se desarrolla la cotidianeidad de la experiencia de fe y que exigen un estudio multidisciplinar como ya he mencionado; por otro lado y, muy particularmente, la dificultad que implica el ser fiel intérprete y traductor de la experiencia de la propia comunidad, sin reemplazar su lenguaje en la siempre presente tentación de amoldarlo a categorías y formatos preestablecidos, con las negativas implicaciones que conlleva esta proclividad.

No es infrecuente el que las experiencias de grupos marginados sean manipuladas y moldeadas para embonar en categorías preestablecidas del discurso teológico, respondiendo a preguntas que nadie se plantea.[26] Así mismo, no es infrecuente el que sean utilizadas tales experiencias para dar forma a planteamientos que son determinados y estructurados precisamente por aquellos que controlan los sistemas sintiéndose con derecho de decisión. El reemplazar el lenguaje propio de los grupos marginados, sin permitir nunca que ellos mismos sean los que propongan las cuestiones, no es otra cosa que una sofisticada manera de silenciarlos.

En tal virtud, una percepción encarnada en la cotidianeidad de este espacio fronterizo, exige entender cómo la cultura, la economía, la estructura socio-política y visión del mundo de la sociedad estadounidense, desde su papel de sistema de dominación en donde se intersectan los prejuicios étnicos, racistas, sexistas y de opresión económica, impacta la experiencia de la comunidad fronteriza binacional en la vivencia de su fe. Así mismo, y de manera primordial, exige engarzar ese entendimiento en la respuesta a dos preguntas fundamentales: ¿Cómo recibe, interpreta y expresa esta comunidad la revelación del Dios de Jesucristo? ¿Qué símbolos y lenguajes ha acogido como suyos desde su "aquí y ahora" para entenderse a sí misma en la angustiante búsqueda de una identidad liberadora que pugna por ser encontrada en medio de instancias de profunda transculturización, resemantización y estructuras jerárquicas de una iglesia que no termina de entender que el camino de Jesus con los pobres exige su seguimiento precisamente ahí donde los pobres hacen camino?

Una reflexión teológica *en* y *desde* la frontera no se limita a los cuestionamientos planteados ni se agota en ellos; tampoco su amplio marco referencial se restringe a los contextos presentados. Bajo el universo del catolicismo popular como elemento epistemológico y hermenéutico de este quehacer teológico, el abanico de elementos que exigen ser analizados rebasa con mucho el restringido campo superficialmente tratado en esta presentación. A manera de ejemplo y, valorando el papel dogmático/revelatorio del catolicismo popular, baste citar la necesidad de una relectura de la revelación desde la mexicanidad,—aunada a su expresión fronteriza— integrada al estudio del dogma, con un análisis de las raíces históricas, las tradiciones, el lenguaje, el pensamiento, la cultura, la piedad y el evento guadalupano, así como también una relectura de la autocomunicación de Dios explicitada desde la perspectiva de la mujer en la experiencia de su cotidianeidad fronteriza.

Conclusión que No lo Es

Tijuana y San Diego, límite y encuentro de dos mundos: tradiciones que se entrelazan, mezcla de orígenes y añoranzas, mosaico multicolor de sueños e ilusiones, caleidoscopio cultural y religioso donde la búsqueda de la identidad choca con el desarraigo. Gente noble que mira hacia atrás o hacia adelante, pero que difícilmente se compromete; religiosidad pobre en formación pero rica en sus raíces y expresiones populares; puente del narcotráfico con su secuela de muerte.

Tierra común con humus de migrantes que dejaron atrás familias, tradiciones, lugares y seres queridos, cargándose al hombro su costal de anhelos y esperanzas en búsqueda de una nueva vida, con mejores niveles de bienestar para unos y final de su propia existencia para otros.

Tijuana y San Diego son el espacio de una historia particular donde Dios se revela y la tarea y el reto consisten en leer el lenguaje de esa historia desde el aquí y el ahora, desde la cotidianeidad de la esperanza y la angustia, la vida y la muerte, desde la cima y el abismo.

Notas

1. Ver, Orlando O. Espín, *The Faith of the People: Theological Reflections on Popular Catholicism* (Maryknoll, NY: Orbis Books, 1997), 93-96; Roberto S. Goizueta, *Caminemos con Jesús: Toward a Hispanic/Latino Theology of Accompaniment* (Maryknoll, NY: Orbis Books, 1995), 191.

2. Ver al respecto el estudio realizado por Fernando F. Segovia, en la introducción al libro *Hispanic/Latino Theology: Challenge and Promise*, eds. Ada María Isasi-Díaz y Fernando F. Segovia (Minneapolis: Fortress Press, 1996), 31-42.

3. Un amplio estudio sobre el catolicismo popular en sus diversas vertientes y manifestaciones, así como la correcta apreciación del *sensus fidelium*, puede encontrarse en el excelente libro de O. Espín (citado en la nota 1).

4. María Pilar Aquino, "Direction and Foundations of Hispanic/Latino Theology: Toward a Mestiza Theology of Liberation," en *Mestizo Christianity: Theology from the Latino Perspective*, ed. Arturo J. Bañuelas (Maryknoll, NY: Orbis Books, 1995), 195. Mi traducción del inglés al español.

5. María Clara L. Bingemer, "Chairete: Alegrai-vos a Mulher no Futuro da Teología da Liberçâo," *Revista Eclesiástica Brasileira* 48/191 (1988): 571, citado en María Pilar Aquino, *Nuestro Clamor por la Vida. Teología Latinoamericana desde la Perspectiva de la Mujer* (San José, Costa Rica: Departamento Ecuménico de Investigaciones, 1992), 190.

6. Allan Figueroa Deck, S.J., "The Spirituality of United States Hispanics: An Introductory Essay," en *Mestizo Christianity* (citado en la nota 4) 227. Mi traducción.

7. Ver, Virgil Elizondo, "Mestizaje as Locus of Theological Reflection," en *Mestizo Christianity*, Ibid., 10-12.

8. Deck, 227.

9. El *Center for the Study of Latino Catholicism* (Centro para el Estudio del Catolicismo Latino), de la Universidad de San Diego (USD), dirigido por el Dr. Orlando O. Espín, tiene proyectado un ambicioso estudio sobre el catolicismo popular en la frontera Tijuana/San Diego, en colaboración con la Universidad Iberoamericana-Noroeste, de la Ciudad de Tijuana.

10. University of California San Diego, "Who Crosses the Border: A View of the San Diego/Tijuana Metropolitan Region," *San Diego Dialogue: Division of Extended Studies and Public Services of UCSD* (April, 1994): 10; y mi propia investigación para corroboración de datos en las oficinas centrales de la carrera de Comunicación de la Universidad Iberoamericana Noroeste, cuyos alumnos colaboraron con la UCSD en la elaboración de este reporte, según el protocolo de investigación entre estas dos universidades.

11. Ibid., 7-8.

12. Ibid., 20-29.

13. Elizondo, 9.

14. Diócesis de Tijuana, *Directorio Eclesiástico de la Diócesis de Tijuana* (Tijuana, B.C: Diócesis de Tijuana, 1997), 102-137, 139-149, 179-195; y mi propia investigación en los archivos electrónicos del Obispado de Tijuana, B.C.

15. Diocese of San Diego, *Catholic Directory of the San Diego Diocese* (San Diego, C.A: Diocese of San Diego, 1997), 1; y mi propia investigación para corroboración de datos e información adicional proporcionada por el Señor Obispo Auxiliar de la Diócesis de San Diego, Monseñor Gilberto Chávez.

16. Ibid.

17. Los datos sobre el Sistema de Inmigración y Naturalización de los E.U.A. se encuentran citados en Raúl Ramírez, "Nueva Política Norteamericana," *Revista Migrantes* 3/2 (1997): 5-7, edición particular de la Casa del Migrante en Tijuana, B.C.

18. Gianni Fanzolato y Raúl Ramírez, "Construyendo el Camino Hacia una Pastoral Migratoria: La Migración Actual en la Frontera Norte de México Vista por la Iglesia Católica," 4. Ponencia presentada en el Foro "Diferentes Rostros de la Migración," convocado por el Museo de la Ciudad de México, D.F., enero 1996.

19. Ibid.

20. Ver, Juan Carlos Scannone, *Teología de la Liberación y Doctrina Social de la Iglesia* (Madrid: Ediciones Cristiandad, 1987), 85-86. Ver también la importancia de la cotidianeidad en la dimensión eucarística y litúrgica, en Joseph Ratzinger, *El nuevo Pueblo de Dios* (Barcelona: Herder, 1972), 99.

21. Scannone, 85.

22. María Pilar Aquino, "Doing Theology from the Perspective of Latin American Women," en *We Are a People! Initiatives in Hispanic American Theology*, ed. Roberto S. Goizueta (Minneapolis: Fortress Press, 1992), 79. Mi traducción del inglés al español.

23. María Pilar Aquino, "Feminismo," en *Conceptos Fundamentales del Cristianismo*, eds. Casiano Floristán y Juan José Tamayo-Acosta (Madrid: Trotta, 1993), 519.

24. En términos similares asi lo expresa María Pilar Aquino, *Nuestro Clamor por la Vida*, 31. Ver también Roberto S. Goizueta, *Caminemos con Jesús*, 195.

25. María Pilar Aquino, *Nuestro Clamor por la Vida*, 32. Ver también, Orlando O. Espín, "Grace and Humannes," en *We Are a People!* (citado en la nota 22), 137.

26. Ver, Juan José Tamayo-Acosta, *Para Comprender la Teología de la Liberación* (Navarra: Verbo Divino, 1989), 14.

Masking the Invisible: Hispanic and Latino Americans in U.S. Religious Historiography

Evelyn A. Kirkley
Assistant Professor of Theology and Religious Studies
University of San Diego

Hispanic Americans are among the fastest growing groups in the United States (U.S.) population. Since the end of the Mexican-American War in 1848, when eighty thousand Mexicans became U.S. residents virtually overnight, the numbers of Latino Americans have steadily increased, from half a million in 1900 to four million in 1950 and 6.9 million in 1960.[1] Since the 1960s, the population has exploded, to 10.5 million in 1970, 14.6 million in 1980, and more than 22 million in 1990.[2] Currently comprising nine percent of the U.S. population, the Hispanic population is predicted to double by 2010, outnumbering African Americans.[3]

"Hispanics" or "Latinos" is a broad and diverse category. The majority are Mexican, Cuban, and Puerto Rican in national origin, with smaller numbers from Caribbean, Central, and South American countries. These national groups have intermarried with Africans, African Americans, and Native Americans, and as a result many Hispanics identify themselves as mestizo, Chicano, or La Raza. Moreover, they vary in terms of class; while many Hispanics are wealthy or middle class, as a group they are disproportionately poor and working class compared to other U.S. Americans. Settled unevenly across the country, they are clustered in New York, Chicago, Miami, and Los Angeles and a broad geographical swath from Texas to southern California, called *la Frontera* or the borderlands. Although increasing numbers of Hispanics are becoming Protestant, most are Roman Catholic. By 1978, they comprised between twenty and thirty percent of the total U.S. Catholic population.[4] By 2050, a majority of Catholics in the U.S.A. will be Hispanic.[5]

Do U.S. religious history textbooks reflect this explosive growth and increasing influence of Hispanic and Latino Americans? To explore this question, I analyzed eighteen textbooks, nine comprehensive surveys of U.S. religious history and nine of Catholicism for their portrayal of Latinos. Dating from 1844 to 1992, these texts are the best-known, widely cited, and most commonly used in undergraduate and seminary classrooms. I argue that although Spanish colonization is treated in most of these books, Hispanic Americans are interpreted in one of two ways: 1) they are invisible, or 2) they are homogenized and problematized. Either they are ignored, or the complexities and ambiguities of their relationship to U.S. religious culture are masked.

Why are Latino Americans portrayed superficially and dismissively? There are at least three reasons. First, they are an ethnic minority, many living in poverty, and therefore subject to discrimination by the Anglo, middle-class majority, from whose ranks most religious historians are drawn. Second, most are Catholic, while the majority of U.S. Americans and many religious historians are Protestant. Anti-Catholic bias has been common in U.S. history, and even since John F. Kennedy's presidency, Catholics are treated with suspicion in many parts of the country. Similarly, Catholics have been routinely marginalized in comprehensive U.S. religious history texts. Third and related to the first two, Latino Americans do not fit the story most religious historians want to tell. They disrupt the interpretive frameworks of both Catholic and non-Catholic historians; therefore, Hispanics are overlooked and ignored. In the following sections, I analyze the development of these interpretive frameworks in comprehensive and Catholic texts, arguing that adequate inclusion of Latino Americans will require a profound shift in the generally accepted paradigms of U.S. religious history. I conclude with suggestions for developing an alternate theoretical framework to highlight the significance of Hispanic and Latino Americans in the tapestry of U.S. religions.

Comprehensive Texts

Texts that survey the entire scope of U.S. religious history tend to underrepresent Catholics because the authors, usually non-Catholic themselves, argue the superiority and/or dominance of Protestantism. While other, Protestant ethnic groups are addressed, Latinos do not further the argument that Anglo-Puritan-Protestants are the most influential religious group in the United States. This theme is evident in two of the earliest surveys, Robert Baird's *Religion in America* (1844) and William W. Sweet's *The Story of Religion in America* (1930).[6]

While Baird refers briefly to Spanish "discovery" of the western hemisphere under Roman Catholic auspices, his main objective is to trace the English Protestant settlement of the eastern seaboard which he considers testimony to divine providence and the "peculiar qualifications of the Anglo-Saxon race for the work of colonization."[7] He attributes democratic government, commitment to freedom, and the separation of church and state to the triumph of Anglo-Saxon Protestantism. The Roman Catholic Church is included in the section on churches which "either renounce, or fail faithfully to exhibit, the fundamental and saving truths of the Gospel."[8] While he acknowledges that Catholics "hold those doctrines on which true believers in all ages have placed their hopes for eternal life," those doctrines "have been so buried amid the rubbish of multiplied human traditions and inventions, as to remain hid from the great mass of the people."[9]

Although Sweet wrote nearly a hundred years after Baird, his argument is virtually the same: the United States was founded by Anglo-Protestant radicals who established "liberation from the restraint of long established institutions, social, political and religious" as the foundation of U.S. American religion.[10] Commitment to freedom and individualism led to westward expansion, frontier religion, and revivalism. Since to Sweet, Catholics do not share this commitment, they receive scant coverage. Spanish mission efforts were displaced by more fervent Puritans. Mexico is mentioned once, along with Italy, Poland, Canada, and Austria-Hungary, in a list of countries that helped create a "polyglot nature of American Roman Catholicism."[11] Neither Baird nor Sweet mentions Spanish-speaking U.S. Americans or Hispanic religious cultures.

Textbooks written since 1970 follow the interpretive framework established by Baird and Sweet, although they significantly nuance it. Like Baird and Sweet, Sydney Ahlstrom's massive two-volume *A Religious History of the American People* (1972), Catherine Albanese's *America: Religions and Religion* (1981, 1992), *Eerdman's Handbook to Christianity in America* (1983), Martin Marty's *Pilgrims in Their Own Land* (1984), Peter Williams' *America's Religions: Traditions and Cultures* (1990), and Winthrop Hudson and John Corrigan's *Religion in America* (fifth edition, 1992) trace the origins of mainstream "American" religion to Puritan New England.[12] While not assuming Anglo-Protestant superiority, the authors argue for its hegemonic influence on U.S. American culture. They ascribe to it democracy, voluntarism, and separation of church and state as well as racism, sexism, and national chauvinism. They also trace the gradual disintegration of Anglo-Protestant dominance due to secularism and liberal-fundamentalist factionalism and the rise of religious pluralism due to immigration and experimentation with new ideas and forms. As a result, they underestimate the significance of Catholicism and narrowly interpret Hispanics and Latinos. Hispanic religious life is portrayed in two contexts: colonial Spanish missions and Latino immigration in the twentieth century.

During the mission period, these six authors identify the same themes. They consider Spanish and French missions as part of America's prehistory, the "European Prologue" to the establishment of Puritan New England.[13] Despite this claim that "New Spain" was somehow not authentic U.S. America, these historians argue that the colonial Spanish mission movement was significant for three reasons. First, it was the first European settlement. According to Ahlstrom, there is a cultural memory "that old imperial Spain occupies in the consciousness of all Americans, though especially of Roman Catholics."[14] At the same time, Williams adds, "the Spanish presence was not a long-term major factor in the political and cultural development" of the U.S.[15]

Second, according to these historians, the friars were zealous evangelists and compassionate toward Native Americans. They worked in harsh conditions against incredible obstacles, particularly "the heavy hand of Spanish colonial rule and the intractability of the Indians."[16] According to Albanese, although missionaries imposed "a kind of shotgun Christianity," they were "also sincerely convinced of a divine command to bring the Christian message to the Indians."[17] According to Hudson and Corrigan, many missionaries tolerated a degree of syncretism, prompting a blend of Catholicism with indigenous religious traditions. The Virgin of Guadalupe is an example of "the supernaturalistic tone and the distinctive emphases of Spanish Catholicism as it developed in the New World."[18]

Third, the missions were a catalyst for English Protestant

settlement as a check for Roman Catholic imperialism. According to these authors, since church and crown were virtually united in Spain, religious and commercial interests were intertwined in "New Spain" and created conflict between missionaries and conquistadors. Although missionaries are praised for their zeal and compassion for Native Americans, the historians note that conversions were only moderately successful. According to *Eerdman's Handbook*, Spanish settlement "led to a brutal oppression and exploitation of the native population, which was decimated by the twin scourges of European disease and European greed."[19] The underlying message is that although it was first, colonial Spanish religious culture was weak and easily displaced by Anglo-Protestantism.

After "New Spain," Latino Americans disappear from these comprehensive texts until the twentieth century. Hudson and Corrigan state that permanent "Spanish presence in the United States came relatively late," after the collapse of the missions.[20] Although these historians note that most Hispanic immigrants came from Mexico, Cuba, and Puerto Rico, they proceed to lump them together indiscriminately and trace two interpretive strands about them as a group. First, Hispanics are characterized as having low allegiance to the Roman Catholic hierarchy. According to Ahlstrom, they "share a common tendency to anticlericalism, and have usually been extremely poor," and "their participation in Catholic church life has been very slight."[21] Practicing a Catholicism that "has never been particularly vigorous," they have taken little initiative to form their own churches, and few Hispanic men enter the priesthood.[22] This anticlericalism, say Hudson and Corrigan, is due to a fractious relationship with church hierarchy; "expanding Spanish-speaking American churches found themselves in a difficult relationship with an Irish-American hierarchy that disapproved of the folk religion aspects of Mexican-American Catholicism."[23]

Second, they are portrayed as having communal solidarity and strong commitment to social justice. Albanese notes that although Hispanic Americans are "least church oriented of any immigrant group," their "community was not theoretical but lived" and "organized religion became culture."[24] According to Ahlstrom, they are the "latest major Roman Catholic constituency to achieve large numerical importance and a degree of self-consciousness."[25] With this cohesive identity, in the 1960s, they organized at the grassroots level to fight economic exploitation and racism, aided by Latin American liberation theology. The example most often given is the work of Cesar Chávez and the United Farm Workers in California and its close relationship with the Catholic church.

The conclusion drawn by these historians is that Hispanic Americans are homogenous and practice Catholicism at odds with church traditions. Hudson and Corrigan put it succinctly: "Hispanic churches continue to manifest a distinctive form of Catholicism, which includes . . . outspoken advocacy for social and economic justice, and a claim of the right to be different over the demand to assimilate."[26] An exception among these historians is Peter Williams, who notes the diversity of religious cultures among Hispanics, that Mexican-Americans practice "Catholicism heavily tinged with folk religion," Puerto Ricans established storefront churches in New York, and Cubans have been more traditional in their practices and loyal to the church.[27] However, in all these texts, non-Catholic Hispanics receive scant attention. Albanese is typical in her single observation that "many turned from their nominal Catholicism to an intense and active pentecostalism."[28]

Of the comprehensive texts surveyed, the most well-rounded portrait of Hispanic Americans is Mark Noll's *A History of Christianity in the United States and Canada.*[29] Published in 1992, this text takes advantage of 1990 U.S. census data documenting the rapid growth of Latino communities. Like other historians, Noll focuses on "the rise and decline of Protestant dominance in the United States"; however, at the same time he "attempts to recover the experiences of common people," especially laity, women, and ethnic minorities.[30] Unlike other texts, Noll devotes a full eight pages to Hispanic Christians, noting that the term encompasses Mexicans, Cubans, Puerto Ricans, Dominicans, Nicaraguans, and other immigrants from Spanish-speaking countries. He also details a more complex portrait of Hispanic religious cultures than other texts. While commenting that Hispanic Catholics have been a "religious but only lightly churched people," he argues that they have spawned two distinct church communities: one led by non-Hispanic priests and bishops that seeks to assimilate Hispanic Americans and a second "oriented more to the masses" that has "sought ways to inculcate the Christian message through, rather than against, Hispanic culture."[31] Without evaluating these two expressions, Noll concludes that as a result of this bipolarity, "Hispanic spirituality tended to focus on the home and on community festivals more than on the official ecclesiastical activities."[32] Moreover, he argues, this community-based spirituality, along with the African American civil rights movement and the base community movement in Latin America, has conscientized Hispanic Americans and radicalized them socially, economically, and politically. This spirituality has also prompted greater attention from the church hierarchy, demonstrated by the formation of the Bishops' Committee for the Spanish-Speaking in 1945, and more participation in clerical leadership, evidenced by 1990 statistics: two Hispanic archbishops, nineteen bishops, sixteen hundred priests, and two thousand nuns.[33] While acknowledging that most Hispanics are Roman Catholic, Noll notes the growth of Hispanic Protestants, especially Methodists, Presbyterians, and the Assemblies of God, and their difficult cultural position. Not only do they have to adjust to Anglo-Saxon religious norms, they also endure accusations from other Hispanics that they are hostile to Catholicism and sell out Hispanic culture to aspire to the American "good life."[34]

More than other authors of comprehensive texts, Noll expresses the complexity and ambiguity of contemporary Latino religious culture. Yet his treatment has three weaknesses. First, he does not place his analysis of contemporary Hispanic religion in historical context. He provides scant background as to why Latinos emigrated to the U.S. and their economic and social status when they arrived. Second, he does not devote sufficient attention to racism and ethnocentrism of Anglo Americans against Hispanics; he does not discuss the impact of discrimination on Latino communities. Third, he does not address the impact Hispanic Americans have had on the larger religious landscape of the United States, both Catholic and Protestant.

Texts on Catholicism

In surveys of Catholicism, as far back as Henry de Courcy's *The Catholic Church in the United States* (1856) and including more recent works such as Theodore Maynard's *The Story of American Catholicism* (1941), John Tracy Ellis' *American Catholicism* (1956, 1969), Andrew Greeley's *The Catholic Experience* (1967), Thomas McAvoy's *A History of the Catholic Church in the United States* (1969), James Hennesey's *American Catholics* (1981), Timothy Walch's *Catholicism in America* (1989), and James Prest's *American Catholic History* (1991), the primary interpretive framework is the meaning of being both Catholic and American.[35] Ellis asks the question concisely: "How 'American' has Catholicism become in America? In what ways has American life been most intimately touched and most largely shaped by Catholicism?"[36] Moreover, these eight historians have addressed the question of reconciling religious and national identities from the perspective of the church hierarchy.

Like comprehensive texts, Catholic texts focus on colonial

Spanish missions and twentieth-century immigration as the loci of Hispanic presence in U.S. Catholicism. Yet they give no more attention to the mission movement than comprehensive texts and in several cases minimize it to stress the British (and therefore more "American") origins of the church. For example, Maynard states his objective is to "give due weight to the Catholic factor" in "the building of America," especially to oppose the claim that "is still from time to time fiercely (or else smugly) asserted that Americanism (*sic*) is basically Protestant and that only Protestantism is truly American."[37] He argues that freedom, democracy, and equality are "distinctively American characteristics in our Catholic history that I hope to draw out along with the distinctively Catholic characteristics of American history"; therefore, "I shall be obliged to reduce my account of French and Spanish missionary and colonizing effort to a bare minimum."[38] Likewise, McAvoy gives only a sentence to Spanish missions because they hinder his argument that the "cultural nucleus of American Catholicism has been the English Catholic group that settled first in Maryland and from there passed on in time to other parts of the country."[39] Regardless of immigration from other countries, according to McAvoy, "Roman Catholicism has been recognized as an American institution just insofar as it has been permeated by the spirit of this Anglo-American group."[40] He begins his history with the founding of Maryland in 1634.

Those six Catholic historians who do discuss Spanish missions echo themes from the comprehensive texts, but with different emphases. First, they proudly claim Spanish primacy in settlement. Hennesey crows that "the oldest colonial power in what is now United States territory was Spain, whose ventures spanned three centuries" from Florida to California.[41] According to Ellis, Spain was "unquestionably the greatest Catholic power of Europe" and "more united in its religious faith, perhaps, than in any other single way."[42] This strength and unity "helped to stamp upon every

Spanish enterprise the seal of Catholic energy."[43] Second, they underscore the courage of the missionaries. "Long before these separatists landed at Plymouth in 1620, and while the English settlers hugged the Atlantic shore, too indifferent to instruct in Christianity the Indians whose hunting grounds they had usurped," De Courcy rhapsodizes, the friars courageously established missions, enduring intense hardship and risking martyrdom.[44] Third, they refute the interpretation that weak missions were displaced by stronger Puritans, emphasizing instead conflict between civil and religious authorities as the primary catalyst for decline. Ellis argues that the close relationship of church and state in Spain was "both the greatest strength and the predominant weakness of Catholicism in Spanish America."[45] According to Ellis and de Courcy, missionaries frequently clashed with the Spanish government since they depended on it for finances and protection.[46] Regarding consequences for Native Americans, Ellis claims that "mission system was the most successful institution for dealing with the aborigines."[47]

In discussing contemporary immigration, Catholic historians consider Latinos one of the many ethnic groups comprising the church, one more immigrant group to be "Americanized" and assimilated. Characterized as resistant to clerical authority, politically dangerous, and syncretistic, they are depicted as neither truly Catholic nor "American" and therefore problematic for the church. The church's response to Latinos is the story told. They are flattened and simplified, melting-potted into the larger story of the immigrant church. According to Ellis, "since World War II the most recent immigrant problem has been created for the church by the entrance into this country of numerous Puerto Ricans, concentrated chiefly in New York and Chicago, for whose special care priests with a knowledge of the Spanish language have been assigned."[48] Hennesey notes that as early as 1943 U.S. bishops recognized the needs of Latino

Americans, stating that they "have a right to expect the full enjoyment of our democratic institutions and that help in social life which is accorded to others."[49] He also mentions the church's involvement against exploitation of Mexican migrant workers sparked by Cesar Chávez and the United Farm Workers.[50]

Undoubtedly the fullest interpretation of Latino religious history among texts on Catholicism in the U.S. is Jay Dolan's *The American Catholic Experience* (1992). Unlike previous historians, Dolan defines the church as the "people of God" and therefore stresses the church's history "from the bottom up."[51] He highlights "the social context in which Catholics lived, an economic and social profile of the community, how the people organized their churches, and what leadership roles they assumed in the local church."[52] This approach means that while Dolan, like other historians, identifies Spanish missions and modern immigration as the primary events in Latino Catholic history, he zeroes in "on the people and not just the prelates, on the experience of religion and not just the development of the institution."[53]

Regarding colonial missions, Dolan focuses on the missionaries' intensity. They embarked on a religious crusade to "abolish 'paganism' and establish a City of God in the Promised Land, where the Christianity of the Old World could reach its perfection."[54] Thus he argues that Spanish missions had similar objectives to New England Puritans. He concludes that "the Catholicism of the conquistador and the friar was a blend of profound spirituality, intense activity, ideological intolerance, and feelings of racial superiority."[55] This spiritual activism prompted compassion and acts of heroism, as well as brutality and hypocrisy toward Native Americans. Unlike other historians who claim the mission system collapsed and became extinct, Dolan argues rather that the "Catholic Church has survived in the Southwest to this day," that "for Hispanic Americans, the Rio Grande area has become a major cultural and political stronghold."[56]

Dolan provides the most thorough topography of Mexican immigration of any of the texts surveyed, comprehensive or Catholic. Identifying Mexicans as one of the largest ethnic immigrant groups of the church in the nineteenth and twentieth centuries, along with Irish, Germans, Italian, Polish, and French Canadians, he focuses on the formation of Mexican Catholic communities in various periods. After the Mexican-American War in 1846-48, the U.S.A. annexed a large portion of Mexico, and eighty thousand Mexicans became U.S. residents. A second influx occurred due to immigration from 1920 to 1960.[57] By the 1950s, Mexicans, as well as Puerto Ricans, were emigrating to urban areas, particularly Los Angeles, Chicago, and New York. However, most Mexican Americans lived in the rural southwest, and many lost control over their land after U.S. annexation. Finding themselves at the bottom of the socioeconomic ladder, men became farm workers or unskilled laborers, while women worked as maids, in garment factories and food-processing plants, as well as in the fields. Often surviving in overcrowded and unhealthy conditions, they had high rates of disease and infant mortality.[58]

According to Dolan, the church was slow to respond to social and religious needs of Mexicans. After the collapse of the mission system, southwestern churches had a critical shortage of priests. This inadequacy created a "church without clergy" in which "Mexican people were forced to improvise their own religious expressions."[59] They built private family chapels and home shrines, celebrated religious festivals honoring Mary and the saints, and formed strong mutual benefit societies and *cofradías*, religious confraternities. "Rooted in devotion to the *santo* and promoted by the religious confraternity," Mexican Catholicism flourished independent of parish churches and schools and nurtured strong family and communal bounds.[60]

Given this Mexican Catholic culture, it is not surprising, Dolan argues, that when bishops assigned new priests to southwestern parishes and sought to exercise discipline, they encountered resistance.[61] As a result, many priests characterized Mexicans as being ignorant of their responsibilities to God and church and sought to convert them to "proper" Catholicism and obedience to clerical authority.[62] Dolan claims that the "clergy's inability to understand and appreciate the religious world of the Mexican immigrants created a cultural chasm between the two groups."[63] Due to ethnocentrism and the language barrier, Mexicans were targets of overt discrimination, in some parishes allowed to attend only one Mass per Sunday and restricted to special pews. They formed their own separate national parishes, isolated and segregated from the Catholic community, except in New York City, where the church sought to integrate Puerto Ricans into bilingual parishes through an array of programs and services.[64]

Gradually, clerical attitudes began to change. In 1945 the Bishops' Committee for the Spanish-Speaking was formed to support Spanish-speaking congregations in the Southwest. The committee became involved in social justice concerns, especially the exploitation of migrant farm workers. Parishes, especially in urban areas, became centers for "Americanization," priests convinced that "in making better Catholics, we shall make them better citizens."[65] Parishes established neighborhood settlement houses and provided recreation, educational programs, and economic aid.[66] After several generations, Mexicans gradually became more integrated into church life in the Southwest.

Although Dolan thoroughly covers Mexican American Catholicism, especially within the limits of a textbook, his analysis has glaring weaknesses. First, he gives scant attention to other Hispanics. Puerto Ricans are mentioned briefly, but he ignores Cubans, Nicaraguans, Dominicans, and other Central and South American immigrants. Second, he does not trace the formation of Latino solidarity as vehicle for self-conscious religious and political activism. He does not interpret the relationship of Catholicism to Hispanic radicalization and empowerment. Third, Dolan does not address the impact of Hispanics to the larger church in the U.S.A., their contributions to paraliturgical devotions, liberation theology, and social justice consciousness. He focuses instead on the internal development of Hispanic parish communities and the role of clerics in supporting and/or hindering that development.

Conclusion

The foregoing analysis makes clear that while comprehensive texts on U.S. religious history and Catholicism have made progress in interpreting Latino/Hispanic American religious cultures, additional work is necessary. However, before making suggestions for that additional work, two caveats should be made. The first is to note that no single textbook can do everything. In a survey, generalizations are unavoidable. Second, the greater success of recent texts in incorporating Hispanic and Latino Americans is encouraging. Historians must continue working to transform dominant interpretive frameworks to incorporate analyses of Latino religious beliefs and practice. Where, then, to continue this transformation in interpreting Latino religious cultures? I have three suggestions.

First, historians need to analyze diversity within Hispanic/Latino communities. It is not monolithic, but multifarious; there is not one Latino religious culture, but a number of cultures. One significant difference, noted above, is national origin. The unique histories of Puerto Ricans, Cubans, and Mexicans must be revealed, as well as those of emigrants from other Caribbean, Central, and South American nations. These stories reveal differences in timing, reasons, and geographical patterns of immigration. They also reveal different attitudes toward Catholicism, other religions, the U.S. Anglo mainstream, and toward each other. In addition to national origin, differences of race, class, gender, sexual orientation, and religion must be explored. Many Hispanics identify themselves as mestizo/mestiza and refuse to reject their mixed racial heritage. Historians inaccurately assume all Latinos lived in poverty, when the first Cuban immigrants were middle-class and wealthy families. Women and men, and lesbians, gay men, bisexuals, and transgendered persons have unique experiences of religion in Hispanic communities. And non-Catholic Hispanics must no longer fall through the cracks.[67]

Second, historians need to interpret the shaping influences of U.S. culture on the formation of Latino American religious communities. How has an Hispanic identity been created, as distinct from Mexican, Puerto Rican, and Cuban nationalities? Hispanics have confronted isolation, ethnocentrism, and discrimination, both inside and outside the church. Torn between marginalization, assimilation, and cultural retention, they have experienced loss, uprootedness, and alienation. They have been negatively stereotyped as prostitutes, gang members, and drug dealers in television shows and movies. How have these experiences contoured their faith? How have their experiences been similar to and different from other ethnic minorities, such as African and Asian Americans?

Third, historians must explore the contribution of Latinos to the religious identity of the United States. In the texts surveyed, Hispanics are often portrayed as problems for clerical leadership. They are depicted as passive, acted upon by the church rather than being agents shaping it with their own theology, experiences, and cultural traditions. Overlooked is the active influence Hispanics have exerted especially on Catholicism: conscientizing Catholics on social justice, initiating more emotional and pentecostal worship, focusing the church on liberation and empowerment, and emphasizing intense spirituality. More broadly, how have Latinos shaped the U.S. religious landscape? And through their influence, is an hemispheric religious landscape being created? What does it look like?

Latino Americans have had a significant impact on the U.S. religious landscape. It is no longer an option to ignore or mask them because they do not fit the story historians seek to tell, whether it be Puritan primacy or Catholic identity. Nothing less than an historiographical paradigm shift must occur for marginalized groups in the U.S. religious landscape to receive the attention they deserve. Anglo-Protestantism must be decentralized, the stories of peripheralized groups told, and the delicate negotiation between mainstream and margin in the U.S. further explored. Fuller analysis of Latino and Hispanic American religious cultures in textbooks will advance these ends.

Notes

1. Jay Dolan, *The American Catholic Experience: A History from Colonial Times to the Present* (Notre Dame, IN: University of Notre Dame, 1992), 134, 360; Moisés Sandoval, "The Church Among the Hispanics in the United States," in *The Church in Latin America, 1492-1992*, ed. Enrique Dussel (Maryknoll, NY: Orbis Books, 1992), 239.

2. Sandoval, 239; Joan Moore, "The Social Fabric of the Hispanic Community since 1965," in *Hispanic Catholic Culture in the U.S.: Issues and Concerns*, eds. Jay Dolan and Allan Figueroa Deck (Notre Dame, IN: University of Notre Dame, 1994), 6.

3. Moore, 6.

4. James Hennesey, *American Catholics: A History of the Roman Catholic Community in the United States* (New York: Oxford University, 1981), 313.

5. Timothy Walch, *Catholicism in America: A Social History* (Malabar, FL: Robert E. Krieger, 1989), 111.

6. Robert Baird, *Religion in America* (New York: Harper and Brothers, 1844); William W. Sweet, *The Story of Religion in America* (New York: Harper and Brothers, 1930).

7. Baird, 23.

8. Ibid., 269.

9. Ibid., 269-270.

10. Sweet, 4.

11. Ibid., 533.

12. Sydney Ahlstrom, *A Religious History of the American People*, 2 vols. (New Haven, CT: Yale University Press, 1972); Catherine Albanese, *America: Religions and Religion* (Belmont, CA: Wadsworth, 1981, 1992); Mark Noll and others, eds., *Eerdman's Handbook to Christianity in America* (Grand Rapids, MI: William B. Eerdmans, 1983); Martin Marty, *Pilgrims in Their Own Land: 500 Years of Religion in America* (Boston: Little, Brown, 1984); Peter Williams, *America's Religions: Traditions and Cultures* (New York: Macmillan Publishing, 1990); Winthrop Hudson and John Corrigan, *Religion in America: An Historical Account of the Development of American Religious Life*, fifth edition (New York: Macmillan Publishing, 1992).

13. Ahlstrom, table of contents, I: 7.

14. Ibid., I: 84.

15. Williams, 146.

16. Noll and others, 12.

17. Albanese, 75.

18. Hudson and Corrigan, 383.

19. Noll and others, 10.

20. Hudson and Corrigan, 2.

21. Ahlstrom, II: 506.

22. Noll and others, 401.

23. Hudson and Corrigan, 384.

24. Albanese, 90.

25. Ahlstrom, II: 506.

26. Hudson and Corrigan, 384.

27. Williams, 379.

28. Albanese, 90.

29. Mark Noll, *A History of Christianity in the United States and Canada* (Grand Rapids, MI: William B. Eerdmans, 1992).

30. Ibid., 4, 1.

31. Ibid., 490, 489.

32. Ibid., 489-90.

33. Ibid., 491.

34. Ibid., 493-94.

35. Henry de Courcy, *The Catholic Church in the United States: A Sketch of Its Ecclesiastical History* (New York: Edward Dunigan and Brother, 1856); Theodore Maynard, *The Story of American Catholicism* (New York,

Macmillan, 1941); John Tracy Ellis, *American Catholicism* (Chicago: University of Chicago, 1956, 1969); Andrew M. Greeley, *The Catholic Experience: An Interpretation of the History of American Catholicism* (Garden City, NY: Doubleday and Company, 1967); Thomas T. McAvoy, *A History of the Catholic Church in the United States* (Notre Dame, IN: University of Notre Dame, 1969); James Hennesey, *American Catholics: A History of the Roman Catholic Community in the United States* (New York: Oxford University, 1981); Timothy Walch, *Catholicism in America: A Social History* (Malabar, FL: Robert E. Krieger, 1989); James E. Prest, *American Catholic History* (Lanham, MD: University Press of America, 1991).

36. Ellis, x.

37. Maynard, ix.

38. Ibid., xi.

39. McAvoy, 1.

40. Ibid.

41. Hennesey, 10.

42. Ellis, 3.

43. Ibid.

44. De Courcy, 12-13.

45. Ellis, 4.

46. De Courcy, 12-13; Ellis, 6-9.

47. Ellis, 9.

48. Ibid., 130.

49. Hennesey, 277.

50. Ibid., 326.

51. Dolan, 9, 10.

52. Ibid., 10.

53. Ibid.

54. Ibid., 16.

55. Ibid., 20.

56. Ibid., 27.

57. Ibid., 360-361.

58. Ibid., 198.

59. Ibid., 176.

60. Ibid., 177.

61. Ibid., 177-178.

62. Ibid., 371.

63. Ibid., 372.

64. Ibid., 378.

65. Ibid., 373.

66. Ibid., 374-375.

67. A number of these issues have been addressed in individual monographs, but not in a narrative survey. A beginning, albeit with limitations, is the Notre Dame History of Hispanic Catholics in the U.S., which has published three volumes so far: Jay Dolan and Gilberto Hinojosa, eds., *Mexican Americans and the Catholic Church, 1900-1965* (Notre Dame, IN: University of Notre Dame, 1994); Jay Dolan and Jaime Vidal, eds., *Puerto Rican and Cuban Catholics in the U.S., 1900-1965* (Notre Dame, IN: University of Notre Dame, 1994); Jay Dolan and Allan F. Deck, eds., *Hispanic Catholic Culture in the U.S.: Issues and Concerns* (Notre Dame, IN: University of Notre Dame, 1994).

A Post-Einsteinian Settlement? On Spirituality as a Possible Border-Crossing between Religion and the New Science

J. Matthew Ashley

Assistant Professor of Systematic Theology
University of Notre Dame

We have all heard of the famous interchange in 1802 between the French mathematician and physicist Simon Laplace and Napoleon Bonaparte. Having listened to Laplace's grand exposition of a closed system of cause and effect which would explain all natural phenomena, the then first consul exclaimed "and who is the author of all of this?" to which Laplace is said to have replied, "I have no need of that hypothesis." The interchange is emblematic of a border between religion and science which, militarized slowly in the course of the eighteenth and nineteenth centuries, and by no means as impermeable as some would have it, has nonetheless become a fact of life in the modern West.[1] Fundamentalists contest it by attacking across it and advocating "biblical science," while liberal and progressive theologians work out some version of a mutual non-aggression pact—handing the natural world over to science, while attempting (with less and less success) to stake the integrity and credibility of both religion and theology on the existence and elaboration of some interior world—the domain of values, morality, or spirituality. Whatever the approach, however, no one interested in the health and integrity of *either* modern science and technology, with the culture they have helped to create, *or* religion, can ignore this border. And both the fundamentalist and the liberal-progressive approaches are becoming less and less tenable.

A rather remarkable and relatively recent development entails a shift of terms in the debate. More and more books have been appearing over the past two decades that argue for convergences, or at least opportunities for dialogue, not between science and *religion*, but between science and *spirituality*. Perhaps the first was Fritjof Capra's *The Tao of Physics*, which appeared in the mid-seventies.[2] That book argued for a close correlation between the implicit ontology of Mahayana Buddhism and that of the new physics: particularly quantum theory. It did not take long, however, for similar claims to emerge concerning various representatives of the apophatic Neoplatonic mystical tradition in Christianity (especially the Rhineland mystics) and recently for Jewish Kabbalah as well. Here we will consider four representative texts: a set of dialogues between Matthew Fox and Rupert Sheldrake, the first the well-known advocate of creation spirituality and theology, the second a revisionist biologist; a similar set of dialogues by Fritjof Capra and David Steindl-Rast, the latter a Benedictine monk; a book by Diarmuid O'Murchu exploring the implications of the new physics for spirituality, theology, and religion; and finally, Daniel Matt's investigation of the "resonances" between Jewish Kabbalah and cosmology.[3]

The selection is by no means exhaustive; the literature is vast, expanding, and evidently very popular. Yet even a selective overview is worth the effort, since the development is not only interesting as a new way of crossing the border between science and religion, but is also indicative of the promise and problems that arise in the field of the study of spirituality in general. It raises questions concerning how to define spirituality, how to study it, and how to determine the relationship between spirituality and religion in general, as well as the relationship between spirituality and theology. As a border-crossing between science and religion it does promise a fruitful way of integrating two ways of understanding our place in the cosmos, two ways which are—at least on the level of everyday life—either in opposition to one another or, at best, dangerously indifferent. However, there is a danger in the specific way that spirituality and science are being brought together in this literature. This new border-crossing bears more than a passing resemblance to the "Newtonian settlement" between science and religion of the eighteenth and nineteenth centuries, a settlement which, as Michael J. Buckley has shown, culminated in Laplace's relegation of God to the status of an unnecessary hypothesis.[4]

Premises and Promise of this Border-Crossing

While I will have some critical comments to make later on it should be stated from the outset that there is much to be gained by this shift of locus in relating science and religion. It is premised on a set of developments in both science and in religion (and their study): richer and more nuanced understandings of the complexities of each, and more honest recognition of the needs each has for the other. As all our authors indicate, science and the technological world it has helped create desperately need the sort of orientation toward the transcendent (with concomitant ethical and aesthetic dispositions) that spiritualities have increasingly come to provide today. On the other hand, if we understand "spiritualities" to be the specific sets of practices—with the worldviews that go with them—by which individuals live out their religious beliefs amidst the concrete possibilities and dilemmas of the everyday, then it is important that the world that science reveals and constructs is one which is compatible with the spiritual practices by which we try to negotiate the challenges, and enjoy the beauty of that world.[5] Here our authors are correct in pointing out that the mechanistic world of Newton, Boyle, Darwin, and Faraday, stripped of inherent meaning, presents a profound challenge for any spirituality predicated on the presence of the divine, to be celebrated as well as nurtured, in our world. How much more meaningful and natural do spiritual practices become when the worldview which they project or imply is, at the very least, not contradicted by, and perhaps even reinforced by, the understanding of the world presented by science? This, for instance, is the primary argument of Daniel Matt's book, which, starting from the crisis of faith in a world not only "after Galileo," but also "after Auschwitz," argues for the coherence between the Jewish mystical traditions of Kabbalah and the cosmology of the new physics and cosmology, and then goes on to give Torah and even Jewish Halakhah (Law) a ride on those ample coattails.

Another premise of this development concerns a more contextualized approach to understanding both science and religion. Almost all of our authors make a great deal of the new historicized understandings of the natural sciences, employing (perhaps too much) Thomas Kuhn's famous notion of paradigms and paradigm shifts. Whatever nuances are required in using this notion, it does, as Stephen Toulmin notes, remind us that we have to study science from within the life-world of the community in which science is practiced, and the meanings of scientific truth-claims produced, argued, and legitimated.[6] It has alerted us to the fact that science makes up a subculture which is embedded within the broader cultures of modern society, and develops in a complex constellation of relationships with those cultures, while forming them in turn. The development of the study of spirituality as a distinct field entails, among other things, a similar claim that we need to study persons' faith in terms of the everyday practices and beliefs by which their religious faith is real and meaningful to them—their "spiritualities." In this light, a spirituality can be understood as the product of the intersection of the more universal creeds, rituals, and mores of religion with the political and economic structures, and the culture and ethos at a particular social location.

Thus, methodologically there seems to be much in common in the new history and philosophy of science on the one hand and the turn to spirituality in the study of religion on the other. Both have felt compelled to exploit the riches and negotiate the difficult transactions involved in interdisciplinary work. A correlation of the results of these different studies promises to open up new and important avenues of considering how "science" and "religion" interact, not in the heads of professional scientists and theologians, but in the minds and hearts of persons who, at least in the United States, live in a society which is profoundly shaped by science and technology, and yet is also deeply formed by a pervasive and perduring religious character.[7] If, as I suggested above, spiritualities are on the front lines of the struggle to incarnate one's religious faith in new and challenging cultural conditions, then it is there that we must seek the *sensus fidelium* in which to ground more abstract theological reflection on the relationship between science and religion.

Besides re-enchanting a world that has been disenchanted by modern science, the literature we are looking at often makes strong claims that certain findings in cosmology and quantum physics, as well as in biology (so-called "deep ecology") cohere with and reinforce key insights of the world's mystical traditions, combining to make a compelling case for a more responsible way of "being in the world," a new ecological consciousness that we so desperately need today. For example, Fritjof Capra argues a certain interpretation of the new physics according to which there are no "primary building blocks," concluding that our experience of individuality is finally an illusion, that relationality, relationships, are more fundamental. "Deep ecology" demonstrates that there is no scientific basis for asserting the superiority (not even in terms of complexity of organization) of human beings over the rest of nature.[8] These scientific findings, he goes on, are in complete accord with a Buddhist ontology, which, on his reading, also asserts the illusory nature of our experiences of individuality and of our separateness from other entities. These reinforce one another not only to support ecological responsibility, but even religious and political tolerance.[9]

David Steindl-Rast, a Benedictine monk, makes a similar argument, drawing most heavily on the mystical traditions of Christian Neoplatonism, particularly the more radically apophatic mystics of the late Middle Ages and the golden age of Spanish mysticism. He asserts that *the* central insight of *all* spiritual traditions around the world is a radical sense of belonging.[10] Environmental responsibility with regard to nature, and working for justice in social and political relations, is the way of acting which corresponds to this primordial insight. He argues, furthermore, that specific spiritual traditions have much to teach us about how we must live in the present world: his own Benedictine traditions of stewardship, for instance.[11] In a more bizarre instance of this form of argument, O'Murchu asserts that evolutionary cycles of mass extinction followed by explosive and creative proliferation of new species are instantiations of the cosmic paradigm of death and resurrection, historically played out on Calvary.[12] His usage is more confusing however, since he uses it both to argue in favor of environmental responsibility and to advocate a disposition which could calmly contemplate the (seemingly quite likely) end of our own species in the near future—dying to rise again in the form of a new "more advanced" one.

The general tendency of these arguments is to use particular interpretations of the specific claims and more general ontological implications of modern science to argue against world-denigrating or world-fleeing spiritualities, while using certain traditions in spirituality to argue against those interpretations of modern science which construe the world either as a cosmic storehouse for our control and consumption, or as a cosmic theater of the absurd—indifferent or even hostile to the meanings and values we attempt to find or create in it. This mixture can make a potent brew, but there is a certain troubling circularity to the argument. We are urged to embrace a certain strand of spirituality, or to accept some "essence" common to all spiritualities, because it coheres with certain interpretations of science (often highly speculative or controversial within the scientific community). These interpretations are legitimated in turn because they agree with what the mystics have allegedly known all along—Mahayana Buddhist monks anticipated the "bootstrap theory" in modern subatomic physics or Meister Eckhart was saying the same thing in the fourteenth century that modern physics teaches today.[13]

Some Critical Questions

This brings me to my critical comments, first and foremost of which has to do with issues of definition. What exactly is spirituality; what is science? The issue of defining spirituality is a thorny one. At times spirituality is defined so broadly that, covering everything, it becomes impossible to delineate or to distinguish from religion or faith or even consciousness in general. This genre is no exception. The definitions of spirituality are very general, and often rather vague: I have already noted Steindl-Rast's definition of spirituality as the "absolute sense of belonging." For Daniel Matt mystics and poets have a profound intuition of the "oneness" of all that is: a oneness that ultimately transcends our (and God's) differentiation into persons.[14] Matthew Fox begins with a promising definition of the spiritual life as constituted by the dialectic of the mystical (our "yes" to life as original blessing) and the prophetic (our "no" to all that restricts or destroys life), but his contributions are almost exclusively oriented by the former, and it is the former that is brought into dialogue with science.[15]

O'Murchu defines spirituality as "the human search for meaning" or as "the relational component of lived experience."[16] On these definitions it is hard to know what would *not* count as spirituality. Not surprisingly, furthermore, given this definition O'Murchu tells us that "spirituality is inherent to the human condition—also to planetary and cosmic growth; in my estimation, religion is not."[17] This brings us to another troubling feature of the way this genre often treats spirituality, a feature that again is too often found in popular literature on spirituality. Spirituality is contrasted, and contrasted negatively, with another reality called "religion." Consider the following telling passage at the beginning of *Natural Grace*:

> We both [Fox and Sheldrake] share an interest in going beyond the current limitations of institutional science and mechanistic religion, and we both believe that as a new millennium dawns, a new vision is needed which brings together science, spirituality, and a sense of the sacred.[18]

This juxtaposing, even opposing, of religion—particularly its institutional and historical elements—to "spirituality" occurs frequently. For example, Thomas Matus asserts that "you can have spirituality without religion, but you cannot have religion without spirituality."[19] He does indeed nuance this view somewhat: religion becomes the institutionalization of a spirituality, which is important because it brings out spirituality's intellectual and social implications.[20] But, in fact, the institutional and historical concreteness of Christianity and Judaism often appear only as an embellishment (or obfuscation) of an already-constituted spirituality. For O'Murchu the same sorts of themes emerge: experience of ultimate unity, the relativity of individuality, a sense of the Universe as a subject. Furthermore, and ironically since he insists that "quantum theology" abhors dualisms of all kinds, he posits a strong dualism between religion and spirituality. Spirituality is inherent to the human condition and always good; religion is something of an aberration, born of the Agricultural Revolution of the ninth millennium before Christ as an attempt to gain control over the sacred.[21] It is part of a phase in our evolutionary development that, in O'Murchu's view, we have outgrown.[22]

In short, spirituality means mysticism, and particularly the most radically apophatic of Christian and Jewish mysticisms, which reduce to the same essential core as that of the world's other spiritual traditions, particularly Buddhism.[23] I have already noted that this selectivity is legitimated because of the correlation with the "new science," in a dangerously fragile circular argument. A further problem with this selectivity, however, is that these authors find it very difficult to deal with the problem of evil. It is not that they are unaware of it. On the contrary, Daniel Matt knows of the challenge posed to Judaism by the horrible evil of the Shoah, and the Christian authors all note with approval the development of liberation theology. Yet the mystical resources they draw on do not allow them to do justice to evil: the ancient and venerable neoplatonic solution of seeing evil as a privation, or the stoic solution of seeing it as an element of the cosmic logos, almost always prevails.

Fox tells us that relating social justice and mysticism has been one of the guiding concerns of all his writings.[24] As already noted, he has something like a mystical-political complementarity in his definition of spirituality as a dialectic of the mystical "yes" to the primordial and primal grace of creation and the prophetic "no" to all that does not correspond to that grace.[25] Yet his dealings with evil almost always collapse the second element into the first. Like O'Murchu, he lapses into a quasi-Hegelian subsumption of evil into a cycle of destruction and creation. He calls this

the Eucharistic law of the Universe: everything in this Universe eats and gets eaten in some form or other. For exam-

ple, the supernova explosion five and a half billion years ago
that birthed the elements of our bodies in its explosive and
generous death, that was a Eucharistic event. Things die but
they pass on their food and nourishment for other moments
of evolution.[26]

David Steindl-Rast and Thomas Matus make the
Kingdom of God central to their elaboration of the proper
response to evil and they have high praise for liberation theology.[27] Yet as one reads their attempt to elaborate these concepts as the social-political correlate of the "sense of
belonging" one misses the sort of passion of a Jon Sobrino,
who insists that the Kingdom is not already-given or does
not simply arrive in a vacuum, but rather irrupts into an
anti-Kingdom. One wishes that they would have treated not
Gutiérrez's first book, but his second book, *We Drink from
Our Own Wells*. There Gutiérrez gives a much more nuanced
definition of spirituality, which insists that a Christian spirituality is a following of Jesus, and one which passes through
not just the dark night of the intellect, but the dark night of
injustice.[28]

For his part, Daniel Matt draws on the notion of *tikkun*
from Kabbalah. Evil is divine energy that has become separated from the divine, and the proper response of human
beings is to mend the world—and mend God—by lifting up
these sparks.[29] It is a manifestation of human consciousness,
derived from disordered desire. Overcoming evil means
reorienting disordered desire by reconnecting its "energy"
with the energies of the divine *Sefirot*, thus returning them to
their primal root in God.[30] But this is not the most fundamental level of Matt's response to the problem of evil. He
knows too well that such a response is not adequate to that
incommensurable instance of evil in this century: the Shoah.
On that level his response is simple, if radical: he joins with
those other post-Holocaust Jewish theologians who argue
that the event of the Holocaust makes the notion of a personal God, who has chosen Israel and entered into a special

covenant relationship with the Jews, makes no sense.[31] Like others in the science-religion dialogue, he invokes scientific theories and concepts like the Heisenberg uncertainty principle or chaos theory to hammer further nails into the coffin in which he wants to inter a personal, provident God. Earthquakes just happen, and moral evil and injustice originate in human beings. It is fruitless asking how God could allow such things to happen. Instead, "Torah commands us to fight the social evil of injustice and to wrestle with the personal evil of selfishness and greed."[32] It is not, however, finally clear where the force of this "commands" comes from, once the reality of a personal God who has given Torah is undermined as radically as it is here.

Each of these attempts to grapple with the problem of evil and sin deserves further treatment on its own. However, one need not question the sincerity of their recitations of the seriousness of environmental degradation and economic-political oppression to observe that their appeal to the experience of the ultimate unity and underlying meaningfulness of all that is, and their identification of spirituality as a deep sense of "belonging to the universe," draws much of the sting and urgency from their ethical-political exhortations. I would suggest that the selectivity in defining and utilizing the resources of spirituality or mysticism has much to do with this. Would it not be crucial here to widen the circle, to bring in other traditions of spirituality? What would it mean, for instance, to consider the liberation spirituality of Jon Sobrino and Ignacio Ellacuría, with its insistence that we stand at the foot of the crucified one and, paraphrasing Ignatius' meditation on sin, ask ourselves: What have I done to crucify the crucified peoples of the world? What must I do to uncrucify them? What must I do for this people to rise again?[33] Then one is much more likely to adopt an approach like Edward Schillebeeckx's, with his insight that consciousness of the Kingdom arises just as much from the negative contrast experience of the *absurdity* of what is, the experience that suffering simply *does not make sense.* Corresponding spiritualities would be nurtured by Job's anguished questioning of God.[34] Admittedly the correlation of *these* spiritualities with science will be more difficult to construct, but until the full depth and complexity of the world's spiritualities are brought into the conversation, the "resonances" between science and spirituality will lack the specificity and substance they need to guide the complex political, economic, scientific, and technological discernments we must make if we are to survive long, or survive humanely, into the next millennium.[35]

A second set of critical concerns centers on the specific correlations that are made between mysticism and science. At least since Capra's first book, advocates of the science-mysticism connection have never ceased pointing out that paradoxical statements are found both in the new science and in mysticism. From different perspectives our authors argue that the recent notion of a quantum vacuum in quantum physics, which is "empty" but yet full of virtual particles coming into existence and annihilating one another, can be compared to the "non-thingness" that Buddhism posits as ultimate, the claim (in, say, Meister Eckhart) that God is both the ground of all being and also beyond being, or the Kabbalistic naming of God as *ayin*—nothingness.[36] The wave-particle duality of subatomic particles is compared to the paradoxical experience of the difference in unity of the personhood of God and the nonpersonal Godhead beyond this God.

These comparisons are problematic because they lift the "paradoxical" statements out of the broader network of discourse—scriptural passages, doctrines, and theological assertions in the case of mysticism, the mathematical formalism of the theory in the case of physics—that gives them their meaning and function, and bring them into direct comparisons, without inquiring into the isomorphism of those discursive contexts.[37] Taking the wave-particle dualism, for instance, there is precise clarity about the status of the entity in question, even though that clarity is expressed in the mathematical formalism of the relevant quantum wave functions. To be sure, there is great difficulty in "describing" that clarity in terms of our experience of the world at our level of perception, but this does not mean that there is "obscurity" or "absurdity" at the roots of things themselves. Similarly, the context of Eckhart's discussion of God's "non-being-ness" is the machinery of scholastic method, applied to the question of predicating transcendentals of God.[38] To lift these statements, which on the surface appear to be similar in making paradoxical or mutually self-defeating claims, out of their broader contexts, is to risk dangerously misleading category mistakes.

A further issue has to do with the *purpose* of these sorts of statements. In science their purpose is often to explain the theory to the educated layperson, or to construct a broader model, or set of complementary models, which the scientist uses to navigate through the abstract formalism of the theory, to suggest new directions for research, and so on.[39] Paradoxes are constructed and tolerated only insofar as they are grounded in, and help make sense of, deeper levels of intelligibility. This is not the case of mystical paradoxes and apophatic "self-negating" speech. There, as scholars like Pierre Hadot and Denys Turner remind us, the aim is not as simple as "describing" some state of affairs so that we can experience it.[40] For at least well into the middle ages the purpose of mystical theology was not to elicit or sustain certain kinds of experiences, but to guide the initiate into the comprehensive transformation that happens when one comes into the unmediated presence of God—the God of Sinai and Zion for Judaism, the God of Jesus the Christ for Christianity. Paradoxical statements and self-annihilating language were first and foremost the linguistic ascesis required for *that* ascent, *that* transformative encounter. They were created and tolerated because they launched the believer on a trajectory, mapped out an *Itinerarium mentis in Deum*, to use Bonaventure's language.

In short, in science the goal is always to resolve ambiguity or paradox, or to use them only to provide a heuristic device for entering that level of mathematical or conceptual discourse at which there is no ambiguity; whereas in spirituality the goal is to exploit the self-negating character of the paradoxes in order to bring a person into the presence of a God who is, in crucial respects, beyond "experience." Of course, proponents of the science-mysticism connection claim that the world revealed by the new science is also "beyond experience," that it cannot be captured using the linguistic categories that we use to describe our everyday experience. The question remains whether "experience" and "beyond" have the same meanings when applied to mystical texts of the late middle ages and to technical scientific papers, and this is precisely the question that is begged when statements from the two genres are lifted out of their linguistic matrices.[41] Not only the differences in linguistic context, but also the ultimate purpose, of these sorts of statements, needs to be borne in mind before we make hasty correlations.

A post-Einsteinian Settlement?

In his book, *At the Origins of Modern Atheism*, Michael J. Buckley points out the contradictory and ultimately self-defeating strategy carried out by Christian theologians and philosophers in responding to attacks on the Christian God—real or imagined—in the early modern period. Ignoring the warrants provided by the religious experience of believers, or the force of the disclosure of God in the person, life, and fate of Jesus, as articulated in the theological disciplines of Christology and pneumatology, they retrieved and revitalized venerable classical arguments for the existence of God, primarily teleological. "Natural theology" drew on a "natural religion" or "religion of reason" which was supported, so it seemed, by the new science of Newtonian physics. As we all know, the argument from design was particularly prominent in these attempts, and particularly vulnerable, as Laplace's famous statement shows. Buckley notes how striking the bracketing of religious experience is, given the fact that it occurred during the flowering of mysticism in Spain and France—but this is all a part of the story of the growing separation between spirituality and theology, a sad story we are all too aware of. "In the absence of a comprehensive Christology and a Pneumatology of religious experience," Buckley writes, "Christianity entered into the defense of the Christian god without appeal to anything Christian."[42] It ended up providing the materials for the theism which was so easily and decisively trumped by the atheisms that swept Europe in the eighteenth and nineteenth centuries.

Of course, this theism is equally contested by the authors we have looked at here. They assert, correctly enough, that it is inconsistent with persons' religious experience, and press for a post-Vatican II (for the Catholics; post-Shoah for Matt) and post-Einsteinian settlement that will overcome modernity's panoply of dualisms. At first blush there is much to recommend a "turn to spirituality" as a way of forging a post-Einsteinian settlement. Its hallmark, after all, is precisely an appeal to religious experience, to "spirituality." But on closer examination one wonders if this turn, or at least the way that it is executed in these texts, is really all that new. There are striking and troubling parallels between this new way of crossing the border between science and religion and the older Newtonian settlement that Buckley has analyzed. Consider the similarities in the way that our authors talk about spirituality and the way that the eighteenth century described the "religion of reason." As we have seen, for our authors spirituality is in essence common to all of humanity, and is contrasted (frequently negatively) with religions—just as the religion of reason or natural religion were counterposed to positive religion two centuries ago.[43] Second, while the content of the Enlightenment's religion of reason was to be established in part by consensus among positive religions, a crucial adjudicating factor for what would or would not be included was the new science. So too, spirituality, as our authors use it, is universal, has one essence, and is warranted by the fact that it "resonates with" or even is supported by, modern science.

As with the earlier period, there is a certain millennial enthusiasm in these books. For all of their criticism of the Enlightenment, they are very much its children, with their confidence in the resources of the human spirit to ascend to previously unscaled heights of scientific-mystical awareness.[44] It will be a new age, which will be post-denominational (Fox), or even post-religious (O'Murchu), but *not* post-spiritual. Of course, an important modification is that there is an apocalyptic edge in the contemporary literature that was not present earlier, but common to both is the sense that traditional "religion" is in some ways outdated, to be transcended by a new spirituality which is coming in with the imminent *novum*, be that *novum* apotheosis or catastrophe—or both together![45]

Continental philosophers, from Spinoza to Hegel, would be right at home with much of this genre. Fritjof Capra is willing to use "God" only in the sense of Spinoza's *Deus sive nature*, or *natura naturans*. While his interlocutors, Steindl-Rast and Matus, are aware of the problems this poses for the concept of a personal, loving God, they propose instead the metaphor of God as "horizon," which does not seem much better.[46] Concluding a chapter in which he argues that "the ego is a marvelous fiction and a necessary illusion,"[47] Matt resurrects Hegel's *Geist*:

> Yet God—the Self behind all selves—is not a passive object of our budding spiritual awareness. By evolving through space-time, by organizing Itself into the complex variety of existence, God grows and learns endlessly, discovering

awareness through each of us—God's countless, inimitable selves.[48]

This brings us to another common denominator: the marginalization of doctrine and explicit theological reflection. Doctrines, and their theological elaboration and defense, must follow the cues of this new "natural religion." As with the eighteenth century, doctrines of original sin and of grace are not well developed, or even flatly rejected. Most fatally, Christology is underdeveloped, particularly one that is sensitive to the historical Jesus.[49] Fox makes no bones about his preference for a "cosmic Christ" which verges on a gnostic Christ.[50] Steindl-Rast and Matus are most consistent in their attempt to stay connected with Jesus of Nazareth, but one cannot but be struck by how quickly they move from the person and actions of Jesus of Nazareth to his "mystical awareness," which is, "the experience of limitless belonging."[51] There is a troubling abstractness in this treatment, and a tendency (like the eighteenth century's) to see Jesus as a great teacher or moral exemplar, but not as the unique and uniquely authoritative revelation of who God is.[52]

The most striking feature of these works is the near abandonment of a personal God, or even of the word "God" in general. Matt has another reason for this, as we saw earlier: "[A]fter Auschwitz, how can we speak of a caring, compassionate, caring God?"[53] He argues that the insights of modern cosmology conspire with the negative force of the Holocaust, as well as with questions raised by feminism, to almost completely discredit the traditional image of God.[54] While he contends that we need to hold together both personal and impersonal images and concepts of God, it becomes more and more clear that the former is subservient to the latter. His final position is that the our awareness of our individuality and the construct of a personal God are sustained by "an ancient, secret covenant, sharing a pact of preservation, conspiring together against a oneness that would overwhelm their separateness."[55] Drawing on

Kabbalah he asserts that the human need for a personal God is fulfilled by the "meditative tools" of the ten *Sefirot*, but the more primordial, more "really God" is *Ein Sof*, the God beyond God.[56] The latter phrase will no doubt remind Christians of Meister Eckhart, and not surprisingly we find this kind of language throughout Fox's dialogues with Sheldrake.[57]

Steindl-Rast and Matus are aware that what is at stake is Trinitarian theology, but they never shake Capra from his Spinozistic notion of God: God is a name for the organizational principles of the universe that govern its self-organizing and self-creating activity: *natura naturans*. God "transcends" the universe only insofar as these organizational principles and processes are not reducible to any set of entities in the universe (even the set of all entities). God certainly does *not* transcend as a personal agent. Capra's two Christian interlocutors try to defend a Trinitarian image of God and a notion of God's personhood in which personhood is defined by relationality, but ultimately their conversation ends in a stalemate, and it is clear that Capra believes that his preference for a non-personal God, for the Buddhist *shunyata*, is the option supported by modern science.

O'Murchu is not at all hesitant to take up Capra's approach as the only one consistent with modern science, using words which simply repeat Laplace's claim that a personal God is an unnecessary hypothesis, both for the new science and the "quantum theology" that takes that science seriously:

> In the quantum view, the reality of our world does not need an external supernatural raison d'être or explanation to uncover what is really real. No, the ultimate rationale is within the creative, evolving process itself.[58]

This is simply an updated version of the "dynamic matter" of Diderot and D'Holbach, by which they rendered the God of Jesus, or of Torah, superfluous.[59] For O'Murchu, this conclusion from modern science is one that human beings have known all along, not through religion, of course, but through spirituality. Here we have another striking parallel with the early Newtonian settlement. The "personality" of the earlier god was defined in terms of abstract qualities of power and autonomy; the "personality" (so far as it is admitted at all) of the new god is defined by an equally abstract "relationality." This is where (for the Christians) the absence of a focus on Jesus of Nazareth, and the absence of spiritualities (like Ignatius') that center on the person revealed therein, result in dangerous abstractness.[60]

Not all of our authors follow all of these moves with equal force. O'Murchu is most radical (to the point of incoherence) and Steindl-Rast and Matt most sensitive to religious particularity and theological nuance. But all of these texts show these tendencies, and the structural similarities are strong enough to make one wonder whether or not, once again, this border-crossing is attempting to render credible in a scientific world the God of Jesus, or of Torah, without appeal to anything specifically Christian or Jewish. To be sure, there is one feature that separates this literature from the debates of the seventeenth and eighteenth centuries: the warrants of individual experience of the divine (spiritual or mystical experience) are now front and center, but if the integrity of the tradition which defines the God who is the *telos* of that experience is to be preserved, then theological reflection is crucial.

For all of their desire to "transcend" the Enlightenment and the dualisms allegedly perpetrated by its arch-villain, Descartes, these authors often end up giving us the mirror image of the settlement between science and religion of the eighteenth century. For, as Buckley notes, what was missing in the earlier period was not just the appeal to persons' experience of the divine, but also the theological articulation of that experience within the social-historical context of the Christian tradition, by means of a thorough-going

Christology and pneumatology of religious experience.[61] To use von Hügel's well-known triad, the earlier settlement focused on the intellectual element (as defined by the science of the day) to the exclusion of the mystical-volitional element and the historical-institutional elements of religion. But this new settlement does not restore the integral unity-in-difference of the three elements, but rather wrenches the mystical-volitional element free of the other two. Will this settlement fare any better? I suspect not. Spirituality alone is not up to the task of providing the materials for articulating the understanding and experience of the God of Jesus within the horizons being opened up by modern science. Indeed, just as the theism of the Newtonian settlement helped to generate the atheism of the eighteenth century, it seems likely that the pantheism of the post-Einsteinian settlement is feeding the vehement atheism of Neo-Darwinians like Daniel Dennett and Jacques Monod.

Conclusions

I have argued here that while the parallels and resonances between many statements made in mystical and spiritual traditions and those emerging from the "new science" (particularly from their populizers) are intriguing and provocative, they cannot be successfully mined without a great deal more hard work in the intellectual "second-order" disciplines proper to both: the history and philosophy of science on the one hand, and theology on the other. The meanings of controversial or paradoxical claims in science and in spirituality need to be resolved within those disciplines rather than prematurely decided on the basis of correlations across the border between them. Those correlations may certainly be weighed, but they must not be allowed to foreclose the conversation within the respective communities (scientific, academic, religious). I am not convinced, for instance, that the results of the new physics compel us toward the sort of impersonal "God beyond God" that many of these authors argue is the "god" experienced in the world's spiritualities.[62] On theological grounds I find it difficult to see how a Christian understanding of God, uniquely and irrevocably given to us in a *person*, Jesus of Nazareth, can make that sort of move without very careful checks and balances within Christology, pneumatology, and Trinitarian theology.[63]

I have also criticized the narrow spectrum of traditions within spirituality and mysticism which has been chosen to make the border-crossing between religion and science. Particularly striking by their absence are those spiritualities belonging to that vital and important genus that arose in the Middle Ages, and which Ewert Cousins has named "mysticisms of the historical event."[64] Including figures like Francis of Assisi—and not just the Francis of the Canticle to Brother Sun but the Francis of radical imitation of the historical Jesus—Bonaventure, and even Ignatius of Loyola, this mysticism has been an important part of the Christian landscape of the past millennium, a crucial counterweight to the more ahistorical and apolitical apophatic mystical traditions. To leave these and other spiritualities out of the picture is a judgment that must be made on grounds other than the relative paucity in them of statements that easily resonate with modern science.

For all of this, however, I would close by repeating the positive comments with which I began. In fairness, it should be noted too that these authors concede that they are just beginning to explore this border-crossing. Furthermore, the dialogue form of some of the books does not lend itself well to careful theological exploration. In any event, this genre has clearly caught the imaginations of many people in the industrialized world, and its potential contributions to a renewed sense of the sacredness of nature should not be underestimated. My primary concern is that the turn to spirituality, here as in other arenas of modern religious life, not end up being a turn away from difficult but crucial theological work.

And what is this work? Gustavo Gutiérrez, a theologian who has given a great deal of thought to the relationship between spirituality and theology, identifies three tasks for theology when it reflects on a spirituality.[65] First, theology must seek to root a given spirituality deeply in the rich soil of Scripture; second it must try to relate it to other spiritualities which are different ways of journeying toward the Father in the Spirit of Jesus; and finally, it must show the social-political implications of a spirituality within a given society. Our authors make a good start on the third task, but not the other two. For Christian theology, the touchstone must continue to be the God revealed in Jesus, the Jesus who is present to us in the Scripture and in the power of the Spirit.[66] Other spiritualities besides the apophatic mystical traditions must be brought into the conversation—particularly those that focus on the historical reality of Jesus of Nazareth, and the historical reality of sin and evil. We must strive to give *thick descriptions* of spiritualities, in terms of their cultural and historical contexts, and in terms of the ways they draw from the deep wells of Scripture and tradition. This kind of work, along with analogous tasks in the history and philosophy of science concerning the *new science*, is absolutely crucial if this new border-crossing does not end up leading once again to the claim concerning the God of Abraham and Sarah, of Moses, and of Jesus of Nazareth, that *we have no need of that hypothesis.*

Notes

1. For a good survey of this process in all its complexity, see John Hedley Brooke, *Science and Religion: Some Historical Perspectives* (Cambridge: Cambridge University Press, 1991).

2. Fritjof Capra, *The Tao of Physics: An Exploration of the Parallels Between Modern Physics and Eastern Mysticism* (Berkeley, CA: Shambhala Publications, 1975).

3. Matthew Fox and Rupert Sheldrake, *Natural Grace: Dialogues on Creation, Darkness and the Soul in Spirituality and Science* (New York:

Doubleday, 1996); Fritjof Capra and David Steindl-Rast, with Thomas Matus, *Belonging to the Universe: Explorations on the Frontiers of Science and Spirituality* (San Francisco: HarperSanFrancisco, 1991); Diarmuid O'Murchu, *Quantum Theology: Spiritual Implications of the New Physics* (New York: Crossroad, 1997); Daniel Matt, *God and the Big Bang: Discovering the Harmony Between Science and Spirituality* (Woodstock, VT: Jewish Lights, 1996).

4. This paper relies on Buckley's work for its understanding of the "Newtonian settlement" between science and religion: *At the Origins of Modern Atheism* (New Haven: Yale University Press, 1987). A summary of the argument may be found in an article by the same author: "The Newtonian Settlement and the Origins of Atheism," in *Physics, Philosophy, and Theology: A Common Quest for Understanding*, eds. Robert J. Russell, William R. Stoeger, S.J., and George V. Coyne, S.J. (Vatican City State: Vatican Observatory, 1988), 81-102.

5. This is not the place for a discussion of the problems involved in defining spirituality, although, as we shall see, these problems do in fact arise in the genre under consideration here. For a broader discussion of the difficulties, as well as an elaboration and defense of the implicit definition offered here, see the first chapter of my book on Johann Baptist Metz: J. Matthew Ashley, *Interruptions: Mysticism, Politics and Theology in the Work of Johann Baptist Metz* (Notre Dame, IN: University of Notre Dame Press, 1998).

6. See Stephen Toulmin, "The Historicization of Natural Science: Its Implications for Theology," in *Paradigm Change in Theology*, ed. Hans Küng and David Tracy (New York: Crossroad, 1981), 233-241.

7. One of the most fascinating, if also ambiguous, features of the contemporary religious scene in the United States is that many persons now articulate the latter influence under the rubric of spirituality. How many times have we heard the following: "I'm not really a religious person, but I am deeply spiritual"? For some brief but provocative reflections by a sociologist, see Meredith B. McGuire, "Mapping American Spirituality: A Sociological Perspective," *Christian Spirituality Bulletin* 5/1 (Spring, 1997): 1-8.

8. Capra and Steindl-Rast, 3-5, 70-77, 83-106, 140.

9. Ibid., 140.

10. Ibid., viii, 14-16. The echoes of Romantic Idealism in general and of Schleiermacher in particular, sound out loud and clear. Steindl-Rast even defines God as "the reference point of our ultimate belonging" (27, cf. 16).

11. Ibid., 169f.

12. O'Murchu, 178-181. This is his own response to the problem of evil and suffering, to which I will return below.

13. Fox and Sheldrake, 116f.

14. Matt, 35-42.

15. Fox and Sheldrake, 27, 112f.

16. O'Murchu, 12; 209, n. 3.

17. Ibid., 13.

18. Fox & Sheldrake, ix.

19. Capra and Steindl-Rast, 12.

20. Ibid. For Steindl-Rast both religion and spirituality are manifestations of Religion, or the religious, which is characterized by a "peak experience" of ultimate belonging, or an insight into the ultimate meaningfulness of all that is (13f.). Spirituality arises when this insight is acted out in everyday life, religion ("small r") is its institutionalization. He refers to Raimundo Pannikar, for whom the distinction between Religion and religion parallels a similar distinction between Language and language. In both cases the former is an abstraction which only exists in the concrete in the latter. There is no such thing as "Religion," but only the concrete religions. The same distinction should, however, be made (but is not) when it comes to spirituality. Further, the question of how one gives content to the abstract noun, and how one moves back and forth between the abstract and the concrete, is left untreated. The whole discussion of the relationship between religion and spirituality in *Belonging to the Universe*, while potentially the most nuanced of the four books, is finally unclear, in part because of the dialogue form of the book. The differences in usage between the different interlocutors are never finally resolved.

21. O'Murchu, 11-12.

22. Ibid., 12; see, 42.

23. See, for instance, Steindl-Rast's list of mystics: Meister Eckhart, Jakob Böhme, Julian of Norwich, and John of the Cross (Capra and Steindl-Rast, 48). In Matus' delineation of Church Fathers who can be called mystics we find such fathers of Christian Neoplatonism as Origen, Gregory of Nyssa and Gregory Nazianzen, Ambrose, Augustine, and Gregory the Great (47). *The* mystic for Fox is Meister Eckhart, although Hildegard of Bingen, Mechthild of Magdeburg, and Teresa of Avila receive some mention. Matt's descriptions of Kabbalah are, understandably, strikingly Neoplatonic.

24. Fox and Sheldrake, 4.

25. Ibid., 27, 112f.

26. Fox and Sheldrake, 50. Elsewhere Fox appeals to the pedagogical value of suffering (48, 115). O'Murchu makes the same point even more radically (and to this reader, obscenely), this time not from Eucharistic theology but from soteriology. Contemplating the end of our species due to environmental ravages or nuclear or chemical holocaust, O'Murchu attempts to put it in a larger evolutionary context by connecting evolutionary cycles of mass extinction and subsequent proliferations of new species, with Jesus' death and resurrection. He warns against failing "to appreciate the larger more wholistic interpretation that this is one of nature's strange and ingenious ways of withholding her creative energy for a new outburst of evolutionary life. Species emerge and become extinct, land masses surface and become submerged, cultures unfold and decline again, but the evolutionary story of creation moves unceasingly on its infinite trajectory" (180). This is the lesson of Calvary. In this breathtaking ontologizing-away of evil, Hegel's slaughter-bench of history has been reforged on a cosmic scale as the slaughter-bench of evolution. For a trenchant critique of this enthronement evolution as modernity's master-myth, see J.B. Metz, "Time without Finale: The Background to the Debate on 'Resurrection or Reincarnation,'" in Johann Baptist Metz and Jürgen Moltmann, *Faith and the Future: Essays on Theology, Solidarity, and Modernity* (Maryknoll, NY: Orbis Books, 1995), 79-86.

27. On the Kingdom of God see Capra and Steindl-Rast, *inter alia*, 56-60, 78f. On liberation theology, see 181-194.

28. See Gustavo Gutiérrez, *We Drink from Our Own Wells: The Spiritual Journey of a People*, trans. Matthew J. O'Connell, intro. Henri Nouwen (Maryknoll, NY: Orbis Books, 1984), 83-89, 129-131.

29. Matt, 51, 80-82, 141-143.

30. Ibid., 145-48.

31. See, *inter alia*, 57, 117-125.

32. Ibid. 142f.

33. See Ignacio Ellacuría, "Las Iglesias latinoamericanas interpelan a la Iglesia de España," *Sal Terrae* 826 (1982): 230, cited in Jon Sobrino, *Jesus the Liberator: A Historical-Theological Reading of Jesus of Nazareth* (Maryknoll, NY: Orbis Books, 1993), 262f. This is a paraphrase of the concluding colloquy of the meditation on sin in Ignatius of Loyola's *Spiritual Exercises* (n. 53).

34. This is the tack taken by Gustavo Gutiérrez's response to the terrible suffering of Latin America's peoples in *On Job: God-talk and the Suffering of the Innocent*, trans. Matthew J. O'Connell (Maryknoll, NY: Orbis Books, 1987). Or see J.B. Metz's parallel attempt to delineate a

mysticism grounded in an awareness of the history of suffering of the world's victims. See, for instance, "Suffering unto God," trans. J. Matthew Ashley, in *Critical Inquiry,* 20/4 (Summer, 1994): 611-622.

35. As a start, one could consider the three fundamental presuppositions of any spirituality (note, *not* the essence of all spiritualities) given by Jon Sobrino, and developed from the perspective of liberation theology: honesty about the real, fidelity to the real, and willingness to swept along by the "more" of reality. Here "reality" includes the facticity of the crucifixion of the world and its peoples. The presuppositions open up into the more concrete spiritualities: including Christian ones. These presuppositions are, in my view, more helpful than the more abstract "belonging to the universe," in part because they have a less impersonal cast (honesty and fidelity are more concretely personal categories) and because they have more room for the negative experience of evil in reality. See Jon Sobrino, "Presuppositions and Foundations of Spirituality," in *Spirituality of Liberation: Toward Political Holiness*, trans. Robert Barr (Maryknoll, NY: Orbis Books, 1988), 13-22.

36. See, for example, Matt, 40f.

37. This problem was noted twenty years ago by Sal Restivo, "Parallels and Paradoxes in Modern Physics and Eastern Mysticism," *Social Studies of Science*, vol. 8 (1978):143-181, esp. 151-55. Unfortunately the critique is just as valid today as it was twenty years ago.

38. For a careful analysis of this issue, and a strong argument for interpreting the radical statements in the vernacular sermons within the context of the Latin scholastic works, see Bernard McGinn, "The God Beyond God: Theology and Mysticism in the Thought of Meister Eckhart," *Journal of Religion* 60 (1981):1-19.

39. For a good treatment of the use of complementary models in science and religion see Ian Barbour, *Myths, Models and Paradigms: A Comparative Study in Science and Religion* (San Francisco: Harper & Row, 1974), 71-91. Barbour warns against overextending the use of complementary models (like the famous wave/particle duality with light).

40. See Pierre Hadot *Philosophy as a Way of Life: Spiritual Exercises from Socrates to Foucault*, ed. with intro. Arnold Davidson, trans. Michael Chase (Chicago: University of Chicago Press, 1995); Denys Turner, *The Darkness of God: Negativity in Christian Mysticism* (Cambridge: Cambridge University Press, 1995).

41. The nexus of the difficulties lies in this word, "experience," one of the most notoriously difficult words to define precisely, in large measure because it is such a crucial word for modernity and its intellectual and cultural project. Bernard McGinn has argued cogently that it has

ceased to be a fruitful category in the study of mysticism, in *The Foundations of Mysticism*, vol. 1 of *The Presence of God: A History of Western Christian Mysticism* (New York: Crossroad, 1992), xvii-xvxx, 314- 326. For a brief but penetrating overview of the word's uses and ambiguities in theology, see George Schner, "The Appeal to Experience," *Theological Studies* 53 (1992): 40-59.

42. *At the Origins of Modern Atheism*, 67.

43. For example, immediately after asserting that denominations are passé, Fox states that "[n]ow more than ever we have to strip down religions to their essence, which is not religion but spirituality" (Fox and Sheldrake, 6).

44. Consider this statement of O'Murchu's: "We are fast approaching the moment when information will be stored, not in any kind of visible, tangible object, but in the realm of consciousness itself . . . As a human species we are much closer than we realize to the point wherein everything we think will *automatically* happen, and every problem we put into words will *automatically* be solved. An exciting but chilling prospect," 155. Our authors often use a distinction that is quite similar to the late eighteenth-century distinction between *Verstand* and *Vernunft*: one being the way science has perceived the world, the other a mystical-intuitive grasp of the ultimate unity behind the appearances, a new way of seeing the world which is allegedly emerging out of the new synthesis of science and spirituality. See, for instance, Capra and Steindl-Rast, 73-77.

45. Fox states that "it is creation's travail and pain, Gaia being crucified, that is the apocalyptic moment which calls us into new forms of spiritual expression, some of which are going to be ancient and some of which are going to be created by our generation out of necessity" (Fox and Sheldrake, 6).

46. See Capra and Steindl-Rast, 97-106.

47. Matt, 66.

48. Ibid., 67.

49. Buckley notes the underdeveloped character of Christology in the arguments against atheism of early modernity, *At the Origins*, 33.

50. Fox and Sheldrake, 32f. To be sure, he asserts that he is offering a "corrective" to traditional and exclusivist focuses on the historical Jesus, but the rest of his remarks make it clear that his is not a corrective but an opposing perspective.

51. Capra and Steindl-Rast, 56f.

52. This is due in part to the authors' laudable commitment to building

bridges to other traditions. It is important, however, that the difficult theological issues involved in ecumenical dialogue not be avoided by moving too quickly into the dialogue between science and religion. Issues proper to each dialogue need to be worked out with at least some degree of independence.

53. Matt, 30.

54. Ibid., 124f. In a sense, Matt's book is an attempt to retrieve Jewish wisdom and practice, Torah and Halakhah, given the demise of a personal God: "If the traditional image of God is basically flawed, how can I pray with the same old words? If God is the energy of the universe, manifesting here and there as matter, what kind of prayer is appropriate or possible?" (125, see 30).

55. Ibid., 65.

56. Ibid., 53-57.

57. See, for instance, Fox and Sheldrake, 44f., 138-160. Some of the most problematic parallels between "science" and "mysticism" are raised in this section: for instance, between the notion of "dark matter" in cosmology or the "darkness" that results in interference patterns between two light waves, on the one hand, and the darkness of God on the other. Fox makes a great deal of the "resonances" (138), but there seem to be no parameters for controlling what these resonances mean outside of Fox's own imagination.

58. O'Murchu, 51. Elsewhere he speaks about "Universal Mind" (105) or "supernatural life force" (107), but then tells us that "[q]uantum theology is not particularly concerned about the nature of God" (107). "The evolutionary/creative process [God?] is a subject for contemplation and mystical comprehension rather than for theological discourse or scientific analysis" (ibid.). Speaking of meditation he tells that it "is a type of tuning-up process, facilitating communication between my being and the 'being' of life in the world around me (God, if you wish)," 157.

59. See Buckley, *At the Origins*, 222-235, 300-301; "The Newtonian Settlement," 96-97.

60. For a telling critique from the perspective of liberation theology of such abstractness, see Jon Sobrino, *Jesus the Liberator*, 14-17, 47-63.

61. *At the Origins*, 66f.

62. For examples of a defense of a more traditional understanding of a provident God within the horizons of modern physics, see Ernan McMullin, "Evolutionary Contingency and Cosmic Purpose," in *Finding God in All Things: Essays in Honor of Michael J. Buckley, S.J.*, eds.

Michael J. Himes and Stephen J. Pope (New York: Crossroad, 1996), 140-162; and Elizabeth Johnson, "Does God Play Dice? Divine Providence and Chance," *Theological Studies* 57/1 (March, 1996): 3-18. My criticism of the particular phrase "God beyond God" should not be interpreted as a rejection of Meister Eckhart's usage of this, perhaps one of his most (in)famous phrases. On the contrary, my hunch is that our understanding of how Eckhart used and intended this kind of language about God (*theology*, in its etymological sense) is distorted when we interpret it as a "solution" to the problem of talking about God in our post-Einsteinian age, rather than as a solution to intellectual and pastoral challenges that the Meister faced, both in Paris and in the Rhineland.

63. Furthermore, while I do not have the expertise to enter that debate, it seems to me that, *mutatis mutandis*, the same must be said of the Jewish tradition, as Buckley notes in *At the Origins*, 362.

64. See Ewert Cousins, "Francis of Assisi: Christian Mysticism at the Crossroads," in *Mysticism and Religious Traditions*, ed. Steven Katz (New York: Oxford University Press, 1983).

65. *We Drink from Our Own Wells*, 52f.

66. This point is made quite well by David Toolan in his reflections on spirituality and science. After describing some of the results of the new science he then goes on to detail the difference these should make for our prayer and our faith: "Let me spell this out—speaking out of faith. News from the Hubble Space Telescope or from a nuclear accelerator will not give you the interpretation that follows. Here, while building on the preceding analysis, I follow the news I get from the Hebrew and Christian Scriptures and from the depth probe of my soul's experience—which in the final analysis reaches farther than scientific apparatus into the secret design of things," in "Praying in a Post-Einsteinian Universe," *Cross Currents* (Winter 1996/97): 458.

Crossing Boundaries and Team Teaching

Francis J. Buckley
Professor of Systematic and Pastoral Theology
University of San Francisco

Team teaching attempts to balance the need for teachers and students to specialize with the opportunity to broaden horizons. Teachers are expected to do research and publication in depth to achieve mastery within a field. Usually this demands narrowing focus onto an area which can be thoroughly understood. Students, too, attempt to understand a whole by breaking it down into parts.

Overemphasis on analysis of smaller and smaller units of reality endangers both teachers and students. Researchers may lose sight of important implications and applications of their work. One-sided approaches give skewed results. The solution: synthesis, putting the pieces back together again, imaginatively asking new questions and discovering new relationships. Students are alerted to the complexity of real-life situations and problems.

How is this done? According to Ira J. Singer, "Two or more teachers, with or without teacher aides, cooperatively plan, instruct and evaluate one or more class groups in an appropriate instructional space and given length of time, so as to take advantage of the special competencies of the team members."[1]

A Single-Discipline Team Teaching

A *single-discipline team* consists of teachers from the same

109

department teaching a common set of students. Team members may or may not have the same specialty within the field, but usually bring different research interests.

Team teaching within a department is a relatively simple way to get experience with the dynamics of a team, since many department members already know and trust one another and may be curious how others approach the material. There is less fear of public humiliation when the limits of their knowledge are revealed. In fact, they can rely on one another to keep the pace of class lively and to supplement data with stories. Just the variety of voices and personalities stimulates interest.

Team teaching within a discipline exposes a teacher's specific talents to twice as many students as in a conventional schedule. It permits a new teacher to work with a veteran in an in-service program. Team members can practice continuous curriculum planning and revision, based on student needs as well as their own assets and interests. They may bring in community resource specialists or use films, tapes, closed-circuit television, self-instruction programs, and other technological learning tools.

The department usually takes overall responsibility for the course objectives—cognitive, behavioral, and affective. These include knowledge of the basic facts together with in-depth familiarity or even mastery of certain areas; skills of analysis, synthesis, and critical judgment; and certain attitudes and values characteristic of the field.

Department members together set the course goals and content, select common materials such as texts and films, and develop tests and final examinations to be given to all students. Within these parameters team members set the sequence of topics and supplemental materials. They also give their own interpretations of the materials and use their own teaching styles. The greater the agreement on common objectives and interests, the more likely that teaching will be interdependent and coordinated.

This approach is comparatively easy to administer and find rooms for, especially if several different teams take turns using the large classrooms.

Teaching periods could be scheduled side by side or consecutively. For example, teachers of two similar classes might team up during the same or adjacent periods so that the teachers can focus on that phase of the course which each can best handle. Sometimes students can meet all together, sometimes in small groups supervised by individual teachers or teaching assistants; or they can work singly or together on projects in the library, laboratory, or fieldwork.

Where all students belong to the same department, class discussions should be able to focus more often on issues of common interest. Students from the same department will also be more likely to share other classes, know one another, and interact more frequently and informally outside the common class. Students from the same department feel freer to bring up what they consider to be conflicts between their own discipline and another, without worrying whether they are wasting the time of students from other departments.

Interdisciplinary Team Teaching

The *interdisciplinary team* has teachers from different departments using a common block of time to instruct a common set of students, often within the general education core curriculum. Within the set time frame classes can be broken into large or small groups of varying sizes, down to individual study. Teachers can plan how to divide the block into daily, weekly, or monthly chunks. They may lecture, lead discussion, field questions, or supervise research or tutorials. Joint planning and evaluation can be built into the schedule.

After a long period of ever-narrowing specialization, university faculty have expressed interest in problems which range across subject-area and even college lines. Nursing professors, for example, are understandably interested in health sciences, but also in psychology, sociology, politics, history, business, law, and ethics. All of these fields have immediate impact on the availability and quality of nursing care.

Another example. Broadening appreciation of a biblical text can come through study of the various meanings of the words used in their original language; of the meanings of those words at different historical epochs; of their use in different situations according to sex, social standing, and cultural assumptions; of citations of the text by other biblical authors; of literary use of the text in translations by writers of other cultures; of interpretations of the text by commentators of different theological traditions over the centuries; of the different purposes and uses of language in general. Philology, history, sociology, psychology, anthropology, literature, communication arts all provide useful insights into what the text meant for its original audience—and for other audiences since. Exclusive use of only one approach impoverishes scholarship—and religion.

A great advantage of interdisciplinary team teaching is demonstrating the relationships between the subject areas studied, opening both teachers and students to new points of view, new questions, and new discoveries. One of the exciting offshoots is joint research projects about problems which surface in class. By suggesting topics, students have direct input in shaping their curriculum. These projects can vary in length and depth from assignments to two or more students for a class presentation or paper to long-term research jointly done by the faculty (and even students) and resulting in scholarly publications. Another benefit of such multifaceted problem-oriented teaching is that it connects learning with real life—which is messy, complex, with many viewpoints and alternative solutions. Prior learning is applied to new situations, reinforced, and stretched. Similarities and differences emerge. Skills develop. Interests grow.

Interdisciplinary team teaching also draws from a larger pool of expertise and teaching styles. Teachers teach one another, along with the students. Opportunities for growth abound. Teachers may develop new texts or videos. For example, the Open University in Britain has teams of teachers design video modules for use in class. Today teachers can be at different sites, linked by two-way video, videoconferencing, using satellites or the Internet. Distance learning certainly expands the potential mix of teachers and students. On the other hand, since several departments are involved, this requires more planning and coordination. More people will have to put in more time. More attention will have to be paid to the possibilities of personality clashes. Where conflict arises, this can be creative. It can also be destructive. Techniques of conflict resolution must be learned.

Exploration and resolution of false conflicts between disciplines should significantly improve students' attitudes toward them. Such conflicts now often go undiscussed in many classes and breed doubts. Classes in which the content is interdisciplinary and related to the student's major will have a greater impact. Such a class builds on already existing interests and deliberately tries to integrate the subject with life. Classes which are team-taught will have even more impact, and the effect will be still higher if the team is interdisciplinary with one of the members related to the students' major. Team-teaching usually involves a variety of approaches to a subject area, thus stimulating interest. Different role-models are offered for imitation which complement one another and appeal to different types of students. Several teachers who share the same attitudes and values, critically arrived at, heighten the plausible importance of those values.

Teaching a Capstone Course

A *capstone course*, drawing together insights and skills derived from the entire core curriculum or even the whole four-year course of study, is interdisciplinary by its very nature. Its position in the curriculum highlights the importance given to it by the university. It is meant to be more important than any other single course. But its time restraints make it less influential than the departmental major cluster of courses or even a set of interdisciplinary courses built into the core curriculum—all of which gradually build mindsets, develop skills, and reinforce values over more than one semester.[2]

A School-Within-A-School Team Teaching
A *school-within-a-school team* has teachers from different disciplines instructing a common set of students over an extended period of time, usually two to four years. This has the advantages of interdisciplinary teams, but also builds an *esprit de corps* among the students. They often eat, play, and pray together as well as study and attend class. Sometimes students and teachers live and have offices in the same halls. Teachers can get to know the students better by observing them in a variety of settings over an extended period of time. Teams of students cutting across disciplines can engage in supervised long-term research projects, growing in both analysis and synthesis skills. Veteran students can become teaching assistants, deepening the quality of their own learning.[3]

Apart from providing information, the impact of such a college within a college on students' attitudes and values varies according to several factors:

1. The frequency of contact with another person or group sharing the same interests and goals.

2. The more areas of shared activity (e.g. living, studying, working, playing, eating, social service; participation in setting and enforcing policy, etc.)

3. The smaller the group sharing the same interests and goals. Small groups encourage all to participate and interact in formal and informal ways, thus exposing members to more challenges to rethink attitudes and values.

4. The more isolated the group, whether physically (dormitories, rural setting) or culturally (self-consciously held values perceived as making the group different from a larger society). This is a ghetto effect, "we-they."

5. The more importance assigned by the group to the values shared.

6. The more cooperation rather than competition within the group (e.g., joint projects; student-to-student teaching or tutoring; involvement in curriculum or course planning and design).

7. The more peer-group and faculty agree on the importance of values and interact with one another frequently, intimately, and in various ways: lounges, libraries; joint committees; colloquia followed by lunch or a visit to the teacher's home; research tutorials where faculty and students learn together.

8. The more integration with life in a program (e.g., integrating work, study, community life, personal experience, and interdisciplinary courses) so long as the project is real, useful, and able to be done by students.

9. The more individual faculty have internalized the goals of the department and/or university.

10. The better the faculty balance. Junior faculty are often more attractive and teach lower division or undergraduate courses; senior faculty provide identification with prestigious models, are more concerned about basic problems of the field and gathering disciples, and lead the students to question values, lifestyle, and job. They also show how to do so rationally and to think before acting.

11. The more teaching, testing, and grading focus on the practice and skills of analysis, synthesis, and critical judgment through experience, discussion, and critical essays, rather than memorizing information. The more active the student, the more learning occurs.

12. The overall climate of a university has more impact than any other departmental subgroup or even the personality of the student.[4] Breaking out of the taken-for-granted single-subject, single-course, single-teacher pattern encourages other innovations and experiments. For example, students can be split along or across lines of major, sex, age, culture, or other interests, then recombined to stimulate reflection. Remedial programs and honors sections provide other attractive opportunities for use of teams to make available appropriate and effective curricula for students with special needs or interests. They can address different study skills and learning techniques. Again, class assignments can be rotated among different student teams to encourage student interaction, build community, and stimulate learning:

- Environmentalists prepare the room and chalkboard before and after class,
- Greeters welcome others graciously,
- Class mood can be briefly set by poetry or prose, music or song, art or film,
- The content of the previous class is covered in a brief report,
- A critique briefly assesses the process of the previous class—what happened, what worked or not and why,
- Connections are highlighted between subject areas,
- Applications to life are made.

Finally, team teaching can offset the danger of imperialistic colonization—imposing ideas, values, mindsets on minorities or less powerful ethnic groups. Teachers of different backgrounds can culturally enrich one another and students. Technology cuts across ethnic and geographical frontiers. It is intrinsically catholic, universal.[5]

Notes

1. Ira J. Singer, "What Team Teaching Really Is," in *Team Teaching: Bold New Venture*, ed., David W. Beggs III (Bloomington: Indiana University Press, 1964), 16-22. This book has several useful graphs and case studies.

2. Horatio M. LaFauci and Peyton E. Richter, *Team Teaching at the College Level* (New York: Pergamon, 1970), 51-52.

3. Singer, "What Team Teaching Really Is," Ibid.

4. For a fuller discussion of these factors, see Francis J. Buckley, "Improving College Students' Religious Attitudes and Values," *Lumen Vitae*, Vol. 31, n. 4 (1976): 455-462.

5. Excerpted with some modifications from, *Team Teaching* (Thousand Oaks, CA: Sage Publications, 1998).

Part II
THE CHURCH
AND BORDERS

Death and the "Hour of Triumph": Subversion within the Visions of Saturus and Polycarp

Zaida Maldonado Pérez
Doctoral Candidate in Historical Theology
St. Louis University

The term "vision" is a protean term that has been defined by psychology and religion in a myriad of ways. In religion it has been broadly defined as a visual imagery believed to be "supernatural in origin and revelatory in significance."[1] The notion of visions as a medium of divine communication that has revelatory significance for the Christian community, nevertheless, remains controversial within most contemporary religious circles. Reasons for this abound. The diagnostic value attributed to visions by psychologists and psychoanalysts in determining personality disorders, for instance, has directly or indirectly helped to fuel this controversy. Also, the connection of visions to ecstatic trances, especially characteristic of the so-called "Dark Ages" has undermined their validity meanwhile fostering their disrepute.

The result is that today many consider religious (i.e. Protestant and/or Roman Catholic) visionaries or seers a residual peculiarity of the western medieval past—anomalies that mark the periphery of modern, scientifically

121

enlightened thought. At the very least, they are looked upon as suspect. Rahner, for example, warns that "weakness of faith and difficulties with regard to faith, as well as the misery of life can drive people to excessive credulity where visions and prophecies are concerned."[2] Although he considers the history of Christianity unthinkable without prophetic and visionary elements,[3] he advises against those who would "strengthen their weakened faith in God by believing in visions, and 'then defend this substitute for faith with the violence of a shipwrecked man fighting for the last plank.'"[4]

This warning is not without merit. The experience of visions too often has been the catalyst for the splintering of religious communities by persons claiming to have had a personal revelation from God. Practices traditionally outside the realm of Christian teachings, such as polygamy, for instance, have been sanctioned through the claim to a divine vision. Even today's charismatic circles, where visions are neither uncommon nor infrequent, preach the New Testament injunction to "test the spirits"[5] and practice discernment. For this reason there are special "interpreters" who are often the pastor and/or an elder of the church.

Despite the negative connotations conjured up by the term "vision," Christian history attests that the notion of visions as a viable and authoritative medium for the revelation of God's will and purpose is, and has always been, a legacy of the life and ministry of the church.[6] Visions, for example, played a particularly important role in the religious life of the formative church of the first century.[7] In the book of Luke, Jesus himself is said to have had a vision wherein he "watched Satan fall from the sky like lightning" (Luke 10:17–18). Stephen, whom tradition calls the first Christian martyr, experiences a vision just before being stoned to death wherein he sees the crucified Christ (the "Son of Man") "standing at God's right hand" (Acts 7:56). The apostle Paul speaks of having experienced many visions and revelations. He especially mentions one vision that left an indelible mark upon his memory but for which he can find no human words.[8] And, we must not forget Peter's vision whose dramatic effects radically altered the course of his and the church's ministry to include even the "unclean" gentiles (Acts 10:9-16,28). The book of Revelation, whose author had been exiled to the island of Patmos because he "proclaimed God's word and bore witness to Jesus," contains yet the largest corpus of New Testament visions. Without question, the presence of visions within the Christian Scriptures underscores the importance of the role of visions within the daily life and ministry of formative Christianity.[9]

The emerging church of the third and fourth centuries continued to view visions as a divine medium of communication. However, visions were most common in situations of imminent martyrdom and the ascetical life.[10] This is likely in keeping with Acts 2:17 where the promise of the outpouring of the Holy Spirit for, among others, the experience of visions is prefaced by that sermon's reference to "the last days"—when the church would be persecuted for her faith.[11] The experience of increasing, and at times severe, persecution heavily influenced the church's developing emphasis on visions and martyrdom and the literature that arose in response. Among the literature that developed and circulated among the Christian communities of mid-second century on, are the famous *Acts of the Martyrs*[12] and the *passiones* (or *martyria*)—stories that narrate the last events, visions (if any), and sufferings of the martyrs.[13] These documents became popular Christian literature and were also incorporated in the liturgy of the church. In *The Acts of the Christian Martyrs*, Herbert Musurillo underscores the extent of the use and spread of the *passiones* in third- and fourth-century Christendom. He states: "The *passiones* arose in different communities in the third and early fourth centuries after Christ and soon spread beyond the confines of North Africa,

Spain, and Pannonia, and *became the common heritage of the entire Latin church.*"[14] In fact, the popularity of the *Acts of the Martyrs* (many of which contained *passiones*) reaches to such heights among the Christians that Augustine finds himself having to warn his flock against placing the *Acts* "on the same level of Scripture"![15]

One naturally wonders how the visions of the martyrs may have been interpreted by the seer/recorder or by the layperson hearing it for the first time at church. What kind of impact might these have had upon their worship, theology, and daily lives? While scholarly work on the *Acts of the Christian Martyrs* abounds, very little has been done concerning the significance of the role and content of the visions of the Christian martyrs. This lack of interest may be attributed to modern biases about visions and seers. Yet, the fact that the *passiones* come to us with these visions, that is, that they were not deleted from the martyrdom accounts, makes their importance evident. This and their widespread popularity among the laity also underscores the Academy's need to take them seriously. And so we must ask: Why were visions important? Why consider them at all? What, if anything, can they tell us about the Christianity of their times, the contexts and the protagonists? For instance, how might the visions of the martyrs of the third and early fourth centuries expand our knowledge and understanding of the emerging Christianity of those times?

Upon a close reading of the visions of the martyrs I was delightfully surprised to discover a metaphorical and symbolic undercurrent suffused with theological and sociocultural nuances that defy their particular historical-theological contexts. I refer to this undercurrent that defies prevailing norms as the subversive dimensions of the visions of the martyrs.

Although medical studies have categorically classified visions by their forms—normal dreams, vivid memories, vigorous imaginings, and so forth,[16] the early church did not concern itself with these distinctions; rather, it focused on the role and significance of the content of the visions for their daily lives. This essay takes as its starting point the early church's understanding of visions as divine revelation. It argues that the visions of the martyrs, when interpreted in relation to the visionary/recorder and their sociocultural political context, reveal a nuanced view of, for example, God, the world, power and powerlessness, death and life that at times subverts what may have been construed as normal or dominant by either church or the Greco-Roman society. It will also show that this nuanced view was very likely reflective of a grass-roots or popular theology not readily available to the modern reader through other early church literature.

On this basis, I propose the following considerations regarding the importance of the role and nature of visions as interpreted by the early church. These emerge from my own reading and understanding of the material. They include the following: First, the authority of visions is supported by the multiple attestations throughout the Christian Scriptures. Visions derived their authority from early Christianity's understanding that they were God-initiated acts over which authorities (church and otherwise) had no control. In addition, the authority of prophetic visions was enhanced through the people's own freedom and disposition to believe them. Second, the *content* of the visions served to affirm or counter dominant beliefs, paradigms, and structures. Third, the social, ecclesial status or gender of the person played no role in who might be chosen to receive a vision. Fourth, the transcendental truth(s) depicted by these visions acted as a transforming power throughout the life of the people of the early church. These presuppositions underlie and will support the development of the argument for the subversive dimension of visions.

For purposes of illustration, I have chosen to analyze visions from two popular works: the *Martyrdom of Polycarp* and the *Passion of Perpetua and Felícitas*. I do so from a historical-theological perspective, thus positing the history and emerging theologies of the times as the natural loci from which to begin to consider their meaning and contribution to present historical knowledge. It is only against this historical-theological curtain—and not through the lens of our own historical and theological advances—that the scandal of the subversive nuances can be fully appreciated.

Finally, this study is my own contribution to the task of reconstructing a history of a particular people whose existence, thoughts, ideas, and particularly their visions, would otherwise not have been recorded or possibly survived the test of time and orthodoxy had it not been for their role as martyrs.

The Vision of Saturus in the
Passion of Perpetua and Felícitas

"A number of young catechumens were arrested . . ."[17] Thus begins the account of the martyrdom of Perpetua, Felícitas, Saturus their teacher, and others, thought to have been compiled soon after their deaths in the year 203 C.E. On the eve of his martyrdom, Saturus had a vision. "We [he and Perpetua, a 22-year-old mother of an infant son] had died, he said, and had put off the flesh."[18] Then they were "carried towards the east by four angels."[19] Upon entering what he described to be a beautiful garden, they were paid homage by four angels "more splendid than the others"[20] who, judging by their excitement, were anxiously awaiting the martyrs' arrival. Saturus vividly goes on to describe their experience before the throne of God,[21] and the meeting of the elders who gave them the "kiss of peace" and bid them "Go and play."[22] As Saturus and Perpetua went before the gates they had an interesting encounter:

> Then we went out and before the gates we saw the bishop Optatus on the right and Aspasius the presbyter and teacher on the left, each of them far apart and in sorrow. They threw themselves at our feet and said: "Make peace between us. For

you have gone away and left us thus." And we said to them:
"Are you not our bishop, and are you not our presbyter?
How can you fall at our feet?"[23]

It turns out that the bishop and his presbyter had been
quarreling between themselves and were still in discord.
Their disagreement apparently accounts for their being outside or "before the gates" rather than inside the gates as
Perpetua and Saturus had been. Much to Saturus' amaze-
ment, both the bishop Optatus and the presbyter Aspasius
throw themselves at his and his catechumen's feet and plea
for their succor, for "it seemed that they [the angels] wanted
to close the gates."[24] Saturus' and Perpetua's questions "Are
you not our bishop, and are you not our presbyter? How can
you fall at our feet?," are revealing. They not only point to
the ecclesiastical codes that dictated the norm—bishops and
presbyters do not kneel before their parishioners and, much
less, ask for their mediation—they indicate that what has
happened is a complete reversal of those codes. Even more
striking is the fact that, according to the vision, this reversal
took place within the heavenly garden, thus setting the
anomaly within the context of divine approval.

The implications of this vision become clear when
explored against its particular historical-theological settings.
By the third century, the time of Saturus, and Perpetua's
martyrdom, there had already developed a gender-exclusive
ecclesiastical hierarchy of which the bishop was the apex,
followed by the presbyter and deacons. Finally, comprising
the floor of the pyramid, were the catechumens and the hear-
ers. In his *Letter to the Magnesians* (c. 107) Ignatius, bishop of
Antioch in Syria, assumes this order:

> Let the bishop preside in God's place, and the presbyters take
> the place of the apostolic council, and let the deacons (my
> special favorites) be entrusted with the ministry of Jesus
> Christ who was with the Father from eternity and appeared
> at the end [of the world].[25]

Writing to the church at Ephesus, Ignatius also exhorted them to "regard the bishop as the Lord himself"[26] and to "heed the bishop and presbytery attentively."[27] Saturus' question to bishop Optatus and Aspasius the presbyter leads us to believe that Saturus may not have been a presbyter as has been previously assumed.[28] Herbert Musurillo, for instance, goes as far as saying that he was a "young catechumen."[29] Other scholars, however, refer to Saturus as a catechist or teacher.[30] Unfortunately, the textual evidence can be used to support either of the latter two conclusions.[31] Space limits me to conclude that the most that can be assumed regarding Saturus is that he was a layperson who was also possibly a catechist.[32] He was definitely not a presbyter. Further, Saturus' question to the presbyter Aspasius and bishop Optatus makes more sense within the context of a layperson. For Saturus, the higher ranking bishop and presbyter's act of humbling themselves before two 'little' ones is puzzling and alarming. (Thus he, with Perpetua,[33] exclaims, "Aren't you our father and you our priest? How then do you throw yourselves at our feet?"). In the vision of this simple teacher the ecclesiastical pyramid which, according to St. Ignatius reflected the celestial economy, is inverted. The earthly ecclesiastical order is subverted by the divine disorder where "the last shall be first" and "the humble shall sit with princesses."

The theological and ecclesial impact of this vision's subversive dimension is perhaps best illustrated by the controversy which arose after the Decian persecution fifty years later.[34] The Carthaginian confessors' act of restoring the lapsed to the communion of the church resonates with the vision's depiction of the inverted pyramid—where bishop and presbyter kneel at the feet of the two martyrs. Popular view held that a martyr's death held atoning virtue for others. In one of his many letters to the martyrs, Cyprian, the bishop of Carthage, affirmed this popular view. According to Cyprian the prayers of the martyrs were more efficacious than his own:

For since your voice [the martyr's] is clearly more efficacious
in petition and your prayers in afflictions more easily obtain
what they seek, pray and ask more eagerly, that the divine
grace may consummate the confession of all of us, that God
may also free us together with you undefiled and glorious
from the darkness and the snares of the world.[35]

In North Africa the "powers of forgiveness universally
ascribed to them [the martyrs], raised their status beyond
that of the clergy."[36] The following request from the confessor Celerinus to his fellow-confessor Lucianus regarding
absolution for two women who had committed the sin of
apostasy supports this claim:

I pray, my lord, and beseech you, through Our Lord Jesus
Christ, to inform and to ask your associates, your brethren,
my lords, that whoever of you shall first receive the crown,
grant forgiveness for their grave sin (of apostasy) to our sisters Numeria and Candida.[37]

According to Cyprian, however, only the bishop possessed the authority to reconcile an apostate to the church.
He tells the confessors and martyrs, "Let them (the priests)
reserve your petitions and desires for the *bishop* and await a
peaceful and suitable time for granting your requests."[38] For
Cyprian, the act of forgiving the lapsed outside of ecclesiastical authority was scandalous—it was a subversion of the
laws of God, an usurpation of the authority of the bishop
and, in the end, endangered the unity of the church. His
struggle to maintain and solidify, what was, in his view, the
"right order in the Church"[39] against the popular view that
elevated the status and authority of the martyrs above that
of the bishop is reflected in several of his Epistles:

The responsibility of our position and our fear of the Lord
compels us, most brave and most blessed martyrs to admon-
ish you by our letter that those by whom the faith of the Lord
is so devotedly kept, should likewise observe the law and

discipline of the Lord. For it is the duty of all of the soldiers of Christ to obey the commands of their supreme commander, then it becomes you still more to be obedient to His orders, you who have become an example to others, both of valor and of the fear of God.[40]

In his letter to a number of apostates who were seeking reconciliation with the church based on letters of recommendation written on their behalf by the martyr Paulus, Cyprian further insists upon episcopal authority in all matters:

> Our Lord, whose precepts we ought to revere and to observe, providing for the honor of the bishop and the order of His Church, speaks in the Gospel and says to Peter: "I say unto you that thou art Peter and upon this rock I shall build my Church, and the gates of hell shall not conquer it, and to thee I shall give the keys of the kingdom of heaven, and whatsoever thou shalt bind on earth shall also be bound in heaven, and whatsoever thou shalt loose on earth shall also be loosed in heaven" (Matt. 16:18f.). According to this, through the changes of the times and the succession in office, the appointment of bishops and the right order in the Church is founded on the bishops and *every act of the Church is governed by these same prelates.*[41]

Saturus' vision, on the other hand, affirms the peculiar status and authority of the martyrs. Given the *Passio's* widespread popularity, it is very likely that it helped to further solidify this popular view among the laity and the confessors. In any case, the result is that the confessors were going over and above the bishop (i.e. Cyprian) and, by their own merits, were receiving back the penitent lapsed into the church. Cyprian's efforts and future councils would later legislate against this practice.

When the person of Perpetua is, even briefly, considered, we realize that the ramifications of this vision extend well beyond the ecclesiastical context. We recall that Perpetua was not only a mere catechumen, she was also a woman and mother. Studies show that by the beginning of the second century, the church had begun to espouse and promote the dominant patriarchal values shared by Jews and Gentiles.[42] By this time, women's social and religious roles were relegated and intricately tied to procreation and motherhood. However, glimpses of this eschatological vision of equality were preserved in the Christian Scriptures and other writings such as the *Apocryphal Acts* and, as we have seen, in the *Acts of the Martyrs* which "held a central place in doctrine and devotion."[43] Against this theological and social backdrop, Saturus' vision of the bishop and presbyter kneeling at this young mother's feet not only implies an inversion of the ecclesiastical pyramid—it poignantly suggests a reversal of the social codes that dictated the norm. To those around her, Perpetua was not primarily a mother; she was foremost "a valiant and blessed martyr . . . called and chosen for the glory of Christ Jesus."[44]

Finally, from Saturus' vision it is possible to surmise that visions probably became powerful carriers of an existential newness characterized by its present—yet still to come—gospel Reign quality.[45] As carriers of this newness, visions helped the reader transcend present circumstances by compelling the Christian to envision and live out of that new interstitial domain manifested in his or her hope of what is and is yet to be.[46] This dynamic ability of the martyr to exist between present-future horizons, in turn, defied all boundaries of time and space, life and death, powers and principalities. The result is a subaltern existence that is uniquely subversive. Saturus' awakening response to the vision of his new life within the heavenly garden provides a pithy example of the visions' power to evoke this subaltern existence:

> And there [in the heavenly garden] we began to recognize many of our brethren, martyrs among them. All of us were sustained by a most delicious odour that seemed to satisfy us. *And then I woke up happy.*[47]

The state of being happy amidst oppressive conditions and impending death clearly subverts the state's attempts at crippling the Christian's resolve to remain faithful. The vision of the believer's promised future with God becomes, through the seer/recorder or reader's appropriation of it, the present that is and yet is not. In his vision, the future breaks into Saturus' present compelling him to enter into that new interstitial domain where happiness is not a mere chimera but a genuine possibility.[48] From the margins of persecution, there emerges a new understanding of existence that overpowers, indeed relativizes, the notion of earthly (pagan) life as the center of what it means to be. It is also from the recesses of this periphery that the contours of time and space become extended—beyond the third century and the Roman empire—to include eternity with God in a universe without oppressive borders. From this "otherwise" than-now-or-later subaltern existence the seer, in this case, Saturus (but also Perpetua and the others), becomes empowered to stand and overcome even the cruelest of deaths.

I alluded in the beginning to these visions' rich metaphorical and symbolic content. It is my contention that the *symbols, images, metaphors,* and *signs* inherent within the visions were interpreted subversively against the prevailing oppressive contexts.[49] But, who would have understood these signs? What are the religious and or cultural codes that would help the reader unlock the meaning(s) referenced by these signs and thus arrive at their subversive nature?[50] The vision of Polycarp discussed below provides an illustration of the role of images, metaphors, and signs in evoking meaning beyond the stated obvious. I also include it here as an example of a story of martyrdom that has remained popular throughout time. Every now and then, from any corner of the world, one can still hear Polycarp's famous words passionately resounding from our churches' pulpits: "For eighty-six years I have been his servant and he has done me no wrong. How can I blaspheme against my king and saviour?"[51] Unfortunately, the depth and power hidden within Polycarp's vision have, for the most part, remained unexplored and therefore, untapped.

The Vision of Polycarp

Early in the second century, the frail and aged Polycarp, Bishop of Smyrna, stood in the amphitheater before a tumultuous crowd and the proconsul. He had been arrested at the irate cry of an angry mob for being, in their view, "the schoolmaster of Asia—the father of the Christians, the destroyer of our gods—the one that teaches the multitude not to sacrifice or do reverence!"[52] While at prayer, "Three days before his arrest he had a vision and saw his pillow blazing[53] with fire, and turning to those who were with him he said, 'I must be burned alive'."[54] The proconsul's failed attempt at sparing his life by persuading Polycarp to "have respect to your age,"..."curse Christ" and "swear by the fortune of Caesar"[55] outraged the crowd who then requested he be burned alive. The narrator writes: "For the vision he [Polycarp] had seen regarding his pillow, had to be fulfilled."[56]

The vision of the blazing pillow had several functions. The first and most obvious one is explicitly given to us in the interpretation, "I must be burned alive." The image of the blazing pillow functioned as a sign of his proximate death by fire. One might even say that the blazing pillow became an icon for death and a metaphor for the manner of death Polycarp would have to suffer.

But, might there be more to this vision that is not directly expressed in his interpretation? For instance, Polycarp's statement that he would be burned alive considers only one part of the sign, that is, the image of the blazes. What about the image of the pillow? If the sole purpose of his vision was for him to know that he would be martyred by fire, then, why a blazing pillow and not a pile of blazing branches, for example? Why is there no direct reference to the meaning of the pillow itself? This leads us to believe that there may be a larger and perhaps even deeper meaning intended by the image of the blazing pillow. Further, that its meaning would possibly have been assumed by its readers. This assumed meaning becomes lucid through the process of literary analysis.

The juxtaposition of *blazing* with *pillow* is purposely puzzling for it clearly denotes a contradiction in terms. For instance, the noun *pillow* was associated with sleep and peaceful rest, with the setting of the sun and the dawn of a new day.[57] The adjective *blazing* or burning, on the other hand, implies fire which, when applied to the human body, is associated with horrible pain and possibly one's demise. A closer look at Polycarp's statements regarding his Christian beliefs will show that this contradiction in terms is only superficial. It will reveal that the burning pillow not only became for him an icon for death but also, and most important, for life—new, eternal life. This is not only implied but assumed throughout the text.[58] Polycarp's prayer supports this claim through its explicit reference to a new beginning through resurrection:

> O Lord, omnipotent God and Father of your beloved and blessed child Christ Jesus, through whom we have received our knowledge of you, the God of the angels, the powers, and of all creation, and of all the family of the good who live in your sight: I bless you because you have thought me worthy of this day and this hour, to have a share among the number of the martyrs in the cup of your Christ, *for the resurrection unto* eternal *life* of both the soul and the body in the immortality of the Holy Spirit. May I be received this day among them before your face as a rich and acceptable sacrifice, as you, the God of truth who cannot deceive, have prepared, revealed, and fulfilled before hand. Hence I praise you, I bless you, and I glorify you above all things, through that eternal and celestial high priest, Jesus Christ, your beloved child, through whom is glory to you with him and the Holy Spirit now and for all ages to come. Amen.[59]

One must admit that a prayer of such length points to a possible reconstruction of what only *may* have been Polycarp's prayer. Nevertheless, it clearly elucidates what was more than likely Polycarp and his community's understanding of death as but a necessary yet temporary means to resurrection unto a better life, that is, an eternal life with God. This belief is heard in the prayer's reference to "*the resurrection unto* eternal *life* of both the soul and the body in the immortality of the Holy Spirit."[60] It is also echoed in Polycarp's response to the governor's demand to "change his mind" and deny Christ. "The fire you threaten me with," Polycarp retorted, "burns *merely for a time* and is soon extinguished."[61]

Thus, the key to the meaning of the paradox of the blazing pillow lies within the prayer and the rest of the text. In them, we find the theological codes whose referent is a well established teleological understanding of life beyond death. This understanding was supported by Christianity's claim of Christ's own death and resurrection.

Polycarp's reference to the fire that "burns merely for a time," (i.e. versus "the fire of everlasting punishment and of judgment that is to come, which awaits the impious"[62]) opens the door to exploring anew his interpretation for the symbolic meaning of the word *blazing*. A fire that "burns merely for a time" implies a blazing, or in his case, a demise that is swift and expeditious. Hence, Polycarp's emphasis on the expeditiousness of his death is signified by his interpretation of the menacing fire as burning "merely for a time." Further, his focus on the ephemeral nature of this fire eclipses any emphasis on the impending anguish produced by the burning of his flesh. This focus throws more light on the role and function of the pillow in his vision.

I have already alluded to the symbolic association between pillow and sleep and the dawn of a new day. Polycarp's expectation of a heavenly resurrection provides the teleological code that expresses an unequivocal connection between pillow and a temporary sleep. This connection allows the pillow in his vision to function as the key metaphorical link between things past and things new. Together, the words blazing and pillow signal a swift transition from a physical, even painful, death to a new heavenly existence. Thus, the presence of the word *pillow* not only softens the metaphor of a pillow blazing, it completes the meaning of the icon.

We must conclude that the opposition between burning and pillow powerfully underscores the temporality of Polycarp's suffering and the expectation of a reawakening of his "soul and body" into a new eternal day. Polycarp and his community's belief in the Christian's immortality after death, would make the step from the burning pillow to its function as an icon for swift death, and life, or new life with Christ, an easy and most natural one. Although not explicitly stated in the interpretation of his vision, Polycarp's hope of resurrection, as shown in the prayer and elsewhere within the text, turns the blazing pillow not only into a divine as well as metaphorical sign of his impending death by fire, it elevates it into an icon for the new life that awaited him, but after a short slumber.

The function of the vision of the burning pillow as an icon for the kind of death that signified a sleeping and reawakening into the dawn of eternal life with God, has subversive dimensions, especially as it pertains to second-century Roman political power. While the state, deeming itself powerful and in control, purported to take Polycarp's life through fire, it in fact provided the means through which the martyr passed from one oppressive, and at times, painful life to the long awaited heavenly existence. Further, "to have a share among the number of the martyrs in the cup of . . . Christ," was, among others, considered a "blessed" and "noble" gift. Thus, for Polycarp and the Christian faithful, the vision of the blazing pillow upstaged and in fact subverted the power of the state to determine the Christian's fate. In addition, his vision was also instrumental in encouraging Polycarp (with others) in his faith, and in strengthening his resolve to die for it. For the Bishop and his community, the vision was not only a sign of his chosenness, but of God's presence with him. As it is written, this 86-year-old Christian named Polycarp stood his ground before the powerful Roman empire and through his death overcame his oppressors.

Conclusion

The formative and emerging church of the first four centuries thought of visions as a viable and authoritative medium for the revelation of God's will and purpose. Some of these visions are contained within the *Acts of the Martyrs*, a genre of literature that is thought to have begun circulating among the Christian communities in the second century with the *Acts of Ignatius*.[63] As shown above, the extensive and widespread use of the *Acts* among the third- and fourth-century Christians gives the historical theologian ample reason to inquire into the content and function of the visions. Our short excursion through the visions of Polycarp and Saturus revealed theological and sociocultural nuances that defied their particular historical-theological contexts. I referred to these nuances or incongruences as the subversive dimensions of the visions of the martyrs.

In the vision of Saturus, for example, the bishop's and presbyter's act of throwing themselves at the feet of the lay teacher and the female catechumen defied the already developed gender-exclusive ecclesiastical hierarchy. It also defied cultural codes that taught that women were inferior—biologically and culturally—to men. Even more striking is the fact that, according to the vision, the reversal of these ecclesiastical (and social) codes took place within God's heavenly garden, setting the anomaly within the context of divine approval. Saturus' vision thus helps us to see what may have been a reconstruction or re-viewing of the social and ecclesiastical power structures as conceived by the laity (e.g. Saturus). The confessors' act of restoring the lapsed to the communion of the church—outside of ecclesiastical authority—after the Decian persecution, is a vivid example of how that popular and subversive view was played out in daily life.

Visions also impacted the quality and the nature of earthly existence, especially in times of persecution. Their ability to evoke an interstitial—here now yet still to come—domain subverted all earthly notions of time and space. For the seer/recorder or reader, the present "reality" was subverted by that new reality represented by the "otherwise" than-now-or-later visual interstice. In this subaltern existence, from this spatio-temporal margin, all other centers of thought and being are minimized, and their persuasive powers relativized.

In addition, the visions of Saturus and Polycarp helped us to reaffirm the existence and impact of a theology that professed life after death. This theology, as noted by the analysis of the vision of Polycarp, was so strong it was assumed by the seer/recorder or (Christian) reader. We also saw in the Martyrdom of Polycarp how a seemingly powerless vision—a blazing pillow—conveyed a powerful message of hope and resurrection. His vision overturned the state's belief and insistence on the primacy of earthly existence by proclaiming and graphically reaffirming the primacy of life in Christ. Polycarp's vision is especially important because it underscores the metaphorical and symbolic power of visions to evoke meaning beyond what is explicitly stated. This gives us all the more reason to consider the import of these visions upon the early church and upon our knowledge of it.

As shown, both visions provide us with a historical and theological basis for arguing on behalf of an underlying grass-roots or popular theology that at times subverted the prescribed theological and sociocultural norms.

Notes

1. Robert Worth Frank, "Visions," in *An Encyclopedia of Religion*, ed. Vergilius Ferm (New York: Philosophical Library, 1945), 815. In *Visions and Prophecies*, Karl Rahner defines visions (referring to the mystical and prophetic) as "all those extraordinary occurrences of divine origin." (New York: Herder and Herder, 1963), 17.

2. Rahner, 7.

3. Ibid., 15.

4. Ibid., 8. Rahner is quoting Adalbert Brenninkmeyer's book, *Traitement Pastoral des Néurosés* (Paris: Vitae, 1947), 145.

5. "Beloved, do not believe every spirit, but test the spirits to see whether they are from God; for many false prophets have gone out into the world" 1 John 4:1 (*New Revised Standard Version*). 1 Thessalonians 5:19–21 is also used.

6. This is also asserted by Rahner, "According to the testimony of Scripture so much at least is clear: the history of Christianity would be unthinkable without prophetic and visionary elements (in the broadest sense). To try to explain all these things by natural or even abnormal human causes, would be logically to deny that any historical activity of the personal God revealing himself in the Word was possible at all. But this would be to repudiate the character of Christianity as an historical supernatural, revealed religion," 15.

7. Visions also have precedence in the Old Testament. For the sake of space I will limit myself to those of the New Testament.

8. "Snatched up to Paradise to hear words which cannot be uttered, words which no man may speak" (2 Corinthians 12:1–4).

9. "It should not be too readily assumed that the prophetic charisma was only a transient privilege of the primitive Church . . . Side by side with the office transmitted by the imposition of hands there must always be in the Church a prophetic vocation as well which is not handed down by humanity. Neither of these two gifts can replace the other." Rahner, 28. (I have used inclusive language).

10. Asceticism in the emerging church of the fourth century onward, was viewed as a form of martyrdom. For example, "Christianity in Egypt became the Christianity of the martyr's substitute, his 'brother' and sometimes his rival, the ascetic." See William H. C. Frend, *Martyrdom and Persecution in the Early Church: A Study of a Conflict from the Maccabees to Donatus* (Oxford: Basil Blackwell, 1965), 541.

11. See Matthew 10:23, Luke 11:49, 21:12, and others.

12. The "Acts of the Martyrs" (*acta* or *gesta* and also known as *acta*

Christianorum) is a genre of literature that is thought to have begun circulating among the Christian communities in the second century with the *Acts of Ignatius*. (Scholars who exclude the *Acts of Ignatius* as inauthentic begin the origin and development of the genre in the mid-second century with the *Martyrdom of Polycarp* [died between 155-177] and the *Martyrdom of Ptolemaeus and Lucius* [died before 160]). According to Gary A. Bisbee, scholarly consensus is that the earliest *acta martyrum* originated as copies of *hypomnematismoi*, the legal term for records of official court discourses between magistrates and martyrs (e.g. the *Acts of the Scillitan Martyrs*, the *Acts of Justin Martyr*). See Bisbee's *Pre-Decian Acts of Martyrs and Commentarii* (Philadelphia: Fortress Press, 1988), 1-17. The church obtained some of these Acts by various means, including bribing the tribunal agents. Daniel Ruíz Bueno, for example, points out that after the last persecution, the Council of Arles (canon 13) used the public Acts to establish who among them were *traditores*, that is, had turned over the sacred books as demanded by Diocletian. See Bueno's introduction to *Actas de los Mártires*, Texto Bilingüe, Segunda Edición (Madrid: Editorial Católica, 1968), 1-168.

13. Other literature that emerged, especially during the mid-second to fourth centuries, include apologetical works aimed at the defense of the faith to non-Christians, and those that focused on encouraging the church. See for example, Origen's "Exhortation to Martyrdom," trans. John J. O'Meara, in *Ancient Christian Writers*, eds. Johannes Quasten and Joseph C. Plumpe (New York: Newman Press, 1954); Tertullian's "On Flight in Persecution," trans. Edwin A. Quain, *Fathers of the Church* XL (Washington, D.C.: Catholic University of America Press, 1959), 275; "The Anonymous," in Eusebius' *Ecclesiastical History*, vol. 1, trans. and intro. Hugh Jackson Lawlor and John Ernest Leonard Outon (New York: Macmillan Co., 1927), v. 16-v. 17, 158-162; ; The "Letter of the Churches of Vienne and Lyons," also in Eusebius, v. 1, 139-149; Hippolytus' *Apostolic Tradition*, ed. Gregory Dix, rev. with corrections preface and bibl. Henry Chadwick (Buntingford, Great Britain: Layston Press Ltd., 1968).

14. (Oxford: Clarendon Press, 1972), lvi. My emphasis.

15. See his *De Natura et Origine Animae* 1.10, 111.9, *Corpus scriptorum ecclesiasticorum latinorum* (Vienna, 1866-). *Nec scriptura ista canonica est.*

16. Frank, 815.

17. *The Acts of the Christian Martyrs*, intro. and trans. Herbert Musurillo (Oxford: Clarendon Press, 1972), 109, ch. 2.

18. Ibid., 119, ch. 11.

19. Ibid.

20. Ibid., 121.

21. The vision does not say "God" but is unequivocal in its implication that the "aged man with white hair and a youthful face" before whom voices endlessly chanted "Holy, holy, holy!," was meant as God, or better still, the God-Christ. See Musurillo, 121, ch. 12.

22. Ibid., 121, ch. 12.

23. Ibid., 121, ch. 13.

24. Ibid.

25. In *Early Christian Fathers*, ed. Cyril C. Richardson (New York: Macmillan Publishing Co., 1970), 95. Brackets are Richardson's.

26. Ibid., 89.

27. Ibid., 93.

28. Frend, for example, refers to Saturus as a "Carthaginian priest." The "catechist Saturus," he continues, "was himself a presbyter," see 363-364.

29. See p. xxvi. Musurillo makes no argument for his conclusion, however.

30. See, Donald Attwater, *Martyrs: From Stephen to John Tung* (New York: Sheed and Ward, 1957), 21; Ruíz Bueno, intro. Spanish version, 400; Cecil M. Robeck says that "it is quite possible that Saturus was the instructor of these new converts, although that position may also have been occupied by the teaching presbyter, Aspasius," in *Prophecy in Carthage: Perpetua, Tertullian, and Cyprian* (Cleveland: Pilgrim Press, 1992), 70; Walter Hayward Shewring says only that Saturus had been the means of the other martyrs' conversion. See his trans. of and intro. to, *The Passion of SS. Perpetua and Felicity and the Sermons of S. Augustine* (London: Sheed and Ward, 1931), xiv.

31. For instance, we recall that Severus' edict of 202 was aimed at new converts and proselytizers. In this light, Perpetua's statement that Saturus had later given himself up of his own accord because "he was not present when we were arrested," can mean either of two things. First, that had Saturus, himself a catechumen, been present among the others, he would also have been arrested. On the other hand, as their catechist, it could mean that Saturus would have been arrested for proselytizing. Either way, it seems to imply that Saturus felt some sense of commitment to, or bond with, his fellow catechumens or students (whatever the case) that compelled him to give himself up and accompany them to their martyrdom. Second, Perpetua's mention of Saturus as the "builder of our strength," (Musurillo, 111, ch. 4) might be used to support the argument for his role as teacher. However,

Perpetua herself is portrayed as building the faith of the other cate-chumens (see, for example, Musurillo, 129, ch. 20.20). Finally, reference to other Christians within the *Passio* seem always to include their eccle-sial (or social) standing. This pattern continues throughout the text. For instance, Tertius and Pomponius (not imprisoned), are identified as "deacons," Optatus as "the bishop" and Aspasius as "the presbyter" (Musurillo, 109, ch. 2, and 121, ch. 13). Saturus, on the other hand, is not called by any ecclesiastical title.

32. In the third century, this function was carried out by the lay, there-fore implying that Saturus was definitely among the laity who also functioned as a catechist.

33. Frend puts the questions to the bishop and presbyter only in the mouth of Perpetua. This is probably in keeping with his view of Saturus as priest. However, in the vision it is Saturus *with* Perpetua who ask the questions to the bishop and the presbyter. Thus, the use of the first person plural "we": "And *we* [that is, Saturus, who is said to have written the vision, and Perpetua who was "at my side"] said to them: 'Are you not our bishop, and are you not our presbyter? How can you fall at our feet?'" Musurillo, 121-123, ch. 13. My emphasis.

34. This point is noted briefly in Frend, 364.

35. I have used the translation given by Edelhard L. Hummel but I have substituted the word "clearly" for the word "evidently," which best translates the Latin word *plane* in this quotation. *Plane quia nunc vobis in precibus efficacior sermo est et ad impetrandum quod in pressuris petitur facilior oratio est, petite inpensius et rogate ut confessionem omnium nostrum dignatio divina consummet, ut de istis tenebris et laqueis mundi nos quoque vobiscum integros et gloriosos Deus liberet.* See *The Concept of Martyrdom According to St. Cyprian of Carthage* (Washington D.C.: Catholic University of America Press, 1946), 157. See also *Epistle 76, 7 (Corpus Scriptorum Ecclesiasticorum Latinorum* [CSEL], Vienna).

36. Frend, 363.

37. Trans. Hummel, 158.

38. Ibid., 168. Translator's emphasis.

39. See Hummel, 169.

40. Trans. Hummel, 170 (*Epistle* 15, 1 [CSEL 3.2 513, 7-13 Hartel]). Translator's emphasis. See also Hummel, *Epistle 27*, 3, and 167-171.

41. Trans. Hummel, 169 (*Epistle 33*, 1 [CSEL 3.2 566, 2-12 Hartel]).

42. See, for example, Clarissa W. Atkinson, *The Oldest Vocation: Christian Motherhood in the Middle Ages* (London: Cornell University Press, 1991), 18-19 and Elisabeth Schüssler Fiorenza, *In Memory of Her:*

A *Feminist Theological Reconstruction of Christian Origins* (New York: Crossroad, 1983), 251-270.

43. Atkinson, 19.

44. Musurillo, 135, ch. 21.

45. See for example, Luke 10:9,11; 17:21. The Reign of God is said to be both "near" and "already in your midst."

46. The word "interstitial," reflects post-colonial theory. I have found it most appropriate for describing the here-not-yetness of God's Reign and the quality of existing within that space which is neither the present nor the future. See Homi K. Bhabha's very insightful use of the term in *The Location of Culture* (New York: Routledge, 1994).

47. Musurillo, 123, ch. 13. My emphasis.

48. By "interstitial" I do not mean an entrenched or staid position of "in-betweeness" but a dynamic existence that, according to the vision, will manifest itself fully and concretely upon martyrdom.

49. See also, Umberto Eco, *A Theory of Semiotics* (Bloomington: Indiana University Press, 1979), 16. For more information on Augustine's semiotic theory see Winfred Noth, *Handbook of Semiotics* (Indianapolis: Indiana University Press, 1990), 15.

50. Alex García-Rivera's book, *St Martín de Porres: The "Little Stories" and the Semiotics of Culture*, has been very helpful in elucidating the role and use of semiotics, specifically in terms of culture (Maryknoll, NY: Orbis Books, 1995), see especially 36-39.

51. Musurillo, 9, ch 9.

52. Ibid., 11, ch. 12.

53. The Greek word for "pillow" is *proskefalaion*. Note the word for pillow in Greek literally means a cushion for the head, pillow.

54. Musurillo, 7, ch. 5.

55. Ibid., 9, ch. 9.

56. Ibid., 13, ch. 12.

57. In Mark 4:38 the word *pillow* or *cushion* is specifically connected to sleep—even in time of peril. According to the gospel of Mark, Jesus and his disciples were on their way to "the country of the Gerasenes" (Mark 5:1) when "a great windstorm arose and the waves beat into the boat, so that the boat was already being swamped. But he [Jesus] was in the stern, *asleep on the cushion*; and they woke him up and said to him, 'Teacher, do you not care that we are perishing?'" (My emphasis). Upon waking up Jesus then rebuked the wind, and calmed the sea. Jesus sleeps restful amidst the peril awaking only to create that new sit-

uation of peace. New Revised Standard Version (New York: American Bible Society, 1989).

58. The notion of death and rest or sleep is also clearly implied in the New Testament Scriptures. In Paul's first letter to the Thessalonians 5: 10 he refers to death as being *asleep*. "He [Jesus Christ] died for us, that all of us, whether awake or *asleep* (*katheúdomen*), together might live with him" (my emphasis). In Luke 8:52, Jesus is recorded as referring to the death of Jairus' daughter as sleeping: "Stop crying for she is not dead but asleep" (*katheúdei*). (See also Mark 5:39, Matthew 9:24; 1 Thessalonians 4:14).

59. Musurillo, 13-15, ch. 14. Musurillo's emphasis.

60. Ibid.

61. Ibid., 11 ch. 11. My emphasis.

62. Ibid.

63. See note 12 above.

The Ecclesiology of Teresa of Avila: Women as Church Especially in *The Book of Her Foundations*

Keith J. Egan

Professor of Theology and Religious Studies
Saint Mary's College, Notre Dame

Ecclesiology had its formal beginnings during the medieval Conciliar movement, and its major architect from the sixteenth until the twentieth century was the Jesuit Robert Bellarmine (1542-1621). Bellarmine, born in the same year as John of the Cross, was a younger contemporary of Teresa of Jesus (1515-1582). The Jesuit cardinal was named a doctor of the church in 1931; the Carmelite nun was declared the first woman doctor of the church in 1970. Bellarmine crafted an ecclesiology that much influenced Catholic theologians for three and a half centuries.[1] On the other hand, Teresa of Jesus composed spiritual texts that have been consulted for their mystical wisdom. However, theologians have not been wont to consult this Spanish nun about her ecclesiology. She more than anyone else would have thought it a waste of time to do so. Teresa left theology, she thought, to the *letrados*, learned men (Teresa used this word to describe theologians).[2] Nonetheless, I suggest that Teresa of Jesus may profitably be consulted about what it means to be church, especially for what it means to be a more contemplative church, perhaps an ecclesial need for the church as it prepares to enter its third millennium.

Recall that Teresa of Jesus said many times on her deathbed, "Finally, Lord, I am a daughter of the Church."[3] In her book known as *The Way of Perfection*, Teresa described the way of life that she inaugurated not least of all to support a church that she felt was under siege by the Protestant Reformation.[4] Prayer on behalf of the church by her daughters was the intent of this foundress.[5] Teresa was, indeed, a reformer but she never wavered in her loyalty to the church despite not infrequent opposition to her plans and activities by leaders in the church.[6]

The Book of Her Foundations

For a sense of Teresa's implied ecclesiology I shall turn mainly to that much neglected work, *The Book of Her Foundations*. Very little attention has been paid to this work in comparison with her much better known acknowledged masterpiece, *The Interior Castle*, or to the oft read *The Book of Her Life*, or even to *The Way of Perfection*, her version of Carmelite contemplative life written as a blueprint of this life for her daughters.

For the sheer delight of meeting Teresa at her most human and colorful self, one turns to the rather large collection of her letters[7] and also to *The Book of Her Foundations*, which shows Teresa at her storytelling best. Teresa had described toward the end of *The Book of Her Life* the foundation of her original reformed monastery, that of Saint Joseph in Avila.[8] The Jesuit Jerónimo Ripaldi who had read her *Life* wanted Teresa to continue what she began there by describing the additional seven foundations that she had made since she initiated her reform of Carmelite life at Avila. She began the composition of *Foundations* on 25 August 1573, a text that she did not complete until the year of her death in 1582.[9]

Foundations is a lively presentation of so much that went

into making foundations since Teresa's primordial foundation at Avila. In all, Teresa founded seventeen monasteries for women, the last two in the year of her death, 1582, besides taking a hand in the foundations by Discalced Carmelite men at Duruelo and Pastrana. In *Foundations* Teresa was mostly interested in showing that these foundations were all God's work, not hers. Nonetheless, she took pains in this text to paint hagiographic portraits of patrons and founding members of these monasteries, and she very engagingly described the ordeals and the joys that she and her daughters sustained in the establishing of these Carmels as they are now called. It is in *Foundations* that one gets a sense of what Teresa was about as she founded her monasteries which served as local churches for her daughters.

Experiments in Ecclesiology

I have long felt that religious orders and congregations are inaugurated as experiments in being church.[10] Through the centuries women and men whom we have called religious have over and over again found new ways to gather together as disciples of Jesus, that is, to become an assembly of Christians. In their original charism these religious inaugurated a lived ecclesiology that preceded a formal or theoretical ecclesiology. From the beginning religious patterned their lives on what they saw as an imitation of the apostolic life of the Christian Scriptures. The use of New Testament texts that inspired the monks, canons, and friars to live this apostolic life has been described by the Dominican M.-H. Vicaire in his little classic *L'Imitation des Apôtres*.[11] Christians have taken much wisdom about being church from the hermits and cenobites of the desert, ever so much from the Benedictine Rule, and later from all the various religious who came after these early models of the Christian ecclesial life. Perhaps that is why it is so crucial that Christians keep an eye on contemporary religious as they try new ways of being religious, rather we should say, of being church. This imitation of ecclesial experiments by religious has consisted in learning from religious forms of prayer, personal and liturgical, ways of ministering, even ways of designing church buildings and much else besides. This paper seeks to name some of the ways in which Teresa's foundations, or little churches (*ecclesiolae* as the word was used in the middle ages), were a vision of what Teresa meant by being church. Monasteries and convents of all kind have through the centuries have been established as local churches offering to neighbors and visitors a vision of what it means to be church locally. There is, I propose, in Teresa's writings wisdom about being church in a new millennium.

Models of Church

As we explore Teresa's ecclesiology, I shall keep in mind the ecclesial models that Avery Dulles discovered in his study of ecclesiology,[12] without, however trying to fit Teresa's experiment too narrowly into Dulles' categories. You will recall that the models Dulles first proposed in 1974 in his book *Models of the Church* consisted in: the Church as Institution, as Mystical Communion, as Sacrament, as Herald, and as Servant. Later, Dulles added what he came to recognize as the guiding ecclesial model, that of the Community of Disciples. I had intended to relate Thomas O'Meara's philosophical models of the church[13] to Teresa's stories of her little houses of God but those models would have taken this paper too far afield into a philosophic milieu not often germane to Teresa's undertakings. I shall confine this paper to a brief inspection of how Dulles' models may be reflected in Teresa's foundations. More to the point of this paper is an exploration of Teresa's descriptions of the local churches that she founded and of what these churches looked like to a woman of action who had no time and little taste for theorizing. *Praxis* was her thing, and it is important to listen to her express that *praxis* though her own reports. In all things Teresa was a pragmatist, but she also knew when it was time to consult others if theory were needed to validate the direction that she was taking.

To begin with, let me say that we do not find in Teresa the well known New Testament images for the church such as the Body of Christ or the church as the Bride of Christ. Teresa used bridal imagery abundantly, but, when she did, she used it about her relationship or that of her individual daughters to Christ. Teresa saw Carmelite nuns individually as the brides of Christ.[14]

Intimations of Dulles' Models in
The Book of Her Foundations

Here I shall indicate briefly the general way in which Dulles' models of the church are reflected in the writings of Teresa of Jesus. Teresa of Jesus took the Church as Institution for granted.[15] She was in no way a disaffected member of the institutional church. She respected ecclesiastical authority and worked within it, but she also knew well how to influence authority so that ecclesiastical authorities would grow to appreciate her point of view. Teresa was an able manipulator of the ecclesiastical institution in the very positive sense of well planned politics.

Teresa perhaps would have been most at home with the Church as Mystical Communion. Hers truly was a contemplative ecclesiology. Her houses of God were founded for the sake of solitude, a solitude that she saw as the ground of contemplation. Teresa saw, as I shall indicate below, that the women who came to her monasteries were there to live fully in presence of Jesus in the same sense that Bernard McGinn has been writing about the presence of God as the paradigm for mystical experience.[16]

Teresa would also have been at home with Church as Sacrament. If anyone ever had a sacramental vision it was this woman whose eyes could discern that "the Lord walks among the pots and pans . . ."[17] Teresa saw her monasteries as places where the revelation of the divine presence occurred. God was, she was sure, manifested in the lives of those who lived in the monasteries that she founded.

Teresa would have had an affinity for the model of the Church as Herald, as gathered and shaped by the Word of God. The life and thought of this woman, whose lack of an education in Latin prevented her from having full access to the Bible, were remarkably shaped by the Word of God which she knew uncommonly well from anthologies, sermons, and the divine office. Teresa was no fundamentalist, but in her own way she was like Francis of Assisi. They both knew when to take the Word of God literally. Teresa of Jesus lived the Word of God, and she wanted her sisters to do the same. She was a herald, a prophet, whose spiritual experience prepared her to bring new vitality to religious life, an endeavor for reform that had been floundering for several centuries.[18]

Teresa could easily identify with the model of the Church as Servant. Service of God was her primary goal in life, a service that included service of her neighbor. In her role as foundress and reformer Teresa exercised a leadership by service. As La Madre to her daughters, Teresa's life of prayer and action was the pattern for their way of life. Teresa of Jesus expended enormous energy on behalf of the reform of her beloved Carmelite Order—a singular service that has benefitted the church to this day and far into the future.

Well known is Avery Dulles' discovery that his 1974 *Models of the Church* lacked what he came to see as the primary and guiding model for the Christian church. He failed in his original book to take note of discipleship as the guiding and connecting model for the church. There surely is a message in this failure when so astute an ecclesiologist as Dulles had to think twice before detecting discipleship as the primary mode of being church. It is indicative that Teresa used this model hardly at all. Explicit references to discipleship are infrequent in her writings although the notion of following and imitating Jesus is an unspoken presumption in Teresa's descriptions of Carmelite life. Perhaps Teresa's experience shows that the loss of a sense of explicit discipleship among Catholics goes back at least to her time and probably beyond. Her most explicit mention of this discipleship occurs in *The Way of Perfection*,[19]

> Draw near, then, to this good Master with strong determination to learn what He teaches you, and His Majesty will so provide that you will learn to be good disciples. He will not abandon you if you do not abandon Him. Consider the words that divine mouth speaks, for in the first word you will understand immediately the love He has for you; it is no small blessing and gift for the disciple to see that his [sic] Master loves him [sic].[20]

This quotation demonstrates what Teresa could have done with discipleship if this model for church had become an habitual symbol for her.

Teresa of Jesus' Descriptions of Her Houses of God
More than anything this paper investigates Teresa's *praxis* of ecclesiology that was manifested in her descriptions of the way she made her foundations. I shall explore chiefly Teresa's *Book of Foundations* as well as her description of the founding of her first foundation, described in *The Book of Her Life*.[21] The focus will be on what wisdom this ecclesial woman has offered her readers about being church in her simple and unsophisticated conversational manner.

Teresa's sense of being church in the first of her foundations, that at Avila (for all that she knew the last of her foundations) contains in an unselfconscious way what she saw her foundations to be and what she wanted them to be. This monastery of San José in Avila became the premier model for all subsequent Discalced Carmelite monasteries for women. Teresa was delighted when she discovered that the sisters at Medina del Campo "were following in the footsteps of the Sisters of St. Joseph's in Avila through complete religious dedication, sisterly love, and spirituality."[22] Before all else, Teresa saw this foundation as God's undertaking and all subsequent foundations as God's work, not Teresa's work.

Her understanding of grace was very Augustinian: the human person can do nothing without God's help. Even more so, in this undertaking Teresa was adamant that this foundation was God's project, a God who made the whole undertaking possible: ". . . it is often made clear that it is not I who do anything in these foundations, but the work is His who is all powerful in everything."[23] Known as Mother Foundress, Teresa wrote:

> It seems our Lord desires me and all others to know that it is only His Majesty who does these works, and that as he gave sight with mud to the blind man, He wants someone as blind as I to do something worth more than mud.[24]

Teresa's little monasteries were God's creation. That is a very strong ecclesial statement. Her foundations were not a human undertaking, not an association of women instigated merely by human design. Listen to her say as much to the Dominican García de Toledo for whom she wrote her *Vida*:

> . . . I beg your Reverence for the love of God that if you think you should tear up what else is written here to preserve whatever pertains to this monastery. And when I am dead, give it to the sisters who live here that when those who are to come see the many things His Majesty arranged for its establishment by means of so wretched and dreadful a thing as myself they might be greatly encouraged to serve God and strive that what has been begun may not collapse but always flourish.[25]

She expressed the same notion in *Foundations*:

> I am growing fearful and want our Lord to make known to everyone how in these foundations we creatures have done next to nothing. The Lord has directed all by means of such lowly beginnings that only His Majesty could have raised the work to what it is now. May He be always blessed, amen.[26]

For Teresa a new monastery was, as I have said, a "house of God."[27] Teresa's ecclesiology was not about a human project but one which God wanted and directed. *The Book of Her Foundations* is filled with Teresa's reports of God's direct intervention in the planning and in the execution of her various foundations. These interventions were often manifested in her visionary experiences. That means that Teresa, though she had moments of doubt, was doing God's will in founding new monasteries. Moreover, the way of life that was adopted therein was also God's will.[28] There is, of course, a great deal of comfort that comes from the conviction that one is doing God's will. Only Teresa's insistence on self-knowledge and humility could save her from the arrogance that so easily emerges from the conviction that one has fully grasped what God's will is.

A Foundress on the Move

After Teresa founded the monastery of San José in Avila, she went on to found fourteen more monasteries for women besides what she did to influence the founding of the men's convents and what she did "at a distance" to found two other women's monasteries. As a woman of the Catholic Reformation Teresa gave no thought to "syneisactism," women and men living the celibate life together as proposed recently by Jo Ann Kay McNamara as an ideal for religious life,[29] nor is there reason to think that Teresa would have thought to do so in another age, even our own. Teresa was, in fact, vigilant about male presence in her enclosed monasteries. She made specific restrictions about the presence of the confessor and the visitator.[30] Teresa can hardly be described as thinking the sexes could intermingle freely in monastic communities. Though, if the truth be told, Madre Teresa left no record that, as a nun, she ever found men a threat to her own commitment to celibacy.

Teresa's monasteries were small local churches. For the sake of solitude she considered the ideal number of sisters in a monastery to be thirteen. To the number twelve made sacred throughout the middle ages as a way of honoring the twelve apostles, Teresa added one member to serve as prioress. However, the number thirteen became too small to support the monastery financially so that Teresa later raised that number to twenty.[31] Teresa's monasteries were to be small enough to insure solitude and large enough to support the community.

Teresa's little churches, houses of God were single-sex small communities devoted to the solitude which Teresa considered necessary for the contemplative life. In a day when *Comunidades Cristianas de Base* and small faith communities find so many proponents, Teresa's strong convictions about the small number needed for solitude has some resonance. The reasons for the small number are not entirely dissimilar when one takes into account Teresa's concern for friendship in her communities.[32] The end of all Christian community may well be the same—to live as a loving community more fully and more consciously in the presence of Jesus.

Teresa of Jesus saw her small communities as eucharistically centered. The Carmelite Rule (to whose observance she was so committed) called for "hearing" mass daily when a priest could be had,[33] not a problem in Teresa's day. At first Teresa was under the mistaken notion that a monastery was not officially established until the Blessed Sacrament could be fittingly reserved. She eventually found out that a foundation was officially established once the eucharist had been celebrated,[34] though she was always much concerned about having the eucharist reserved in her monasteries. In regard to the eucharist, one may recall how often Teresa speaks of her spiritual experiences as occurring after the reception of Holy Communion. In Teresa's era Carmelite nuns would have received communion more often than the laity but usually not daily. Teresa's Constitutions have the following specifications for the reception of communion.

> Communion will be received every Sunday, on feast days, and on days honoring our Lord, our Lady, our Father St. Albert,

and St. Joseph, and on other days that the confessor designates in accordance with the devotion and spirit of the Sisters and with the permission of the Mother prioress. Communion will also be received on the titular feast of the house.[35]

Contemporary and patristic theology says that the celebration of the Eucharist makes the church present. Teresa would not have argued with that theory. Eucharist was at the heart of Teresa's spirituality and ecclesiology as it surely is in all Catholic Christian ecclesiology.

Teresa's little churches were quite devotional by post-Vatican II standards but quite modern by the norms of late medieval piety. Note her influential devotion to Saint Joseph. Western affinity for the foster father of Jesus may in large measure be attributed to Teresa of Jesus and Francis de Sales.[36] Coincidental to the theme of this paper Saint Joseph was declared patron of the Universal Church in 1870 by Pius IX. Some will remember that Joseph's name was added by John XXIII in 1962 to the list of saints in what we now call Eucharistic Prayer I. Teresa who placed so many of her monasteries under the patronage of Joseph would have been pleased by the honors paid to the saint she loved so dearly. Let me add that Teresa took a strong stand against prioresses who added prayers and observances to the life of the nuns.[37] Teresa of Jesus spoke often of wearing the habit of Our Lady and of her order as Mary's own. This devotion to Mary is sprinkled all through her writings. Teresa took great pride in belonging to "the Order of Our Lady of Mount Carmel."[38] John Paul II's predilection for Mary as the Mother of the Church would have met with Teresa's approval.

Teresa wanted, with divine sanction,[39] to have her houses founded in poverty, that is, without income. However, she saw that, in areas of small populations, monasteries could be indigent without income. So some of her monasteries were, as she said, "founded in poverty" or "with an income."[40] Teresa was much influenced in this regard by her Franciscan friend St. Peter Alcántara.[41] Teresa's heart in the matter of poverty lay with the Franciscan tradition. Teresa, moreover, grew in her love for poverty: "From then on my desire to be very poor increased. And I felt freedom in having so little esteem for temporal goods, for the lack of these goods brings an increase of interior good. Certainly, such a lack carries in its wake another kind of fullness and tranquillity."[42] Teresa's ideal for her monasteries was as a local church living in a solidarity of goods like the Jerusalem community of the Acts of the Apostles (2:44; 4:32). The prevailing wisdom in Teresa's time tended toward requiring women to have an income on which they could count for sustaining a decent way of life.[43]

Teresa also took pride in foundations that lived not only in poverty but in the austerity that was so congenial to the monastic reform movements of the sixteenth century, especially those in Spain. But Teresa was no extremist, and she did not want her nuns to be enmeshed in austerities when she had a more important ideal in mind, that of solitude and prayer.[44] Teresa was a very balanced monastic reformer. While she was in awe of the rigorous penances of some about whom she wrote in *The Book of Her Foundations*, Teresa admired much more the moderation that she found in her dear friend Jerónimo Gracián, about whom she wrote: "In his first visitation of the friars, he arranged everything with such moderation and harmony that it indeed seemed he was helped by the Divine Majesty and that our Lady had chosen him to help her order."[45] Gracián and Teresa shared a common vision of Carmelite life, a vision later challenged by Nicholas Doria, a provincial obsessed with an austere, even rigid, notion of Carmelite asceticism.[46]

Teresa's primary ideal was that her houses of God be, in fact, places of solitude where prayer is the primary activity of the nuns. The Carmelite Rule, which was Teresa's principal guide after the Scriptures, makes prayer the central activity of Carmelite life: "Let each one remain in his [sic] cell, or near it, *meditating day and night on the law of the Lord and keeping vigil in prayer* unless occupied with other lawful duties."[47] Teresa was enthusiastic about the progress in contemplative prayer made in her foundations, and this enthusiasm is a refrain in *Foundations*.

> . . . the favors the Lord grants in these houses are so many that if there are one or two in each that God leads now by meditation all the rest reach perfect contemplation. Some are so advanced that they attain to rapture. To others the Lord grants a favor of another kind, giving them, along with rapture, revelations and visions that one clearly understands to be from God.[48]

Teresa of Jesus could have paraphrased Karl Rahner's now famous saying with her vision of Carmelite life: the Carmelite of the future will be a mystic or she will be nothing at all.[49] Yet, Teresa fully realized that mystical favors do not constitute holiness: "Well do I understand that sanctity does not lie in these favors, nor is it my intention to praise only them . . ."[50] On the other hand, Teresa felt confident that those who followed her way of self-knowledge, detachment, and recollected prayer could ordinarily expect God's special favors in prayer.

> And, in my opinion, there is no reason why entrance even into the final dwelling place should be denied these souls, nor will the Lord deny them this entrance if they desire it; for such a desire is an excellent way to prepare oneself so that every favor may be granted.[51]

Teresa pictured her monasteries as "little dovecotes" where God sends abundant mystical gifts.

> Well, as these little dovecotes of the Virgin, our Lady, were beginning to be inhabited, the divine Majesty began to show His greatness in these weak little women, who were strong though in their desires and their detachment from every creature. When practiced with a pure conscience, such detachment must be what most joins the soul to God. There is no

need to point this out because if the detachment is true it seems to me impossible that one offend the Lord. Since in all their dealings and conversation these nuns are concerned with Him, His Majesty doesn't seem to want to leave them. This is what I see now and in truth can say. Let those fear who are to come and who will read this. And if they do not see what is now seen, let them not blame the times, for it is always a suitable time for God to grant great favors to the one who truly serves Him. And let them strive to discern whether there is some failure in this detachment and correct it.[52]

Teresa did not see contemplation as some abstract, ethereal state for which her nuns prepared themselves. Rather for her contemplation was love. Toward the end of *The Way of Perfection*, Teresa wrote that "with contemplatives there is always much love, or they wouldn't be contemplatives."[53] Union with God in love expressed in love of neighbor was what Teresa's little churches were all about, a love which culminated for her in what she saw as spiritual marriage. She puts that spiritual marriage in what I take to be a paraphrase of the Beatitudes when she was about to conclude *The Interior Castle*, that is, love lived at the service of God and neighbor.[54]

Teresa's vision for her local churches has much to say to the church of the twenty-first century if that church seeks to be a more contemplative church, that is, a church which fully embraces its humanity and at the same time accepts the Holy Spirit as its animator. As the churches of Latin and Central America and the Hispanic churches of North America become ever more vigorous, I believe they will find in Teresa, as in her collaborator John of the Cross, an ecclesiology purified in the dark nights of suffering and deepened by a profoundly contemplative approach to the way they follow Jesus in the new millennium. Teresa's communities were to be places where the joy of the Christian life was to be manifest among those who were gifted with union with God so that those so gifted would experience "overwhelming joy and delight, which reaches so extraordinary a peak that indeed, the soul, I think, swoons to the point that it is hardly kept from leaving the body..."[55] As one of Teresa's poems reads: "Oh, my Beloved, what joy/To be oned to You!"[56] Wherever Christian communities will be formed in the new millennium, Teresa's wisdom, preserved in her writings, about praying communities that share goods and live poorly with God at the center of their lives, will be worth consulting.

Notes

1. Richard P. McBrien, "Ecclesiology," in *HarperCollins Encyclopedia of Catholicism*, gen. ed. Richard P. McBrien (HarperSanFrancisco: San Francisco, 1995), 448.

2. The word *letrados* does not appear in Cobarruvias' 1611 Spanish Dictionary. See Sebastián de Covarrubias Horozco, *Tesoro de la Lengua Castellana y Española* (Madrid: Real Academia Española, 1611).

3. Efrén de la Madre de Dios and Otger Steggink, *Tiempo y Vida de Santa Teresa*, second ed. (Madrid: La Editorial Católica, 1977), 983-984.

4. Teresa of Jesus, *The Way of Perfection*, vol. 2 of *The Collected Works of St. Teresa of Avila*, trans. Kieran Kavanaugh and Otilio Rodríquez (Washington, D.C.: Institute of Carmelite Studies, 1980), ch. 1. In this paper W=*The Way of Perfection*, in the same volume IC=*The Interior Castle*; F=*The Book of Her Foundations*, vol. 3 of *The Collected Works* (1985); L=*The Book of Her Life*, vol. 1 of *The Collected Works* (1976).

5. W 4, 1. See L 40, 12; IC, Epilogue 4.

6. See Keith J. Egan, "Teresa of Jesus: Daughter of the Church and Woman of the Reformation," *Carmelite Studies* 3 (1984): 69-91.

7. For her letters see *The Letters of Saint Teresa of Jesus*, 2 vols., trans. E. Allison Peers (1951; London: Sheed and Ward, 1980). Kieran Kavanaugh, O.C.D., is presently working on a translation of the letters for the Institute of Carmelite Studies.

8. See *The Book of Her Life* 32, 33, 35 and 36.

9. *Collected Works*, vol. 3, p. 5.

10. Keith J. Egan, "Dom David Knowles, 1896-1974," *The American Benedictine Review* 27 (1976): 235.

11. (Paris: Les Éditions du Cerf, 1963). English translation: *The Apostolic Life*, trans. William E. DeNapale (Chicago: Priory Press, 1966).

12. Avery Dulles, *Models of the Church* (Garden City, NY: Doubleday,

1974). For Dulles' addition of a "guiding" model, discipleship, see Dulles, "Community of Disciples as a Model of Church," *Philosophy/Theology* 1 (1986): 99-120; and "Imaging the Church for the 1980s," in Avery Dulles, *A Church to Believe In: Discipleship and the Dynamics of Freedom* (New York: Crossroad, 1982), 1-18.

13. Thomas O'Meara, "Philosophical Models in Ecclesiology," *Theological Studies* 39 (1978): 3-21.

14. See Paul S. Minear, *Images of the Church in the New Testament* (Philadelphia, PA: Westminster, 1960); for imagery in Teresa see Elizabeth T. Howe, *Mystical Imagery: Santa Teresa de Jesús and San Juan de la Cruz* (New York: Pater Lang, 1988).

15. See note 12 for the various models delineated by Dulles.

16. Bernard McGinn, *The Foundations of Mysticism*, vol. 1 of *The Presence of God: A History of Western Christian Mysticism* (New York: Crossroad, 1991), xvii-xix.

17. *Foundations* 5, 8.

18. See Henry Outram Evenett, *The Spirit of the Counter-Reformation*, ed. John Bossy (Cambridge: University Press, 1968), 25.

19. The word disciple does not occur frequently in Teresa's writings; sometimes it is used in a very general sense. See e.g., *The Way of Perfection* 24, 3, 5; 26, 10; IC 5.1.1.

20. W 26, 10.

21. See note 8.

22. *Foundations* 9, 1.

23. F 29, 5.

24. F 29, 24.

25. *The Book of Her Life* 36:29.

26. *Foundations* 13, 7.

27. F 25, 14; 27, 10.

28. For Teresa's expression of the details of this new Carmelite life, see "The Constitutions," 319-333, in *The Book of Her Foundations*.

29. Jo Ann Kay McNamara, *Sisters in Arms: Catholic Nuns Through Two Millennia* (Cambridge, MA, London, England: Harvard University Press, 1996), 6 and passim.

30. Teresa of Avila, "On Making the Visitation," in *The Book of Her Foundations* 15, 16, 39, 45, 47.

31. F 1,1 and note 2; *The Way of Perfection* 2, 9, note 5 in vol. 2 of *The Collected Works*; *The Book of Her Life* 32, 13; 36, 19.

32. W ch. 4-15.

33. *The Rule of Saint Albert*, n. 10; see *Albert's Way*, ed. Michael Mulhall (Barrington, IL: Province of the Most Pure Heart of Mary, 1989).

34. *Foundations* 19, 3 and 9. See *Collected Works*, vol. 3, 417, n. 12.

35. "The Constitutions," n. 5, 320.

36. *The Oxford Dictionary of the Christian Church*, ed. F. L. Cross, third ed. E. A. Livingstone (New York: Oxford University Press, 1997), 901.

37. "On Making the Visitation," n. 22.

38. *Foundations* 27, 10.

39. *The Book of Her Life* 35, 6.

40. "On Making the Visitation," n. 11. See Jodi Bilinkoff, *The Avila of Saint Teresa: Religious Reform in a Sixteenth-Century City* (Ithaca and London: Cornell University Press, 1989), 123-127.

41. "Introduction," *Foundations* 38. (See index to this work). See Teófanes Egido, "The Economic Concerns of Madre Teresa," *Carmelite Studies* 4 (1987): 151-172.

42. F 15, 15.

43. See "Decree on Regulars and Nuns," Council of Trent, in *Decrees of the Ecumenical Councils*, vol. 2, ed. Norman Tanner (London and Washington, D.C.: Sheed and Ward and Georgetown University Press, 1990), 777.

44. "Introduction," *Foundations* 29-35.

45. F 23, 13.

46. Joachim Smet, *The Carmelites: A History of the Brothers of Our Lady of Mount Carmel*, vol 2 (Darien, IL: Carmelite Spiritual Center, 1976), 104, 126.

47. *The Carmelite Rule*, n. 7.

48. *Foundations* 4, 8.

49. Karl Rahner, *Theological Investigations*, vol. 7, trans. David Bourke (New York: Herder and Herder, 1971), 15.

50. *Foundations* 8.

51. *The Interior Castle* 3. 1. 5.

52. *Foundations* 4, 5.

53. *The Way of Perfection* 40, 4.

54. *The Interior Castle* 7, 3.

55. IC 6. 11. 11.

56. *Collected Works*, vol. 3, 382.

Ethnic and Racial Diversity and the Catholicity of the Church

Bradford E. Hinze
Associate Professor of Theology
Marquette University

The Roman Catholic Church is in the midst of a transition from a Eurocentric to a global and multicultural understanding of the church.[1] The Second Vatican Council was a decisive impetus for this change, but other social and ecclesial forces in the United States and around the world have also served as catalysts. This transition invites, indeed necessitates, reflection on how ethnic and racial diversity can be conceived as a constitutive feature of the church's identity and traditioning process.

What comprises ethnic and racial identity is not entirely agreed upon.[2] In contemporary usage, ethnicity commonly refers to specific human traits and traditions that have their origins in national affiliations, whereas race refers to human traits, especially skin pigmentation and physical characteristics, and traditions that are based on a group's origins within a geographical context.[3] It is difficult to deny that ethnic and racial differences are related to ancestors and genetic codes, biologically based human characteristics, so-called phenotypes. But attempts to define such differences are elusive, imprecise, and debated. The efforts to reduce such distinctions to essential biological traits and to develop a hierarchy or comparative valuation of these differences have been repudiated as scientifically deficient and socially destructive. There is, however, widespread agreement that ethnic and racial differences and their significance, are socially constructed and historically situated, that is, selectively chosen and interpreted modes of human representation. These differences are conveyed by the cultural transmission of communal beliefs and practices in the form of narrated memories, stories of origins, language, rituals, music, and food.[4]

The ongoing social historical constructions of ancestral and biological heritage that comprise ethnic and racial differences are constitutive dimensions of the mystery of human being. The question at hand is how do these differences bear upon our understanding of a church that identifies itself as catholic? The aim of this paper is to explore ways in which ethnic and racial diversity bears upon the very substance of a fundamental and systematic theology of the church, and should be included as a necessary component in ecclesiological treatises and in college and graduate courses on the church. I have chosen to set my reflections on the catholicity of the church within the context of the local church in the United States quite deliberately. There is much discussion these days about ethnic and racial diversity in the setting of theologies coming from Latin America, the Caribbean, Asia, Africa, and in the reunited Europe, and as an ingredient in interreligious dialogues. These findings are valuable, indeed indispensable, for the larger purpose of my paper. But frequently too little time and attention is devoted to the diversity in our own backyard. It seems easier to confront "the other" when they are halfway around the world and we can approach them with a certain abstractness and detachment. In the end, however, the theology we live will be judged not primarily by how we have treated the stranger on the other side of the globe, but by how we have formed community with those who are different in our parishes, neighborhoods, and cities. The factors that are contributing to our new awareness of ethnic and racial diversity are manifold. It may be helpful to call to mind a few. (1) As previously mentioned, the teachings of the Second Vatican Council mark a shift in official Catholic doctrine away from a uniform vision of Catholic cultural identity, sometimes referred to as Christendom, to a growing sensitivity to ethnic, racial, and religious others; in the aftermath of the council we have witnessed the emergence of liberation theologies, inculturation theologies, and myriad efforts at interreligious dialogue.[5] (2) A number of historical events and social movements over the last thirty years in the United States have heightened our awareness of ethnic and racial diversity, even though such diversity has been a constant feature of the United States. Since the 1960s we have witnessed the civil rights movements, the black consciousness and chicano movements, and an ethnic revival among European descendants. And add to these the ongoing "second wave" of immigration from Latin American, Caribbean, and Asian countries. (3) Globalization is the term being bandied about recently to describe a coalescence of social forces that has brought about an increasing international interdependency of financial markets and commercial and political relations between companies, consumers, and nations. The social forces that have contributed to these economic and political arrangements include global communication, the growth of the entertainment and news media industry, and international transportation, all of which have shrunk the world and brought us face to face with ethnic, racial, and religious others from the far corners of the world. The cumulative effect of these developments is that debates about the politics of identity and multiculturalism are widespread.[6]

Many today recognize ethnic and racial diversity as human issues that touch upon family, educational, political, and economic life. But they also affect every level of the church's existence: how we worship, catechize, preach, and live together, and how members of the church in various ministries learn from each other and witness to the gospel. What does this new awareness of ethnic and racial identity contribute to our ecclesial identity? To put the question in its starkest form: does this new awareness of ethnic and racial diversity threaten the unity, identity, and persuasive power of the Catholic church and its tradition? Or does it provide an important opportunity to come to a deeper appreciation of the catholicity of the church and its still unfolding tradition? Could it be both a threat and an opportunity, a danger and a gift? Indeed this essay will argue that it is both, and that cultivating our ability to think about it in a constructive way, purified of unnecessary posturing and subterfuge, is very important for the ongoing vitality of the church.

My argument will proceed in several parts. Part one examines features of the ethnic and racial history of the United States (U.S.) church as resources for ecclesiology. Second, the concept of catholicity and its usage will be considered. Third, I will examine how earlier in the twentieth century the doctrine of the mystical body of Christ, based on an incarnational ecclesiology, supported an argument in favor of catholicity against racist and ethnocentric ideologies. Then, in an effort to move beyond the limitations of this earlier mystical body and incarnational ecclesiology, I will explore how a trinitarian ecclesiology, which is decisive for understanding the church as a dialogical communion, provides a more promising way to address the issues of ethnic and racial diversity in the church.

The Ethnic and Racial History of the Church
in the United States as a Resource for Ecclesiology

The history of the Catholic church in the United States offers important resources for a theology of the church. This national expression of the church exhibits a remarkably rich and complex set of relationships between Catholics of European descent, and Native Americans, African, Asian, Caribbean, and Hispanic Americans.[7] Indeed, the conviction voiced on occasion in the United States that there is something providential and messianic about this nation that is not based on an ethnic or racial identity, but on the idea of freedom that draws together people of different ethnic and racial cultures, has commanded the attention of many, including most recently Jürgen Moltmann.[8] And while it is true that this multicultural context holds much promise, the succession of encounters, confrontations, and negotiations between peoples of diverse ethnic and racial identities in the United States shows the difficulty that the Christian church, and specifically the Roman Catholic Church has had in realizing this promise. The series of important steps forward has been accompanied by missteps and missed opportunities. A review of this history is not in order here, but several episodes and features of the twentieth century can suggest how important this history is for ecclesiology.[9]

The confrontation between Catholics from European descent and people of African descent in the United States reminds us of the admirable efforts and deplorable failures of people to live up to their catholic identity. John T. McGreevy in his recent book, *Parish Boundaries: The Catholic Encounter with Race in the Twentieth-Century Urban North*, chronicles the migration of African Americans from the south into the neighborhoods and churches of northern Catholics.[10] Drawing from archival materials from numerous northern urban dioceses, McGreevy's social history builds on the older story of resistance and assimilation of Catholic ethnics into a United States dominated by Anglo-Saxon Protestants as told by Philip Gleason and others. He shows that earlier in this century the "lines between 'race' and what is now considered 'ethnicity' were unclear. The assumption that Celtic, Polish, [Italian,] and German races existed was common; as was the belief that differences between these races and the 'Anglo-Saxon' race were deep and enduring."[11] But "for Catholics to bracket African Americans as simply another 'immigrant' group . . . ignored the way in which Euro-Americans claimed a shared identity."[12] A Brooklyn pastor made this observation in 1938, "The presence of Negroes contributes to the rapid exodus of the Catholic Whites." And McGreevy explains: "Irish and Germans . . . became 'Catholic Whites' only in the context of African-Americans moving in large numbers to a particular area. Ethnicity was flattened into race. These developments—neighborhood change, a growing distinction between 'black' and 'white' and a blurring of lines between Euro-American Catholic groups—were slowing occurring across the urban North."[13] There were certainly brave individuals in parishes who were hospitable to migrating African Americans and who fostered the formation of hybrid cultural communities. But the U.S. Catholic hierarchy was tardy in its response to the issues of slavery and racism, and in many cases Catholic parishes were ineffectual in the midst of this newly changing social context.

One of the most important U.S. Catholic critics of racism was the Jesuit priest John LaFarge (1880-1963), long associated with the Jesuit journal *America*, beginning as a journalist in 1926 and then working as editor in the early 1940s. David Southern has recently offered a helpful history of John LaFarge's advocacy of interracial justice through education, clerical paternalism, and the establishment of interracial councils.[14] LaFarge's 1937 book *Interracial Justice: A Study of the Catholic Doctrine of Race Relations* was his most influential statement.[15] Pope Pius XI was so impressed with this book that he personally asked LaFarge to write an encyclical for him on the subject. LaFarge with another Jesuit, Gustav Gundlach, the German social ethicist teaching at the Gregorian University in Rome, drafted in 1938 an encyclical *Humani Generis Unitas* (The Unity of Humankind), which was never adopted because of certain Vatican resistance and the death of Pius XI in 1939.[16] LaFarge's critics and rivals are also important as we shall see. The African American Catholic Dr. Thomas Turner (1877-1978), a biology professor at Howard University and a leader of the Federation of Colored Catholics, argued that racism was not simply an error to be corrected through education, as LaFarge had stressed, but a sin to be challenged, requiring black leadership and initiative. Father Paul Hanley Furfey (1896-1992) offered a more confrontative alternative to LaFarge's polite public argument and incrementalist practical proposals. A sociology professor at the Catholic University of America, and outspoken advocate of the Catholic Worker movement, Furfey wrote frequently and eloquently against racism, as in *The Mystery of Iniquity* (1944) and in *The Respectable Murderers* (1966).[17] We will return to LaFarge, Turner, and Furfey later.

An immense amount of research is being done on the history of U.S. Hispanic Catholics,[18] but let me highlight one person and one particular feature of contemporary Hispanic theology that are particularly important for our topic. The person is Virgilio Elizondo, born in 1936 in Texas of Mexican descent, a diocesan priest who has devoted himself to addressing the challenges of Hispanic Catholics.[19] I wish to suggest that Elizondo merits comparison with John LaFarge. Both are important advocates in their own generation of interracial and interethnic justice. Both have combined writing careers appealing to broad audiences, and have espoused practical programs—LaFarge's interracial councils and Elizondo's Mexican American Cultural Center. Both have spoken out prophetically against Eurocentric exclusion of others—African Americans and Hispanics—in parishes and in social and economic life in the United States. And both have emphasized the importance of education in addressing the issues of ethnic and racial exclusion or discrimination.

The differences between LaFarge and Elizondo are equally important. While Elizondo would not deny the arguments espoused by LaFarge about the dignity of the human person, human equality, human rights, and the need for social unity, he has a deeper analysis of the social, historical, and cultural dimensions of ethnic (and by extension racial) diversity as features to be both cherished and evaluated.

Moreover, Elizondo's focus on the experience of Mestizo, that is, of intermarriage between people of different cultural heritages and of the children born of different parentage, combines an important category for social description with a theological interpretation of this phenomenon that is not in evidence in LaFarge's work. Both LaFarge and Elizondo address broad publics; LaFarge was directed primarily to the cultural elites and establishment, whereas Elizondo has broad populist appeal both in San Antonio, Texas and through his televised masses in Hispanic households around the United States. And while LaFarge reflects the then common paternalistic clerical paradigm, Elizondo's post-Vatican II view of priestly ministry promotes lay leadership. Finally, Elizondo speaks as an Hispanic who has experienced being marginalized, while LaFarge is one who speaks for blacks out of deep concern but from a position of privilege.

One feature of contemporary Hispanic theology also deserves consideration here: the emphasis given to popular religiosity. The significance of popular forms of piety among Hispanic theologians is multifaceted. It provides a way to recover the experience of God, the self, and the community in everyday life and spirituality. It offers a way to see how ancient traditions have become incorporated into the common experiences of people. Moreover, it supplies a means of resistance to the perceived hegemony of modern, scientific, liberal ideology in North America. Various social sciences, but especially ethnography, have proved to be helpful new tools for interpreting these local traditions. Likewise, popular piety has fostered a renewed appreciation of the aesthetic and practical dimensions of these practices. In terms of ecclesiology, popular religion raises challenging questions about the *sensus fidelium* and reception, the threat of syncretism and superstition, and the role of ideology critique within the hermeneutics of Christian beliefs and practices.[20]

What about Catholics in the United States of European descent? It seems that precisely when African Americans are reclaiming a lost and repressed past, and Hispanics are forced to be defensive about their heritage even while they are asserting its importance for the United States, people of European descent are in the midst of a transition in terms of their ethnic identity. But what is the nature of the transition? It is commonly recognized that the ideology of the melting pot and cultural assimilation has never squared well with the experience of Catholic immigrants.[21] But with the decline of many language-based ethnic parishes—Polish, Italian, and German— what are we witnessing now? Has the strength of ethnic traditions among first and second generation European Americans been permanently eroded by social mobility, geographical migration, and ethnic intermarriage? Is concern for ethnicity limited to lower and working class people, and once individuals are upwardly mobile, does ethnicity become decreasingly important? A number of commentators have argued that in the 1960s and 70s there was an ethnic revival among European Americans, evidenced in the rise of ethnic festivals and the celebration of ethnic cuisine in the 1980s. The experience is complex and varied. Some, like my parents, second and third generation descendants who were not upwardly mobile, seem to exhibit ethnic disinterest, amnesia, and possibly shame. For my father and his German ancestors, after World Wars I and II, there was a conscious act of ethnic cloaking, disguise, and amnesia motivated in part by shame. For others like my Lithuanian mother, there was a feisty resistance to relishing things about "the old world," and a firm profession: "I am American." However, among numerous Italian and Irish Americans it seems that ethnic traditions were regularly invoked, celebrated, and maintained.

The study of European Catholics in the United States reveals many things about ethnic identity: disinterest, amnesia, defensiveness, assertiveness, nostalgia. Historical and social studies of ethnic parishes and neighborhoods are important here for they provide evidence of how the church provided a safe place for ethnic traditions to be defended against Protestant criticism, and a place for ethnic pride and assertiveness as social mobility occurred, but sadly it also provided a bunker mentality when African Americans migrated to the North and in relation to Protestant neighbors. Herbert Gans, and following him, Richard Alba, have spoken about the emergence of "symbolic ethnicity," as an "ethnicity of last resort," in which there is a "gradual, albeit inevitable withering of ethnic differences among Americans of European ancestors." As one historian put it: "Because of widespread social mobility and intermarriage, ethnic differences have become increasingly peripheral to the lives of Americans of recent ethnic origins. But they do not relinquish ethnic identity altogether; rather, they adapt it to their current circumstances, selecting from an ethnic heritage a few symbolic elements that do not interfere with the intermix socially, turning ethnicity thereby into an occasionally practiced avocation."[22] Are we witnessing a new social construction of a homogenized European ethnic identity propelled by ongoing intermarriage, or are the distinctive European ethnic heritages undergoing their own ongoing selective appropriation in light of changing experiences in the United States? Neither interpretation can suffice.

The history of official U.S. Catholic social teaching offers one more important piece in the puzzle of ethnic and racial diversity in the U.S. church. Against the backdrop of Roman documents, from Pius XI's letter condemning racial hatred, *Mit Brenneder Sorge* in 1937 to the Pontifical Justice and Peace Commission's 1989 document, "The Church and Racism: Toward a More Fraternal Society," the U.S. bishops' statements, including the writings of black bishops, need to be set in their proper place and scrutinized.[23] What began slowly and cautiously has developed in depth of insight and in force of expression.

A catholic ecclesiology must learn from the complex experience of ethnicity and race in the history of the church in the United States. This entails being mindful of the church's rich ethnic and racial diversity; lauding the promotion of ethnic and racial harmony and justice and the defense of immigrants and migrant workers, as well as lamenting the church's blindness, tardiness, and inconsistency in advancing these causes. We should call to mind with gratitude the many evangelists of previous generations, but we must also critically and fairly evaluate their views of Catholic cultural identity in light of recent insights into the dynamic relationship between evangelization and inculturation. Finally, we cannot underestimate what Virgilio Elizondo has claimed, that "the future is Mestizo"; that through intermarriage and through the birth of babies born of parents with diverse ethnic and racial identities a new reality is coming into existence.

Rethinking the Catholicity of the Church

How are we to think and speak about the catholicity of the church in relation to ethnic and racial diversity? What are the basic Christian beliefs that intellectually justify and affectively motivate a firm affirmation of and vital commitment to the catholicity of the church that is neither monolithic and Eurocentric nor fragmented by polycentric ethnic and racial factionalism? What are the doctrinal and communal implications of this catholicity for our understanding of the nature of the church?

The term catholic, which was affirmed as one of the notes of the church at the Council of Nicea, provides a starting point and frame of reference for this argument. The catholicity of the church is drawn from various theological currents in ancient Christianity.[24] It conveys the fullness of God's wisdom as a gift bestowed in Jesus Christ and received in word and action. This Christian wisdom is catholic because it is comprehensive, but also because it is universal in intent, destined to be communicated to all the corners of the world. As a result the Christian assembly, the *ecclesia*, is to be universal, a gathering of people from every national, ethnic, and racial grouping.

In accordance with the ministry of Paul and the verdict of the Council of Jerusalem, we see in the transition from the first to the second and third generations of Christians in the Mediterranean world a growing recognition that the gospel of Jesus Christ and the gift of the Holy Spirit were available to and being received by all people and not just the Jewish audience that constituted Jesus' original companions. But it is equally clear that in order to be universal, to be catholic, the church had to break out of a narrow conception of what it meant to be Christian. That expansion of vision took time to realize; the entire New Testament gives evidence of the earliest struggles to promote a Christian identity that was genuinely catholic.

Paul's invocation to catholicity-in-unity has echoed down through history: "There is no longer Jew or Greek . . . for all of you are one in Christ Jesus."[25] The term ethnic derives from the Greek word *ethnos*, which is found in the New Testament, where it serves as an ancient Greek synonym for the word *gentile* that comes to us from Latin (*gens/gentilis*) and designates a non-Christian and non-Jewish pagan (cf. Hebrew *goy*). Although gentile has sometimes been used in translation for Greeks or Hellenists in the New Testament, Greeks could also refer to a species of the genus ethnos or gentile.[26] In relation to Jews and Greeks, Christians were said to form a "third race" (*triton genos*),[27] which, according to Orthodox theologian John Zizioulas, "was only to indicate that it was a 'non-racial race,' a *people* who, while claiming to be the true Israel, declared at the same time that they did not care about the difference between a Greek and a Jew once these were members of the Christian Church. This attitude which transcended not only social but *also natural* divisions...was portrayed in the eucharistic community *par excellence.*"[28]

The use of Paul's phrase, "no longer Jew or Greek," and the term "third race," which Zizioulas interprets as a "nonracial race" gives rise to a question. Does this new oneness and reconciliation in Christ Jesus imply an obliteration of ethnic and racial differences through baptismal initiation? This in turn leads to two larger historical questions, which must be left unanswered here. In what ways were the cultural contributions of various converted peoples affirmed, celebrated, and incorporated into the catholic identity? And to what extent did the versions of catholicity that emerged in the Roman empire, in the high middle ages, and in the late nineteenth and early twentieth centuries with the rise of neoscholasticism and ultramontanism, inadvertently deny or suppress the values and contributions of diverse ethnic and racial groups in the interest of the unity of the Empire, Christendom, and the Holy Catholic Church?[29] What is needed is a detailed historical description and an accounting of how various European ethnic traditions were sometimes incorporated and at other times rejected by the church in order to work toward a fair and accurate understanding of the contributions of various Mediterranean and European ethnic groups in the formation of a vision of Christendom. Then mindful of the cultural amalgam of European-based traditions that helped shape classical Christendom, we would be able to appreciate the interethnic and interracial history of missionary activities in Latin America, the Caribbean, Asia, and Africa. Those rich and complex histories have a direct bearing on understanding and realizing the catholicity of the church, but not on our immediate argument.

What is of central and abiding importance, however, is that the catholicity of the church has demanded a universal outreach to peoples of various ancestral backgrounds and cultural traditions. This is the lasting legacy of the missionary impulse of nascent Christianity rooted in the prophetic anointing of the Spirit impelling Christians to witness to the gospel of Jesus Christ.

The call to catholicity was significantly transformed in the twentieth century into a moral standard for communal living in response to the scandals of genocide in Germany and racism in North America, in both situations where Christians, including Catholics, were sadly complicitous.[30] In 1938 Pius XI, responding to the situation in Germany and the United States, stated, "Catholic means universal, not racist, not nationalistic in the separatist meaning of these two attributes . . . There is only one human, universal, 'catholic' race . . . and with it and in it, different variations . . ."[31] A similar kind of argument about catholicity can be found expressed in the very different approaches of Turner, LaFarge, and Furfey. In 1919 African American Thomas Turner wrote to the U.S. bishops to decry "race prejudice" which he identified as "the outstanding sin of the present age." He urged the bishops "to inculcate the spirit of the Church's Catholicity."[32] Jesuit John LaFarge wrote in *America* in 1926 that "black Catholics represented a challenge to the genuineness of . . . catholicity."[33] And Catholic sociologist Paul Hanley Furfey stated in 1944: "Our attitude toward men of other races is a crucial test of our catholicity."[34] The demands of catholicity require now not only a universal evangelistic outreach to those of any ethnic and racial group, but also the rejection of racist and ethnocentric ideologies. This is a profound development in the church's understanding of catholicity, but take note that this formulation does not imply that catholicity requires a multicultural sensibility. This kind of argument against racism and genocide reflects a neoscholastic ecclesiology that was incarnational and at times harbored ultramontanist proclivities. This governing ecclesiology promoted a vision of Catholic cultural identity that tended to be homogeneous and monolithic, providing a bulwark of resistance in the face of errors and temptations attributed to Protestantism and modernity.

That being catholic means being multicultural, in the sense of being alert to the contributions of people of diverse ethnic and racial traditions in their reception of the gospel, was definitively articulated at the Second Vatican Council and combined with an implicit repudiation of a Eurocentric Christendom model of catholicity. Without a doubt there are many precursors and contributing factors to this decisive breakthrough: the experience and insights of countless missionaries from the sixteenth to the twentieth centuries; the official recognition of the value and validity of different liturgical rites from Eastern churches;[35] the German romantic appreciation of the individuality of social and linguistic cultures through the concept of *Volksgeist*, despite its pernicious applications;[36] other theologians, like U.S. Benedictine Virgil Michel who championed in the early twentieth century the importance of inculturating the gospel and liturgy;[37] and finally one should mention Pius XII's *Evangelii Praecones* of 1951 which urged a new "respect for native civilizations, for the individuality of the different peoples and for all the elements of truth that Christianity may find in them."[38]

There are many precursors, but the Second Vatican Council[39] marked the official recognition of the value of the diversity of cultures, which includes by implication the diverse ethnic and racial sources of culture. *Lumen Gentium* stated, "It has come about through divine providence that, in the course of time, different Churches, set up in various places by the apostles and their successors, joined together in a multiplicity of organically united groups which, whilst safeguarding the unity of the faith, and the unique divine structure of the universal Church, have their own discipline, enjoy their own liturgical usage and inherit a theological and spiritual patrimony . . . This multiplicity of local Churches, unified in a common effort, shows all the more resplendently the catholicity of the undivided Church" (n. 23.4). And in *Gaudium et Spes*, culture is recognized as a social and historical reality. As a result, it is said that "we can speak about a plurality of cultures. For different styles of living and different scales of values originate in different ways of using things, of working and self-expression, of practicing religion and of behavior, of establishing laws and juridical institutions, of developing science and the arts and of cultivating beauty" (n. 53). Responding to this diversity of cultures, "the Church has been sent to all ages and nations and, therefore, is not tied exclusively and indissolubly to any race or nation, to any one particular way of life, or to any customary practices, ancient or modern. The Church is faithful to its traditions and is at the same time conscious of its universal mission; it can, then, enter into communication with different forms of culture, thereby enriching both itself and the cultures themselves" (n. 58.2). These official statements reflect a new multicultural dimension of the catholicity of the church. This deeper appreciation is restated with forceful simplicity in the 1984 statement by the U.S. black bishops: "To be Catholic is to be universal. To be universal is not to be uniform. It does mean the gifts of individuals and of particular groups become the common heritage shared by all."[40] The many cultures of the Christian community are a part of the common catholic heritage.

The call to be catholic means to be universal in our evangelization, it means repudiating racist and ethnocentric ideologies, and it means realizing the multicultural identity of the one, holy, catholic, apostolic church. But difficult questions still remain. If in the past the catholicity of the church was united to a certain degree of uniformity in cultural expression, the question is where do we go from here? If efforts to unite the church restricted the catholicity of the church in its self-realization, would a more genuine realization of the catholicity of the church require an expanded notion of its unity? On the other hand, if polycentricism flourishes will it not threaten the unity of the church by means of syncretism and group rivalry at regional, national, and international levels?

Neither Homogenization nor Balkanization

Let me propose, then, that the challenge for a genuinely catholic ecclesiology is to avoid two extremes. On the one hand, a theology of the church that is authentically catholic must repudiate cultural homogenization in the church. This error can be characterized as a version of ecclesiological monophysitism wherein unity in Catholic culture, which has been defined by a hierarchical teaching office that has been predominantly Eurocentric in outlook, is promoted at the expense of diversity of ethnic and racial cultures in local churches within the global church.[41]

On the other hand, in order to be truly catholic a theology of the church must also condemn the illusory advantages of balkanization, wherein ethnic and racial distinctions are the cause for separateness and isolation. Such ethnic and racial elitism or sectarianism, can be identified as a version of ecclesiological nestorianism, wherein ethnic and racial diversity and distinctiveness are accentuated at the expense of a dynamic unity and collaboration in the church.

As an alternative to ecclesiological homogenization and balkanization, the nature and mission of the church must be articulated in such a way that ethnic and racial identities are neither ignored nor idolized, but rather that ethnic and racial cultural traditions are viewed as important assets and charisms in the church, offered for the common good and for mutual enrichment. At the same time, these cultural traditions are not immune from blindness and sin. They can be destructive of both those inside and outside the designated group, and as a result, a need for mutual discernment emerges from the church's dialogical communion.

In order to be genuinely catholic, our vision of the church must be neither monophysite nor nestorian. Mindful of the

Chalcedonian heritage, we must be able to affirm that without confusion or identification, without division or separation, the distinction of ethnic and racial groups is never abolished by their union in the church, but the character proper to each ethnic and racial group is preserved as they come together in the one, holy, catholic, and apostolic church. Now I realize that this transposition of the classic Chalcedonian formula merits further scrutiny in order to determine the precise nature of the analogical predication being proposed and its limitations. Moreover, this theological proposal must take into account the evolutionary and eschatological character of ethnic and racial identities. But I believe this formula offers a way of thinking about unity and diversity in the church that respects enduring and evolving distinctions, and that also posits a vital union.

Corpus Christi Catholicity

How is this fuller understanding of the catholicity of the church as multicultural to be theologically warranted and promoted? Earlier in this century the doctrine of the mystical body of Christ served this purpose and was used to repudiate racism and to advance racial justice and harmony in the local church.

John LaFarge anchored his understanding of the catholicity of the church to the doctrine of the mystical body of Christ. In his book *Interracial Justice* he argued that "Through the institution of His Church as a universal, perpetual, supra-national Society, all mankind was offered participation in a unity infinitely higher than that which the mere fact of common creation and common anthropological origin afford. This higher unity is symbolized in the figure of the Mystical Body of Christ. As members of the one Body of which Christ is the Head the children of God enter into a unique relationship not only with one another but with the whole of mankind as well."[42] Later in that same work he says, "The theological doctrine of the *universality* or catholicity of the Church [is] the doctrine that races and nations and peoples and conditions of mankind are embraced in the Church of Christ and in His Mystical Body."[43] LaFarge drew inspiration from the passage on the mystical body motif in Pius XI's encyclical *Quadragesimo Anno* (n. 90) and from the broader theological currents in Europe and in the United States that culminated five years later in 1943 with Pope Pius XII's *Mystici Corporis Christi.*[44] David Southern observes that "Although LaFarge related black rights to natural rights and American values, he argued that basic human rights for Catholics derived first and foremost from God and could be extrapolated most strikingly from the doctrine of the Mystical Body of Christ."[45]

Another proponent of the doctrine of the mystical body as an indispensable component of Catholic social doctrine was Paul Hanley Furfey, who, along with Virgil Michel, was an advocate for the Catholic Worker movement in the United States. Since Furfey was affiliated with the Catholic Worker Movement, it may be tempting to emphasize the fact that Furfey was not an enthusiastic supporter and apparently was even critical of LaFarge's kind of arguments against racism and of his promotion of interracial councils.[46] Indeed, LaFarge's mixed natural law and mystical body of Christ argument seems temperate in its call for radical transformation and its resistance to complicity with racism when compared to Furfey's writings. However, Furfey was never explicitly critical of LaFarge, and indeed later in his life he commended LaFarge for "making the Christian social ideal concrete."[47] Nevertheless, Furfey denounced with great passion other policy makers and fellow Catholics who were conformists, assimilationists, who lived by a mediocre standard, and who avoided speaking in the language of Catholic doctrine and liturgical practices and living in the heroic manner this faith required.[48] In his own words, if a Catholic speaks about "Negro-white relations in the United States and fails to mention the supernatural aspects of the problem . . . The remedies he proposes [may be] sensible and sane. He may even quote papal condemnations of racism. But he has nothing to say about the ultimate basis of such condemnations. He has nothing to say about the great duty of Christian charity which requires us to love all men with an intense supernatural love. He neglects the inspiring doctrine of the Mystical Body of Christ and its tragic violation by interracial hatred."[49] For Furfey, belief in the doctrine of the mystical body of Christ requires participation in, we would say solidarity with, the suffering of others. "One may say 'It's too bad these Negroes in the slums are dying off like flies from tuberculosis; but after all, it's not my responsibility. I'm not affected.' A man may talk such non-sense, but it doesn't alter the cold fact that 'if one member suffers anything, all the members suffer with it.'"[50]

Furfey goads his readers, challenging their complacency. It never occurs to people who speak about various social ills, like race relations, that the remedy lies in the mystical body doctrine and in participation in the Eucharist.[51] With biting sarcasm, he would also indicate the repercussions for taking his word to heart. "If we want to keep our reputation for sanity and common sense, we would do well to join in the usual American persecution of the Negro . . . But suppose we should begin to take Catholic doctrine at its face value. Suppose we should treat Negroes as though we really took seriously the Mystical Body. Suppose we showed our contempt for the nasty doctrine of white supremacy in sensational, dramatic ways? What would be the answer to that? A lynch mob, possibly. A noose at the end of a rope. Martyrdom for a Catholic doctrine perhaps. Not an alluring prospect to flesh and blood. But we would be right!"[52]

While we can easily find evidence that the human dignity of each person and human equality have been theologically based on the conviction that each person is created by God in the image of God, it was the mystical body doctrine that provided a common focal point during the first half of the twentieth century. This doctrine of the mystical body of Christ was nurtured and undergirded by an incarnational model of ecclesiology that grew in influence during the second half of the nineteenth century and the first half of the twentieth century and that has proved to be quite versatile.[53] This incarnational ecclesiology nurtured the pious sacramental imagination of the Catholic faithful to live good and holy lives. It also justified a clerical, institutional, legalistic, and ultramontanist approach to church identity, authority, and mission. At the same time, it supported the social mission of the church and promoted programs of social action, such as Catholic Action and Catholic Worker. Moreover, its versatility in application is seen in the fact that LaFarge could combine it with loosely neoscholastic forms of argument that could appeal to Catholic and non-Catholic audiences, while Furfey used it to speak in a specifically doctrinal and liturgical idiom, devoid of natural law forms of argumentation.

But what seems noteworthy, and really not surprising looking back over the last thirty years, is that the body of Christ ecclesiology was used at the time to defend the equality of blacks and whites, their common humanity, their universal identity, and as a result the need for blacks and whites to work together for unity. It was not used, as far as I have been able to determine, to identify the different contributions of the various ethnic and racial parts in the whole body of Christ. The proponents of the mystical body of Christ saw it as a key doctrinal vehicle for advancing a prophetic critique of racism, but it seems not to have occurred to them, or contrary to their inclination, to employ it to affirm the importance of cultural differences as gifts to be envisioned as parts of the church's living body.[54] For example, LaFarge considers whether there are racial differences between blacks and whites—physical, mental, and moral, but his argument is directed against any racial inferiority. He is not concerned with distinctive cultural contributions. Identifying and celebrating ethnic and racial diversity was not a part of this incarnational ecclesiology. The criticisms of LaFarge's approach to race relations in the church by the Catholic African American Thomas Turner demonstrate the painful limits of LaFarge's version of an incarnational and mystical body ecclesiology: besides being clerical and paternalistic, it was unable to recognize and cherish the important cultural contributions and leadership of African Americans to the life of the church.[55]

Trinitarian Catholicity

Since the heyday of the mystical body ecclesiology in the first half of the twentieth century, the christological arguments employed to advance the catholicity of the church have changed.[56] Over the last thirty years Catholic theology is slowly moving beyond the stalemate between a high and low christology, a descending and ascending christology to a more comprehensive christology that draws strength from the plurivocity of New Testament witnesses, as well as from creedal and other theological authorities. As a result, the christological resources for clarifying the nature and the mission of the church have been enriched.[57] The doctrines of the incarnation and the body of Christ will remain central abiding resources for ecclesiology, but they must now be set in a larger and more thorough frame of reference provided by the various christologies in the New Testament and the history of doctrine.

There are now many other christological arguments employed to address ethnic and racial diversity in the church. Besides the parable of the good Samaritan, which has long served as an indicator of the catholic outlook of Jesus, attention is now frequently given to various aspects of Jesus' initially Jewish-oriented renewal mission. Jesus transgresses social boundaries to reach out to various marginalized groups through his teachings, healings and exorcisms, and table fellowship. Jesus appealed to those beyond the borders of traditional piety, and he also confronted those who had a narrower, more exclusivist understanding of Jewish identity. Jesus' death is the human outcome for disturbing the social and religious order in the interest of reaching out to more, and his resurrection is God's vindication of this person and mission. This greater appreciation for the catholicity of Jesus' announcement of the reign of God is important for ecclesiologies in its own right, and people like Virgilio Elizondo employ this focal topic with great effectiveness.[58] Indeed, retrieving these deep currents in the synoptic portrayals of Jesus can shed fresh light on the deep bonds between Jesus' mission and Paul's gentile mission. Moreover, the recovery of these profoundly catholic impulses in Jesus' ministry can surely contribute to a fuller accounting of the doctrine of the incarnation and the Pauline doctrine of the body of Christ as they bear on the nature and the mission of the church. Perhaps for many a more developed approach to Jesus will provide a sufficient way to address ethnic and racial diversity. Indeed this stereophonic christology provides a necessary ingredient for affirming a multicultural ecclesiology; necessary, indeed, but not sufficient.

The larger implication of the Second Vatican Council is that an ecclesiology based on the doctrines of the incarnation and the mystical body of Christ has abiding significance, but that it is deficient: a genuinely catholic understanding of the church and tradition is made possible not only by a more comprehensive christology, but also by a robust pneumatology, and a recovery of God's glorious activity in the pluriform creation, within a doctrine of the Trinity. As George Tavard puts it: "The Trinitarian framework of the ecclesiology of Vatican Council II is of great importance even though it has not had much of an impact on subsequent developments in the Church's life."[59] This must change. In particular, we need to discover how the doctrine of the Trinity, which constitutes our most cherished beliefs in their most comprehensive parameters, provides a proper mode of discourse for articulating an ecclesiology able to affirm the value of ethnic and racial diversity and to motivate work in history toward an eschatological unity in God. A trinitarian ecclesiology enables us to reject homogenization and balkanization. Let me offer a few indications of what this might mean.

The doctrines of God's creation and the Holy Spirit complement a christological approach to ethnic and racial diversity in the church. God's action in creation has been heralded throughout modern Catholic social teaching as the strongest pledge of the dignity and equality of human persons, created in the image of God, and as the basis for the teachings on social justice and human rights. But if our common humanity has been affirmed by the doctrine of creation, we have yet to fully explore God's creation of the human person into linguistic and historical communities and how the gift of creation with its genetic codes and environmental influences contributes to an understanding of the ethnic and racial particularity of the person and community. God has created each individual with a human identity and a freedom that is destined for God. This identity reflects the divine purpose and the very glory of God. Human identity includes ethnic and racial features transmitted biologically and communally that can serve as means for the discovery of God, community, and the self. But the human person is often lured to things less than God, and through human freedom sin corrupts what is given as gift and passed on in language, community, and custom. God's creation is not an established structure, but an eschatological journey underway.

The doctrine of the Holy Spirit also provides an indispensable resource for affirming the importance of ethnic and racial diversity for the church's identity and for promoting the dynamic flourishing of unity amidst diversity. With the sending of the Spirit at Pentecost, people from various languages and cultures were empowered to receive the gospel and thrive as temples of the Spirit. Indeed, it is the Spirit of

God that inspires and empowers the early Christian missionaries to reach out to people of all languages and cultures. With this reception of the Spirit, the project identified with the tower of Babel can be toppled.[60] No longer is ethnic and racial diversity something that must be overcome and denied in the interest of ascending to God through the imposition of cultural ecclesial control. Instead, there is the divine directive to be open to the Spirit's distinctive gifts given to various groups not simply for ornamentation and style in the body collective, but as vital contributions for the common good of the church and the world. Through baptism Christians are given a share of the Spirit that binds them together through the *instinctus fidei*, but this Spirit also cooperates with diverse Christians in reception and toward a more genuinely catholic *sensus fidelium*.

It is ultimately through a fully trinitarian ecclesiology that the catholicity of the church will be realized. This is because through the doctrine of the Trinity we learn that each individual's identity and mission are discovered and fulfilled in communion, and that greater interdependence and greater freedom coincide. This dynamic interplay of persons, identities, and missions in the Trinity provides the deepest and most profound bases for thinking about our life together. Together God's agency in creation, in Jesus Christ, and in the Spirit enables us to envision a person's distinctive identity as a reflection of the abundance of God's life-giving love, as a reflection of the glory of God, which must be celebrated and reverenced. The creation of human identity, which includes ethnic and racial dimensions, is not an eternal structure, but is rather an historical and eschatological reality, which can be corrupted by sin. Ultimately, however, human identity is a gift and a mystery, which must be accepted, purified, and elevated by participating with the Trinity in history.

The most basic reason why a trinitarian ecclesiology is so important for the topic of ethnic and racial diversity in the church is because it provides the deepest reasons for the church's commitment to dialogical communion. The Roman Catholic Church is moving from an incarnational ecclesiology that often supported a descending and legalistic model of hierarchical authority to a trinitarian ecclesiology of dialogical communion. This trinitarian viewpoint provides the most comprehensive way to address a wide variety of classical issues in ecclesiology: the relationships between office and charism, between teaching and learning in the church, between the communicative actions of consultation, collaboration, exercises of the church's teaching office, and reception, between the local church and the universal church, and the dynamic relationship between unity and diversity. So too, a trinitarian ecclesiology offers reasons for why a commitment to catholicity requires dialogical communion among people of diverse ethnic and racial groups.

Much more needs to be said about how a commitment to dialogical communion can help address the issues raised by ethnic and racial diversity. But the following remarks will have to suffice.

It used to be debated whether ethnocentrism and racism were based on ignorance or were a manifestation of personal sin and social sin.[61] We do not need to choose. Pope John Paul II has helped us to recognize the importance of dialogical communion in situations where there are destructive patterns of discourse and behavior.[62] Dialogue, he has argued, can serve as an examination of conscience in which individual and social sin can come to light, and repentance and reconciliation can take place. This is a mandate for a genuinely catholic church. Equally important for this catholicity is that we need to learn from each other, not only so that we can appreciate the gifts that come from people of other ethnic and racial traditions, but also so that our own understanding of the Catholic faith can benefit from diverse receptions of the gospel of Jesus Christ. Forgiveness and learning must take place together in order to overcome sin and ignorance so that a genuine catholicity can emerge.

It has been argued in the past by Thomas Aquinas and others that the Jews were chosen as a part of God's peda- gogical purpose.[63] Now there is certainly room here for a critical evaluation of how the Jews were viewed as a part of God's plan of education, but it was at least implied that as a part of God's pedagogy the Jews have taught (and we would add can continue to teach) those far beyond the Jewish bor- ders including those within Christian churches. Thomas also taught that the divine plan of history required that the gospel be spread to all the corners of the world.[64] In eigh- teenth- and nineteenth-century Germany, Gotthold Ephraim Lessing, Johann Gottfried Herder, and Johann Sebastian Drey argued that by the church spreading the gospel to all nations, God is involved in a process of educating the human race. For rationalists like Lessing this meant that specific Christian beliefs and practices would be distilled into a reli- gion of reason and moral practice, whereas for romantics and orthodox Christians like Herder and Drey there were more complex processes of divine pedagogy at work.[65] It has been clear for quite some time that we are not reduced to a choice between a Christendom paradigm of the divine ped- agogy and a rationalist paradigm. However, thanks to the developments over the course of this century, we are now in a position to realize that previous efforts to develop a peda- gogical view of history offer only part of the truth. At the end of this millennium, we are now coming to a fuller eschato- logical realization that the proclamation of the gospel to all ethnic and racial groups is indeed a part of God's pedagogy. But it is not only that various peoples from the diversity of ethnic and racial groups will receive and be transformed by the gospel, but also that Christians throughout the world can and need to benefit from these diverse receptions of the Gospel. The European reception of the Gospel has had a pro- found influence on how we have understood Christianity in the past to which we are all indebted, but in the future Christianity will be enriched by the reception of the Gospel among the diversity of peoples on the earth. This is the learning church and the teaching church actively realizing its multiethnic and multiracial constitution.

In the end, if we were to imagine the heavenly banquet, extrapolating from the glimpses provided by the prophet Isaiah (25:6), by Jesus' parable of the great banquet (Luke 14:15–24) and his table fellowship, and most profoundly by the eucharistic banquet, what might we find? We would have to expect that there would be choice foods and beverages from all the ethnic and racial cultures of the world and the sounds of the great diversity of language and music in the air. Genuine dialogue and ecstatic dancing would be in abundance. This will be possible because the grace of dialogical communion and catholicity will bring us to a more profound profession of our trinitarian faith, giving us all the more reason to celebrate and worship the God that has brought us together.

Notes

1. I wish to thank a number of people for their help on this essay: M. Shawn Copeland in a special way for her wisdom on this subject and for research leads and encouragement, and Christine Firer Hinze, Mary Ehle, and Dennis Doyle for their reactions and recommendations.

2. For an overview of concepts and theories of ethnicity and race with bibliography, see John Hutchinson and Anthony D. Smith, *Ethnicity* (Oxford: Oxford University Press, 1996); Michael Omi and Howard Winant, *Racial Formation in the United States: From the 1960s to the 1990s*, Second edition (New York and London: Routledge, 1994); Thomas F. Gossett, *Race: The History of an Idea in America* (Dallas: Southern Methodist University Press, 1963); Ian Hannaford, *Race: The History of An Idea in the West* (Washington D.C.: The Woodrow Wilson Center Press and Baltimore: The Johns Hopkins University Press, 1996).

3. It is currently debated whether racial diversity should be equated with ethnic diversity. Orlando Patterson, a Harvard University sociologist, argues that race is a scientifically meaningless category in "The Race Trap," *The New York Times*, Friday, July 11, 1997, A, 21. But Omi and Winant contend that to equate ethnicity and race would be to obscure the common social perception of racial differences that so pro-

foundly affects peoples' lives, and to ignore the further differentiation afforded by ethnic affiliation (e.g., Ghanaian blacks and Jamaican blacks, Filipino and Japanese Asians); Omi and Winant, *Racial Formation in the United States*. In my judgment theologians and pastoral ministers, like social scientists and politicians, cannot simply ignore racial differences (to be "color blind") or reduce them to ethnic differences. This would be to deny the ongoing social impact of racial differences. Various social and cultural modes of analyses are important for investigating both ethnic and racial differences.

4. Ethnic and racial identities intersect with national affiliations, but ethnicity and race are conceptually distinguishable from national identity because of migration and blended national populations. There are also deep historical affiliations between certain ethnic and racial groups and specific religions (e.g., Judaism and Buddhism), but religious conversions transgress group boundaries and create hybrid communities.

5. The extent to which a monolithic understanding of Catholic identity is classical or a construct of modern Catholicism merits consideration. For the later viewpoint, see Joseph Komonchak, "Modernity and the Construction of Roman Catholicism," in *Modernism as a Social Construct* Papers for the working group on Roman Catholic Modernism, eds. George Gilmore, Hans Rollman, and Gary Lease (Mobile, AL: Spring Hill College, 1991), 11-41.

6. On the politics of identity, see Iris Marion Young, *Justice and the Politics of Difference* (Princeton: Princeton University Press, 1990); a sampling of the recent debate about multiculturalism, see Arthur M. Schlesinger, Jr. *The Disuniting of America: Reflections on a Multicultural Society* (New York: W. W. Norton & Co., 1992); Robert Hughes, *Culture of Complaint: The Fraying of America* (New York: Oxford University Press, 1993); Nathan Glazer, *We Are All Multiculturalists Now* (Cambridge, MA: Harvard University Press, 1997), and Martin Marty, *The One and the Many: America's Struggle for the Common Good* (Cambridge, MA: Harvard University Press, 1997). For a theological assessment of globalization, see Robert J. Schreiter, *The New Catholicity: Theology Between the Global and the Local* (Maryknoll, NY: Orbis Books, 1997).

7. M. Shawn Copeland offers a moving description of the various national, ethnic, and racial groups in the United States in "Self-Identity in a Multicultural Church in a Multicultural Context," in *The Multicultural Church: A New Landscape in U.S. Theologies*, ed. William Cenkner (New York/Mahwah, NJ: Paulist Press, 1996), 5-23.

8. Jürgen Moltmann, *The Coming of God: Christian Eschatology* (London: SCM, 1996), 168-178.

9. The Lilly Endowment funded what was to be a three-part study done under the auspices of the National Conference of Catholic Bishops on African, Hispanic, and Asian American Catholics. Two of the three parts appeared. The first part appeared in 1993, *Strangers and Aliens No Longer: The Hispanic Presence in the Church of the United States*, ed. Eugene F. Hemrick (Washington, D.C.: United States Catholic Conference, 1993), and part two came out in 1996, *Keep Your Hand on the Plow: The African American Presence in the Catholic Church* (Washington D.C.: United States Catholic Conference, 1996). The third part on Asian American Catholics has not appeared and may be stalled. In 1990 there was published "A Catholic Response to the Asian Presence" prepared by the National Catholic Education Association. It is difficult to find writings on Asian Americans in the Catholic church. There is no Asian presence as such, but only specific Asian communities: Filipino, Japanese, Korean, Chinese, Vietnamese, Laotian, Thai, and Cambodian. I wish to thank Guy Wilson and Trish Stevanich from the United States Catholic Conference for pertinent information.

10. (Chicago: University of Chicago Press, 1996).

11. McGreevy, 30. In 1920s the Carnegie Foundation spoke of "racial churches" to describe the parishes of ethnic Europeans, 10f.

12. Ibid., 34.

13. Ibid., 36.

14. David Southern, *John LaFarge and the Limits of Catholic Interracialism 1911-1963* (Baton Rouge: Louisiana State University Press, 1996).

15. (New York: America Press, 1937). The book combined: a discussion of the concept of race; an exposition of the Catholic doctrine of the dignity and equality of each person, of human rights based on this dignity, and the correlative need for unity in the human community; a treatment of the practical problems of security, segregation, prejudice, and intermarriage; and a proposal to address these issues through education and catholic interracial councils.

16. Southern, 214-242. A study of *Humani Generis Unitas* with the French version of this encyclical draft has been prepared by Georges Passelecq and Bernard Suchecky, *L'encyclique cachée de Pie XI: Une occasion manquée de l'Église face à l'antisémitisme* (Paris: Éditions la Découvertre, 1995); English translation, *The Hidden Encyclical of Pius XI*, trans. Steven Rendall (New York: Harcourt Brace, 1997).

17. *The Mystery of Iniquity* (Milwaukee, Wisconsin: The Bruce Publishing Co., 1944); *The Respectable Murderers: Social Evil and Christian Conscience* (New York: Herder and Herder, 1966). Furfey also directed a dissertation by Thomas Harte, which included an analysis of

LaFarge's Catholic Interracial Council of New York. He criticized it for being too hierarchical and too wordy, and insufficiently confrontative of power structures and patterns of behavior. See Southern, 210-211.

18. See, for example, Allan Figueroa Deck, *The Second Wave: Hispanic Ministry and the Evangelization of Cultures* (New York: Paulist Press, 1989); Jay P. Dolan, gen. ed., *The Notre Dame History of Hispanic Catholics in the U.S.*, 3 volumes, including Allan Figueroa Deck, ed. *Hispanic Catholic Culture in the U.S.: Issues and Concerns* (Notre Dame, IN: University of Notre Dame Press, 1994).

19. See especially, Virgilio Elizondo, *Galilean Journey: The Mexican-American Promise* (Maryknoll, NY: Orbis Books, 1983); Idem., *The Future is Mestizo: Life Where Cultures Meet* (Bloomington, IN: Meyer Stone, 1988).

20. See Roberto S. Goizueta, *Caminemos Con Jesús: Toward a Hispanic/Latino Theology of Accompaniment* (Maryknoll, NY: Orbis Books, 1995); Orlando O. Espín, *The Faith of the People: Theological Reflections on Popular Catholicism* (Maryknoll, NY: Orbis Books, 1997).

21. Philip Gleason has often addressed the subject of Catholic European ethnics, see *The Conservative Reformers: German American Catholics and the Social Order* (Notre Dame, IN: University of Notre Dame Press, 1968); "American Identity and Americanization," in the *Harvard Encyclopedia of American Ethnic Groups*, ed., Stephan Therstrom (Cambridge MA: Belknap Press, 1980), 31-58; "Immigrant Past, Ethnic Present," and "Immigrant Assimilation and the Crisis of Americanization," in *Keeping the Faith: American Catholicism Past and Present* (Notre Dame, IN: University of Notre Dame Press, 1987), 35-81; *Speaking of Diversity: Language and Ethnicity in Twentieth-Century America* (Baltimore: Johns Hopkins University Press, 1992).

22. Richard D. Alba, *Ethnic Identity: The Transformation of White America* (New Haven: Yale University Press, 1990), 29; Also see Herbert J. Gans, "Symbolic Ethnicity: The Future of Ethnic Groups and Cultures in America," in *On the Making of Americans: Essays in Honor of David Riesmann*, ed. Herbert J. Gans, et al. (Philadelphia: University of Pennsylvania Press, 1979), 193-220.

23. Pope Pius XI, *Mit Brenneder Sorge* (On the Church and the German Reich), in *The Papal Encyclicals 1903-1939*, ed. Claudia Carlen, IHM (Wilmington, NC: McGrath Publishing Company, 1981), 525-535; Pontifical Justice and Peace Commission, "The Church and Racism: Toward a More Fraternal Society," *Origins* 18 (February 23, 1989): 613-626; *Pastoral Letters of the United States Catholic Bishops*, ed. Hugh J. Nolan (Washington, D.C.: National Conference of Catholic Bishops,

United States Catholic Conference, 1983); in *Pastoral Letters*, vol. I, 1792-1940, see "Pastoral Letter" (1852), 203-204; "Pastoral Letter" (1919), 289; "To the German Hierarchy" (1837), 419-420; in *Pastoral Letters*, vol. II, 1941-1961, see "Discrimination and Christian Conscience" (1958), 201-206; "Protest Against Bigotry" (1960); 232-233; in *Pastoral Letters*, vol. III, 1962-1974, see "On Racial Harmony" (1963), 17-19; "Statement on National Race Crisis" (1968), 156-160. See also David Gibson, "Black Catholics in America: A Documentation Overview," in *Keep Your Hand on the Plow*, 1-8 (cited in note 9); David Gibson, "Hispanic Ministry," in *Strangers and Aliens No Longer*, 21-29 (cited in note 9).

24. See Avery Dulles, *The Catholicity of the Church* (Oxford: Clarendon Press, 1985); John D. Zizioulas, "Eucharist and Catholicity," *Being as Communion* (Crestwood, NY: St. Vladimir's Seminary Press, 1985), 143-169.

25. See Galatians 3:28; Colossians 3:11; 1 Corinthians 12:13; following Zizioulas, 151; neither adult nor child, see Matthew 19:13; 14:21; neither rich nor poor, see James 2:2–7; 1 Corinthians 11:20f.

26. Hutchinson and Smith, 4. The term *ethnos* was used in a variety of ways by ancient Greek writers indicating a collectivity—band, tribe, race, caste. But in the New Testament and church fathers, *ta ethne* refers to gentile peoples. So according to this usage, Christians and Jews are not ethnics, everyone else is. However the term gentile Christians and gentile Christian churches can be found in Paul's writings (e.g., Romans 16:4; Galatians 2:12; Ephesians 3:1). Also see *A Greek-English Lexicon*, eds. H. G. Liddell and R. Scott (Oxford: Clarendon Press, 1968); Walter Bauer, with W. F. Arndt and F. W. Gingrich, *A Greek-English Lexicon of the New Testament and Other Early Christian Literature* (Chicago: The University of Chicago Press, 1958).

27. The Pontifical Justice and Peace Commission says "third race" is an expression of Tertullian and cites *Ad Nat.* 1.8, PL 1, in "The Church and Racism," 625. Thanks to the research of Martin Albl I have learned that the term *Triton Genos*, which has been translated as the third race or third kind or third people, is found in its first form in the second fragment from the early second-century document *The Preaching of Peter*, which is found in Clement of Alexandria's *Stromata*: "Learn then, you also, holily and righteously what we deliver to you and keep it, worshiping God through Christ in a new way. For we have found in the Scriptures, who the Lord says, 'Behold, I make with you a new covenant, not as I made (one) with your fathers in Mount Horeb.' A new one has he made with us. For what has reference to the Greeks and the Jews is old. But we are Christians, who as a third race worship him in a new way," Clement of Alexandria, *Stromata*, in *The Ante-*

Nicene Fathers, vol. 2, eds. A. Roberts and J. Donaldson (Peabody MA: Hendrickson Publishing, 1994), 6. 5. 39-41. The emphasis here seems to be on three kinds of worship. This formula, *Triton Genos*, according to Albl, probably influenced the *Apology of Aristides*, which may date to the time of Hadrian (117-138), and there it does suggest Christians are a distinct people in an ethnic sense (2.1; 14.1). Also see the *Epistle to Diognetus* (circa second or third century), and Heracleon's *Commentary on the Gospel of John* (circa middle of the second century). Martin Albl, "Christians as a Third Race: The Meaning of Triton Genos in the Preaching of Peter" (Unpublished manuscript, paper read at the North American Patristic Society Convention, May 1997); *The Apology of Aristides* is found in *Ante-Nicene Fathers*, vol. 9, ed. Allan Menzies (Peabody, MA: Hendrickson Publishers, 1994), 269-279; Henry G. Meecham, *The Epistle of Diogenetus: The Greek Text with Introduction, Translation, and Notes* (Manchester: Manchester University Press, 1949); Elaine Pagels, *The Johannine Gospel in Gnostic Exegesis: Heracleon's Commentary on John* (Nashville: Abingdon Press, 1973).

28. Zizioulas, 151.

29. Yves M.-J. Congar, *The Catholic Church and the Race Question* (Paris: UNESCO, 1953). Congar maintains that Christianity, the Graeco-Roman world, and the Roman Empire offered no race doctrine and were all "fundamentally aracial" (33). The Fathers relished the unity of different peoples in one body. Opponents of Christianity were heretics and infidels: Jews, Arab Moors, Islam, the Teutonic knights against the Balts and Slavs, and Turks; "no race sentiment entered into any of these struggles." But Congar also admits that "Roman universality sometimes involved too much uniformity, too much submission, too much neglect of proper national particularities" (34). Congar prefers to speak about the diversity of peoples and civilizations and not of a diversity of races. Adaptation to local language and customs, artistic form, and native clergy were gradually affirmed during the twentieth century as important (41).

30. Whether we can identify the usage of catholicity as a moral standard in an earlier period and in response to other acts of racism and ethnocentrism seems dubious.

31. Cited by Pontifical Justice and Peace Commission, "The Church and Racism," 624, n. 11. The quotation is taken from a speech delivered to members of the College of the Propagation of the Faith, which appeared in *l'Observatorio Romano*, July, 30, 1938, and included in *Documentation Catholique* (Paris: Bayard Press, 1938), 579-580.

32. See Cyprian Davis, *The History of Black Catholics in the United States* (New York: Crossroad, 1990), 220.

33. Cited by Southern, 92; originally in "Hardcover," *America* 36 (November 13, 1926): 109-111.

34. Furfey, *The Mystery of Iniquity*, 138.

35. On the different rites, see A. G. Mortimort, ed. *The Church at Prayer*, vol. 1, *Principles of Liturgy* (Collegeville, MN: The Liturgical Press, 1983), 27-43; *Anàmnesis*, vol. 2, *La Liturgia*, panorama storico generale (Genova: Case Editrice Marietti, 1978).

36. Johann Sebastian Drey speaks of the importance of individual nations and peoples in "Vom Geist und Wesen des Katholizismus," a four-part essay published in *Theologische Quartalschrift* 1 (1819): 8-23, 193-210, 369-391, 559-574; it also was reprinted in *Geist des Christentums und des Katholizismus*, ed. J. R. Geiselmann (Mainz: Matthias Gruenwald, 1940), 193-234. Johann Adam Möhler's *Die Einheit in der Kirche* (1825) also acknowledged the principle of individuality and diversity as a factor contributing to the church's vital unity, see Johann Adam Möhler's *Die Einheit in der Kirche*, ed. J. R. Geiselmann (Cologne and Olten: Jakob Hegner, 1957). Johann Gottfried Herder and Friedrich Schleiermacher too affirmed the importance of individuality when assessing the diverse peoples and communities in their understanding of the history of the church, see Herder, *Reflections on the Philosophy of the History of Mankind* (Chicago: University of Chicago Press, 1968) and Schleiermacher, *Brief Outline of Theology as a Field of Study* (Lewiston, NY: The Mellon Press, 1988).

37. "The Church of Christ was founded for all times and peoples. *In her embrace there is room* not only for personal differences among individual men, but also *for national customs and traits, for varying cultures and civilizations* . . . The true Christian spirit is too rich in its treasures and possibilities to be confined within the limits of any single national culture. To the development of the fullest Christ-life all nations are called to contribute, each in its own way. Each distinctive nationality is capable of a different expression of the total spirit of Christ. All will agree in the essentials of the Christ-life, but in their variety they will also help to contribute towards making up together the fullness of the stature of Christ." This quotation is taken from Virgil Michel's *The Christian in the World* (Collegeville, MN: The Liturgical Press, 1939), 174-175, and is cited in *The Full Stature of Christ: The Ecclesiology of Virgil Michel OSB*, by Sister Jeremy Hall, OSB (Collegeville, MN: The Liturgical Press, 1976), 167.

38. n. 58-62 cited in Congar, 41.

39. My quotations from Vatican II are from *Vatican II: Conciliar and Postconciliar Documents*, ed. Austin Flannery (Northport, NY: Costello Publishing Co, 1975).

40. "What We Have Seen and Heard," *Origins* 14 (October 18, 1984): 275.

41. The term ecclesiological monophysitism was used by Yves Congar, and early in the nineteenth century was implied by the criticism of Johann Adam Möhler's ecclesiology offered by Friedrich Marheinecke and F. C. Baur. My own usage is different from Congar's in that I am emphasizing the rigid unity of catholic culture implied by ecclesiological monophysitism. However, it draws from Congar's usage in that this vision of catholic unity assumes the unity of the divine and the human nature of the church to the point of confusion of the two natures at the expense of the contribution of human nature. Ethnic and racial diversity is a matter of human nature that must be envisioned working in concert with divine agency in the church.

42. LaFarge, *Interracial Justice*, 59-60.

43. Ibid., 173, see also 85-86.

44. "If the members of the social body are, as was said, conconstituted, and if the directing principle of economic-social life is restored, it will be possible to say in a certain sense even of this body what the Apostle says of the mystical body of Christ: 'The whole body (being closely joined and knit together through every joint of the system according to the functioning in due measure of each single part) derives its increase to the building up of itself in love," *Quadragesimo Anno* (On the Reconstruction of the Social Order), in *The Papal Encyclicals 1903-1939*, 429 (cited in note 23); Pope Pius XII, *Mystici Corporis Christi* (On the Mystical Body of Christ), in *The Papal Encyclicals 1939-1959*, ed. Claudia Carlen, IHM (Wilmington, NC: McGrath Publishing Company, 1981), 37-63.

45. Southern, 207. In 1933 George Hunton put forth eight resolutions derived from LaFarge's writings, one of which was "To recognize that the Negro shares my membership in the Mystical Body of Christ and the privileges that flow therefrom and to conduct myself in accordance therewith," 203. Also see McGreevy, 43-44, 52, 69-70.

46. On Furfey's views of LaFarge, see Southern, 210-212. Furfey's student Thomas J. Harte wrote a dissertation under Furfey's direction, published as *Catholic Organizations Promoting Negro-White Relations in the United States* (Washington D.C.: Catholic University of America Press, 1947).

47. Paul Hanley Furfey, *The Respectable Murders*: "Father John LaFarge did much more than talk about interracial justice in general; he applied general principles to the concrete Negro-white situation in the United States," 150. It is also noteworthy that he was quite salutary toward

John A Ryan in the same context. Also note that Virgil Michel, who combined a mystical body theology with a social Catholic vision, in two reviews strongly commended both Furfey's book *Fire on the Earth* and LaFarge's *Interracial Justice*, in *Orate Fratres* 11 (1937): 45, 332-333.

48. This kind of argument is made often by Furfey, for a discussion of mediocrity and heroicism, see *Fire on the Earth* (New York: The Macmillan Company, 1936), 17.

49. Furfey, *The Mystery of Iniquity*, 45. "Catholic conformists can render themselves more or less acceptable to unbelieving social thinkers and publicists by maintaining a disingenuous silence about the mystery of iniquity and the whole supernatural aspect of the Church's social doctrine . . . The fact of the Mystical Body is a fact in just as real a sense as a population curve or an immigration law—and it is infinitely more important," 65.

50. Paul Hanley Furfey, *This Way to Heaven* (Silver Spring, MD: The Preservation Press, 1939), 150, read 148-151. See also *Fire on the Earth*, 39-59.

51. This style of argument can be found in Furfey, *The Mystery of Iniquity*, 31.

52. Ibid., 66.

53. On the revival of the mystical body motif in ecclesiology, see Avery Dulles, "A Half Century of Ecclesiology," *Theological Studies* 50 (1989): 419-423. An incarnational ecclesiology became quite commonplace during this century and was the basic point of consensus among theologians like Henri DeLubac, Karl Rahner, Edward Schillebeeckx. An earlier, influential formulation of the church as an "ongoing incarnation" is found in the work of Johann Adam Möhler. See Bradford E. Hinze, "The Holy Spirit and Catholic Tradition: The Legacy of Johann Adam Möhler," in *The Legacy of the Tübingen Theologians: The Relevance of Nineteenth Century Theology for the Twenty-First Century*, eds. Donald Dietrich and Michael Himes (New York: Crossroad, 1997), and Michael J. Himes, *Ongoing Incarnation: Johann Adam Möhler and the Beginnings of Modern Ecclesiology* (New York: Crossroad, 1997).

54. It should be noted that *Quadragesimo Anno* did draw attention to Thomas Aquinas' teaching that "Order. . . is unity arising from the arrangement of a plurality of objects; hence, true and genuine social order demands various members of society, joined together by a common bond" (paragraph 90; citing *Contra Gentiles* 3, 71; *Summa Theologiae* I, Q. 65, A. 2). This doctrine was meant to foster vocational groups, along the line of medieval guilds. LaFarge did not extrapolate from this teaching.

55. See Southern, *John LaFarge* and Marilyn Wenzke Nickels, *Black Catholic Protest and the Federated Colored Catholics 1917-1933: Three Perspectives on Racial Justice* (New York: Garland Publishing Co., 1988).

56. The mystical body of Christ continues to be utilized as a valuable root metaphor in Catholic theology, but now with as much emphasis on diversity as on unity in the church. But after *Lumen Gentium*, the mystical body doctrine received less attention, while a sacramental vision of the church, which draws from many of the same doctrinal tenets and theological sources, took pride of place.

57. It should be noted that there are recent efforts to talk about inculturation in terms of "incarnating" the gospel. The incarnational model is used to describe the relation between the gospel and culture. Such an approach is consistent with an incarnational ecclesiology. The challenge in using such a model is to avoid monophysite and nestorian tendencies.

58. For broader christological approaches to the catholicity of the church and ethnic identity, see Elizondo, *Galilean Journey*, and Roberto S. Goizueta, *Caminemos con Jesus*.

59. George H. Tavard, *The Church, Community of Salvation: An Ecumenical Ecclesiology* (Collegeville, MN: The Liturgical Press, 1992), 29.

60. On the tower of Babel and the reception of the Spirit at Pentecost, see Miroslav Volf, *Exclusion and Embrace: A Theological Exploration of Identity, Otherness, and Reconciliation* (Nashville: Abingdon Press, 1996), 226-231; Bernhard Anderson, "The Babel Story: Paradigm of Human Unity and Diversity," in *Ethnicity*, eds. Andrew M. Greeley and Gregory Baum (*Concilium* 101; New York: The Seabury Press, 1977). The overcoming of the disunity of Babel through the power of the Spirit was a pivotal motif in the ill-fated encyclical drafted by LaFarge and Guntlach for Pius XI. While the mystical body doctrine is mentioned, consistent with LaFarge's previous position, the Spirit takes on a greater role in this document, which may indicate Guntlach's influence, see the draft text in George Passelecq and Bernard Suchecky, *L'Encyclique cachée de Pie XI*, on *Babel and the Spirit*, see n. 14, 26, 67-71; the church as "la continuation de la vie du Christ," n. 122, 2; mystical body of Christ, n. 129.

61. For LaFarge's early argument that it was based on ignorance, not sin, see Southern, 78, 93, 302.

62. See Bradford E. Hinze, "Pope John Paul II on Collective Repentance," *The Ecumenist* 3 (1996): 49-53.

63. St. Thomas Aquinas, *Summa Theologica*, trans. Fathers of the English

Dominican Province (Westminster, Maryland: Christian Classics, 1981), I-II, Q. 91, A. 5: The divine law is divided into the Old Law and the New Law according to the distinction between a child and a grown-up, or a schoolboy under a tutor and an adult who does not need one.

64. Ibid., I-II, Q. 106, A. 4, ad. 2: "The preaching of the Gospel throughout the earth can be understood to refer to its full realization, when the Church has been founded in each of the peoples of the earth. In this sense as Augustine says [Epist. 199], the Gospel has not yet been reached through the earth, but once this has happened there will come the consummation of the world." Also see earlier in the body of the argument where he speaks of "a diversity of places and times and persons, where the grace of the Holy Spirit is received in a greater or lesser degree."

65. Bradford E. Hinze, *Narrating History, Developing Doctrine: Friedrich Schleiermacher and Johann Sebastian Drey* (Atlanta, Georgia: Scholars Press, 1993), 76-82.

Communion Ecclesiology on the Borders: Elizabeth Johnson and Roberto S. Goizueta

Dennis M. Doyle
Professor of Theology
University of Dayton

Communion ecclesiology by definition embraces a significant degree of diversity.[1] Its unity is not to be a mere uniformity imposed from above. The church universal is formed in and out of the local churches, just as the local churches are formed in and out of the universal church. If communion ecclesiology is to be what it is supposed to be, it must be traceable not only in the mainstream and the established and the well-heeled, but also on the fringes, the margins, the borders. In this article I examine one recent work by each of two Catholic theologians who identify themselves as operating on the margins: feminist theologian Elizabeth Johnson and Hispanic theologian Roberto S. Goizueta. I want to explore the extent to which concerns associated with communion ecclesiology, such as *ressourcement*, Trinitarian spirituality, iconic awareness, and a sacramental vision of the church might be found in these works.

Neither of the works that I will examine are, strictly

speaking, ecclesiologies. Johnson's *She Who Is: The Mystery of God in Feminist Theological Discourse* offers a feminist perspective on talk about God.[2] Goizueta's *Caminemos con Jesús: Toward a Hispanic/Latino Theology of Accompaniment* offers a U.S. Hispanic perspective on fundamental questions in theology.[3] But each of these recent books has the combination of being both representative of an identifiable approach and yet groundbreaking in its own right. Each book can serve as a good test case of whether the category of "communion ecclesiology" can be useful for understanding voices on the margins.

In both cases I will be especially interested in a comparison with figures associated with communion ecclesiology, such as Johann Adam Möhler, Henri de Lubac, and John Zizioulas. Because Hans Urs von Balthasar is so associated with the contemporary communio movement, I will pay special attention to connections with his work. I will also bring into the discussion the document on communion ecclesiology of the Congregation for the Doctrine of the Faith (CDF) in order to explore whether Johnson and Goizueta might offer something of value to complement the CDF's approach.[4]

Elizabeth Johnson's *She Who Is*

She Who Is can legitimately be read as a Catholic theology of communion. In terms reminiscent of Zizioulas' *Being as Communion*,[5] Johnson claims that "being in communion constitutes God's very essence."[6] Johnson finds a relatedness at the heart of all reality, "a mystery of personal connectedness."[7] The Triune God emerges in the conclusion of *She Who Is* as the indicator that relatedness, mutuality and equality, and the outpouring of compassionate, liberating love lie at the core of all.[8] The "isolated patriarchal God of the Enlightenment" is overcome by a community in diversity whose mutual interaction can be imaged as a *perichoresis*, like a joyous, revolving dance.[9] Understood in this way, the

Trinity can function "as a model of mutual love stressing the equality of all persons."[10] To be a person is to be a person in relationship; relationship is understood as being ontological, not as an add-on to a previously complete reality.[11] Johnson detects not a detached, above-it-all God, but a God who is related, a compassionate God who suffers.[12]

Johnson's approach is similar to the combination of *ressourcement* and *aggiornamento* associated with Henri de Lubac.[13] De Lubac himself in *Catholicisme* was exceedingly clear that any *ressourcement* must be performed very critically. There is much in the church fathers that cannot simply be retrieved without a lot of hard sorting and editing.[14] And de Lubac also argued explicitly that any retrieval must take place in dialogue with the particular questions of a particular time.[15] Johnson is not merely going beyond a scholastic synthesis to retrieve scriptural and patristic sources, but she is reading the entire range of Christian sources with the intention of working through its patriarchal garb toward a revelation of a God of mutuality and equality. She employs the feminist hermeneutical key of asking how a particular source of revelation contributes to "the emancipation of women toward human flourishing."[16] She thus uncovers a sometimes hidden communion of relationality and mutuality interwoven in traditional sources.

Although Johnson does not dwell for long on the church either as spiritual community or as institution, she can be read as one who applies the categories of trinitarian communion directly to the human community.[17] Most current versions of communion ecclesiology begin with the church and then move on to consider the world. In contrast, Johnson finds trinity, community, relationality, and the grace that leads to human flourishing present in the world. She explores deeply the implications of communion for human solidarity. Furthermore she tackles the critically important issue of the communion between women and men, which *Gaudium et Spes* called, "the first form of the communion of persons,"[18] yet which is often neglected in current versions of communion ecclesiology.

A Von Balthasarian Critique and Appreciation of Johnson
Johnson cites von Balthasar several times in *She Who Is*, always favorably, though in one instance she adds to one of his insights the feminist position that maleness is not constitutive of the essence of the Christ.[19] She certainly does not pick a fight with him, though given her analysis of the patriarchal difficulties that come from men's theological speculations concerning gender, one suspects that von Balthasar could have been game for a good drubbing. I am thinking in particular of the way that Johnson speaks of the limitations and oppressiveness of romantic idealizations of motherhood and of constricting women's roles by confining them symbolically to motherhood and virginity.[20] But the majority of Johnson's references draw upon von Balthasar quite accurately as a defender of the ultimate incomprehensibility of God and as a promoter of the analogical nature of God-talk.[21]

That Johnson's approach could be subjected to a von Balthasarian style critique will be obvious to all who know the work of both of them.[22] I do not wish to belabor the obvious here, but merely to point out a few general lines along which such a critique might travel. Johnson could be depicted as one who commits the cardinal sin of subjecting the revelation of God to merely human, subjective criteria.[23] She places a feminist vision of utopia over and above it. She explores at length the implicit presence of the Holy Spirit in the world and in human experience before ever treating the explicit presence of the Spirit in Christianity. She could be accused of minimizing the extent to which the sources of revelation themselves, although always as bearers of the melody and not the melody itself, reveal the melody through their very concrete particularities. To edit out anything as non-revelatory that may appear patriarchal may prevent one from appreciating the way in which distinctive gender roles can be liberating. Revelation is not to be authenticated according to whether it matches our own ideas of what we think it should be. More authenticating would be the evidence that revelation itself has shattered one's categories, had brought to bear the unexpected, had taught one the true meaning of love.

I want to be clear that I am in no way claiming that von Balthasar himself would have said these things specifically about Johnson, though I have to suspect that a few of them might have crossed his mind in her regard. But to simply leave it at that would represent a one-sided reading of Johnson that would not be characteristically von Balthasarian. I raise these charges because as I point to areas of convergence between Johnson and von Balthasar, I do not want to be perceived as suggesting that a full reconciliation of their positions would be easy or even possible. But I do find connections between the two that are real and important and that reflect concerns commonly associated with communion ecclesiology.

Although Johnson's critique of the Kantian turn to the subject is not as final as von Balthasar's, she maintains her distance from that turn, citing its restriction of theological knowledge to human phenomena and its inattention to what Metz has called the "Alps experience" of being enraptured by the beauty of nature. And, although it is true that Johnson can be read as holding feminist criteria over and above Christian revelation, she could also be read more sympathetically and with some accuracy as using the impact on women's flourishing as a tool for freeing Scripture and tradition from cultural baggage that binds them, in order to unleash their transcendent, revelatory power. Johnson uses her feminist criterion not simply to stand over and judge the sources, but as a standpoint from which to enter into the sources to open up what they have to offer. In spite of obvious differences, it is quintessentially von Balthasarian to mine the tradition in a way that upsets conventional understandings.

It is in her playful and adventurous exploration of images that Johnson is most reminiscent of von Balthasar. And although she draws upon extra-ecclesial human experience perhaps more significantly than von Balthasar would like, when she turns her attention to the tradition she meets some of von Balthasar's most important criteria. She is trinitarian to the core, and in her christology she reads the event of Jesus always against the background of the Old Testament. She is interested not in abstracting images from their historical context, but in exploring "the whole theological significance of what transpires in the Christ event."[24] She finds in the New Testament a Jesus who shatters our preconceived categories about what the mystery of God's love is like.[25] And she discovers a Spirit who is both immanent and transcendent, one that is "not amenable to human manipulation of exploitation."[26] Her feminist retrieval of traditional sources involves a fresh reading of images as applied to God such as Sophia and Mother.

Johnson's description of the *perichoresis* of the Trinity has something of a von Balthasarian flare:

> Casting the metaphor in yet another direction, we can say that the eternal flow of life is stepped to the contagious rhythm of spicy salsas, merengues, calypsos, or reggaes where dancers in free motion are yet bonded in the music.[27]

In a recent article, Johnson names approvingly a wide range of the types of metaphors that are increasingly being used to talk about God. Again, the von Balthasarian flavor is evident:

> God is like a master theatrical improvisor in live performance, amplifying and embroidering each theme as it presents itself; like a choreographer composing steps in tandem with the creative insights of the whole dance troupe; like a composer of a fugue, starting with a simple line of melody and weaving a complex structure by endlessly folding it back

upon itself; like a jazz player, inspired by the spirit of the audience and the night to improvise riffs upon a basic melody; like a designer who sets the rules of a game that includes wildcards and then lets it play.[28]

What is common here between Johnson and von Balthasar is not just their penchant for exploring images in connection with divine revelation but their particular manner and style of doing it. Their appropriation of traditional images is creative and daring and fascinating.

Von Balthasar is known for a certain liberty, even a purposeful looseness, in his interpretation of images and in his openness to new revelatory insights mediated by the human imagination when sufficiently open to the transcendence of the Word. And this opening up of the universe of religious images over against academic approaches that often tend to be dry and mundane is a project in which von Balthasar and Johnson share. As Johnson, puts it, ". . . sister scholars uncover alternative ways of speaking about divine mystery that have long been hidden in Scripture and tradition."[29] It is a key element in the development of a communion ecclesiology that pays serious attention to the mystery of God.

Roberto S. Goizueta's *Caminemos con Jesús*

Like Elizabeth Johnson's *She Who Is*, Roberto S. Goizueta's *Caminemos con Jesús* can be read as a contemporary Catholic theology of communion. At first glance it might appear to contain elements in sharp contrast to a von Balthasarian approach, for Goizueta offers what could be labeled a theology of liberation. In the final analysis, however, the points of comparison with von Balthasar are significantly stronger. Goizueta's perspective as a U.S. Hispanic theologian, which he defines in many ways as "in between," serves also as a corrective to some Latin American versions of liberation theology. This corrective, I will argue, moves distinctly in the direction of von Balthasar.[30]

Identity Yet Difference with Liberation Theology
Goizueta's liberation approach is most evidenced in his final chapter where he argues passionately for a preferential option for the poor. The universality of God's love calls for the recognition that, if God truly loves all, God must have a special concern for those who are suffering and impoverished. Without justice, which must include the overcoming of economic oppression, there can be no authentic pluralism based on a dialogue of equal parties.

Goizueta, however, while recognizing that liberation theology itself exists in many forms, gently criticizes those versions that he thinks tend to be too influenced by Enlightenment concepts of rationality and by Marxist concepts of praxis. For some, liberation becomes too exclusively limited to the material realm and is seen as something that can be produced or achieved by human action. As Goizueta puts it, "To reduce human action to social transformation is to reduce it to productive activity, which is to reduce it to technique; and to reduce human action to technique is to reduce the human person to but a passive object, a mere instrument of production."[31] Some liberation theologians, moreover, have tended to undervalue popular religion. As Goizueta makes these critiques, he acknowledges that many liberation theologians have been growing beyond these difficulties, and he quotes theologians such as Gustavo Gutiérrez, not as examples of the problems but as examples of how liberation theologians are themselves wrestling in positive ways with these issues.

A Theology of Communion
Still, Goizueta holds that his own U. S. Hispanic standpoint offers a distinct perspective. Some of that distinctiveness lies in his treasuring of popular religion; in his clear affirmation of a positive link between popular and institutional expressions of religion; in his giving central place to beauty and to a theory of aesthetics; in his inclusion of not just material

deprivation but also cultural alienation among the forms of poverty to be addressed; and in his focusing not just on economic liberation but also on liberation as the fostering of personal relationships among human beings with God. It is this focus on relationships that provides the main connection between Goizueta's theology and communion ecclesiology. Like Johann Adam Möhler in *The Unity in the Church*,[32] Goizueta places his initial emphasis on the relationship among God and human beings that exists within local liturgical communities. The unity in the church is first of all the bondedness in love that values rather than erases diversity. In a way reminiscent of Möhler's depiction of a love that grows organically as it expands to create more communities, Goizueta focuses on the love that exists in concrete, particular, local communities. He finds connections with the universal grounded always in the ability of local communities to recognize commonalities in and through their own particularities.

To illustrate this last point, Goizueta poses the question of how one can come to know what marriage is.[33] It would not be by engaging in as many marriages as possible in order to arrive at a universal notion abstracted from one's many experiences. The way, rather, would be to enter as deeply as possible into one marriage, and to come to know the universal through the experience of the particular. From the depth of one's own marital relationship one can recognize commonalities with other marriages, and thus come to know more profoundly what marriage is.

Like Zizioulas (with Möhler still in the background), Goizueta sees the Trinity as representing the communal nature of God; "personhood" is not prior to community but is achieved within it.[34] The model holds true also for human relationships. Goizueta argues against the tendency of the dominant U.S. culture to see individuality as a primary reality that exists prior to any relationships. In Goizueta's U.S. Hispanic perspective, community precedes individuality.

Authentic individuality is achieved only within the context of a community which precedes one and from which one draws one's identity.[35] True freedom is found not in a struggle to be a completely autonomous self-made person, but only in relationships.[36] From the particularity of his own perspective, Goizueta, like Elizabeth Johnson, affirms Zizioulas' understanding of "being as communion." Interrelatedness as persons lies at the very heart of reality.

Like Möhler and de Lubac, Goizueta promotes an inclusive "both/and" approach to what it means to be Catholic. But his initial point of entry to this position is not the inclusiveness of the patristic authors, but rather the cultural experience of U.S. Hispanics as being always "in between." U.S. Hispanics live in between the communities of their past and the communities of their present, in between being exiles and being aliens, in between being Latin American and "American," in between being marginal and having opportunities, and in between anger and gratitude. This experience, claims Goizueta, has led U.S. Hispanics not to being either-or dichotomizers, but to being people of the "both/and," people who are as bridges and whose instincts lean toward inclusion. It is an approach sensitive to analogy and paradox and sacrament, a way of being Catholic.

Goizueta's sacramental approach to faith, his focus on inculturation, and his stress on social justice show many similarities with the work of de Lubac. De Lubac was a pioneer who forged links between the sacramental and social aspects of Catholicism. It is true that Goizueta does not explore ideal images that represent the church universal as does de Lubac. Yet the church universal, considered in its relational aspects, does play a significant role in Goizueta's work as the communion of saints. He does not dwell on the communion of saints as an abstract theological concept, but he describes concretely how one's community is comprised not just of those alive now but also of those who have gone before us in death.

Goizueta illustrates how for U.S. Hispanic Catholics, two persons who dwell in the very center of the community are Jesus and Mary. When Hispanics in San Antonio act out the Passion, they are truly walking along with Jesus. It is really Jesus who is being nailed to the cross as they look on. When an Hispanic woman kisses the feet of Jesus on a cross, she is really interacting with Jesus. When Hispanics celebrate the feast of Our Lady of Guadalupe and recount her story, they know that they are accepted as fully dignified human beings by this blessed lady. One cannot know one's own identity as an Hispanic Catholic without being in relation with Jesus and Mary, who are sacramentally and thus really present through ritual and story. For Goizueta, such concepts as the church as the communion of saints or the church as the body of Christ are not abstract idealizations but concrete descriptions that arise from a phenomenology of the U.S. Hispanic experience.

The Jesus who is thus present is one who knows what it is to suffer, and into whose suffering the poor can enter. The Mary thus present is one who loves the poor and who helps them to recognize their dignity as her special ones. Goizueta, who is in many ways grounded in liberation theology, on this point distinguishes his approach from that of many liberation theologians by insisting that this sense of personal dignity is not necessarily attached to a socially transforming practice. It is a dignity that has its own intrinsic value.

Some Parallels with Von Balthasar

Goizueta, in a move that might be described as an Hispanic Catholic *ressourcement*, illustrates the intrinsic value of human dignity by drawing upon the aesthetic theory of the Mexican philosopher José Vasconcelos. There are some interesting parallels between the philosophy of Vasconcelos and the theology of von Balthasar. Over against positivist and reductionist philosophies popular in Mexico in the opening years of the twentieth century, Vasconcelos held that aesthetics is the key category for interpreting human action. In the "special pathos of beauty" can be found a principle that unifies the intellectual, the moral, and the aesthetic.[37] The experience of beauty entails an "empathic fusion" of subject and object by which the subject becomes caught up and loses him or herself in the experience. Such aesthetic union is the basis of love, in which people lose themselves in a union that transcends each. The human desire for aesthetic union is in itself "the yearning for communion with the divine nature."[38] As with von Balthasar, God, love, and beauty present themselves through objective forms that captivate the being of the subject. Aesthetics must precede ethics. Where von Balthasar held that contemplation was superior to action, Vasconcelos finds a priority for play, recreation, and celebration in relation to practical action.

Goizueta uses these points from Vasconcelos to critique the tendency among liberation theologians to settle for the Marxist meaning of *praxis* as socially transforming activity. When measured against the classical understanding of *praxis* in Aristotle, this definition of practical activity sounds as though it better fits *poesis* or even the more specific *techne*. Goizueta argues that *praxis* in Aristotle had to do not with making (*poesis*) or technical activity (*techne*), but with activity done for its own sake. He gives the example of the difference between making a guitar and playing a guitar. The activity of making a guitar is *poesis*; the activity of playing a guitar is *praxis*. The playing of a guitar has an intrinsic value that can be appreciated without reference to some practical external goal.[39]

Goizueta detects in the Marxist meaning of *praxis* a reductionism that subordinates the dignity of persons and the meaning of celebrations to the achievement of political ends. Those who cannot contribute to liberation can come to be perceived as useless. Goizueta is not at all opposed to the transformation of unjust political structures, and indeed the bulk of his book bears out his commitment to such projects. He holds, however, that concern for beauty and concern for justice must be combined. He does this by arguing that the aesthetic dimension of human action is always mediated by the ethical-political; it is lived out within the ethical-political as the deepest sense of the ethical-political.[40] The dignity and the love that constitute the deepest dimensions of human lives are lived out always within concrete social contexts. It is important that these contexts reflect as much as possible this dignity and this love in a real way. But the aesthetic dimension of human activity is never to be reduced to or subordinated to the ethical-political. It is distinct, prior, and even superior.

Goizueta's corrective to liberation theology can serve as one response to the call made by von Balthasar himself in a 1977 lecture at the Catholic University of America.[41] In this reconciling talk, von Balthasar spoke of three theological methods—the anthropological approach, liberation theology, and his own "way of love"—as limited but potentially complementary approaches that each need the other for their completion. He said:

> In conclusion I might point out that the three theological directions outlined here do not contradict each other in their positive aspects. They complement each other, in that each contributes something which the others do not stress sufficiently or are in danger of forgetting. None of the three sets itself up as absolute, but all recognize the whole of "Catholica."[42]

Goizueta holds that where the main concern for Latin American liberation theologians is Justice, the corresponding concern for U.S. Hispanic theologians is Beauty. Goizueta's reliance upon Vasconcelos' aesthetic theory to carve out a realm that is sacrosanct and not to be subordinated to those dimensions of reality studied by the social scientists parallels von Balthasar's reliance on Goethe (and also on Barth) to identify the objectivity of the aesthetic form as that which draws the subject outside of him or herself. The overlap with von Balthasar is striking when Goizueta says:

> When one travels, for instance, through the Rocky Mountains, one is caught up into their majesty and splendor. The extraordinary vistas raise the hairs on the back of one's head and send a chill down the spine. Such a reaction is not merely arbitrary and subjective, but an appropriate subjective response to an external, objective reality: the overwhelming natural beauty of the mountains. Not only a "meaningful experience," aesthetic, or empathic fusion is also a revelation of self-transcending truth.[43]

Von Balthasar himself described liberation theology sympathetically and suggested that criticism be limited to the point where "it comes close to giving absolute priority to the political dimensions."[44] That is precisely the point at which Goizueta provides his corrective, one based on aesthetic theory.

Goizueta treats Hispanic ritual and narrative in ways that are perhaps not unlike von Balthasar's treatment of scripture, patristic writings, and the visions of Adrienne von Speyr.[45] There is a strong confidence in the revelatory power present in the form, and a freedom to allow the imagination to engage these forms with a trust that the revelatory power will guide it. And when attending to their respective sources, both Goizueta and von Balthasar place heavy emphasis on the celebration of the Triduum and on the person of Mary. Goizueta's U.S. Hispanic approach and von Balthasar's aesthetic theology share much indeed.

Points of Comparison with the CDF's Statement

Several points of intersection have been uncovered between the theologies of Johnson and Goizueta and a range of concepts commonly associated with communion ecclesiology. Both theologians focus on the connection between relationality in God and relationality among human beings. Both operate with an explicitly sacramental appreciation of life. Both engage in a style of *ressourcement* theology. Both value an aesthetic approach to theological sources. And both affirm the positive links between popular, local religion and the church universal. Yet one wonders how their approaches might line up with the vision of communion ecclesiology expressed in the Congregation for the Doctrine of the Faith's "Some Aspects of the Church Understood as a Communion."[46]

One suspects that if either Johnson or Goizueta tried to produce an official-style document on communion ecclesiology, their starting points would run counter to those of the CDF. They would likely stress the local and the particular so strongly that the institutional elements of the church universal might seem relatively neglected. Neither has any opposition to the institutional elements of the church universal, and in fact they both seem to see them as functioning, at least potentially, in a positive and complementary fashion within the very fabric of popular, local religion. But as the CDF emphasizes the priority of the church universal, Johnson and Goizueta tend to emphasize the priority of the local and the particular.

Still, a strong point of comparison could be developed starting with the CDF's notion of the "mutual interiority" characteristic of local churches that provides the basis for recognizing the common faith that exists among them. The document states:

> In order to grasp the true meaning of the analogical application of the term *communion* to the particular churches taken as a whole, one must bear in mind above all that the particular churches, insofar as they are part of the "one church of Christ," have a special relationship of "mutual interiority" with the whole, that is, with the universal church, because in every particular church "the one, holy, catholic, and apostolic church of Christ is truly present and active."[47]

What this means is that each particular church contains microcosmically within itself the entire church universal. One example the document gives of this is that the office of the papacy is not simply exterior to each particular church, but exists as an intrinsic dimension.

Although Johnson and Goizueta would come at "mutual interiority" from a different direction than that of the CDF, the kernel of a potential synthesis is present in the concept. Recall Goizueta's example of how one comes to know what "marriage" is through the experience of one's own marriage and the recognition of analogous elements in other marriages. For the CDF to highlight "mutual interiority" is to open for consideration the potential fruitfulness of approaches that begin from the local and the particular, even as the CDF denounces movements that are said to arise from the base in opposition to the institutional elements of the church universal.

The strongest potential intersection between Johnson and Goizueta and the CDF's focus on communion ecclesiology lies in their emphasis on the relational aspects of the Catholic faith and their ability to link the experience of intimacy and solidarity in small forms of community with the universal elements of God and the shared tradition. If communion ecclesiology is to be recognized as the one, basic Catholic ecclesiology, then it must include this major thrust in Catholic theology today that focuses on context, social location, and the process of inculturation. It is understandable that the CDF document would take the church universal and church unity as its central concerns; the equally important matters of diversity and the role of local churches, however, cry out for more attention. It is precisely in this critical aspect of communion ecclesiology that Johnson and Goizueta have valuable contributions to make.

Notes

1. "Communion ecclesiology" is a much-used term today, but its meanings are varied. It can refer to a vision of church presupposed by the

writers of late Christian antiquity; to the vision of church appropriated by the *nouvelle theologie* authors whose works helped to bring about Vatican II; to the ecclesiology of Vatican II itself; to the vision of the current communio movement; to the vision of church associated with Eastern Orthodoxy; and to any view of church that stresses community more than institution. For the purposes of this article, I use the term in a broad sense intended to be inclusive of this variety of meanings.

2. *She Who Is: The Mystery of God in Feminist Theological Discourse* (New York: Crossroad, 1996).

3. *Caminemos con Jesús: Toward a Hispanic/Latino Theology of Accompaniment* (Maryknoll, NY: Orbis Books, 1995).

4. "Some Aspects of the Church Understood as a Communion," *Origins* 22 (June 25, 1992): 108-12.

5. *Being as Communion: Studies in Personhood and the Church* (Crestwood, NY: St. Vladimir's, 1985).

6. Johnson does not cite Zizioulas in *She Who Is* (227), but she does cite theologians whose work evidences contact with Zizioulas, such as Catherine LaCugna and William Hill.

7. *She Who Is*, 228.

8. Ibid., 216.

9. Ibid., 220-221.

10. Ibid., 196.

11. Ibid., 216.

12. Ibid., 251.

13. For an exploration of these terms, see Marcellino D'Ambrosio, "*Ressourcement* Theology, *Aggiornamento*, and the Hermeneutics of Tradition," *Communio* 18 (Winter 1991): 530-555. For a comparison of de Lubac with Zizioulas, see Paul McPartlan, *The Eucharist Makes the Church: Henri de Lubac and John Zizioulas in Dialogue* (Edinburgh: T&T Clark, 1993).

14. *Catholicisme, les aspects sociaux du dogma* (Paris: Les Éditions du Cerf, 1938), 173; *Catholicism: Christ and the Common Destiny of Man* (London: Burns and Oates, 1950; Universe Books edition, 1961).

15. Ibid., 174.

16. *She Who Is*, 30.

17. I find a similar application of the terms and concepts of communion ecclesiology directly to the human community in Michael Himes and Kenneth Himes, *Fullness of Faith: The Public Significance of Theology* (New York: Paulist Press, 1993). See Dennis M. Doyle, "Communion

Ecclesiology and the Common Good: A Comparison of Cardinal Ratzinger and the Brothers Himes," in *Religion, Ethics, and the Common Good*, The Annual Publication of the College Theology Society, vol. 41, eds. James Donahue and M. Theresa Moser (Mystic, CT: Twenty-Third Publications, 1996). This characteristic of Johnson is found also in "Does God Play Dice? Divine Providence and Chance," *Theological Studies* 57 (1996): 3-18, where she says: "The universe, in other words, is a sacrament. Every excellence it exhibits is a participation in that quality which supereminently exists in the incomprehensible mystery of God," 11.

18. *Gaudium et Spes*, n.12, as found in *Decrees of the Ecumenical Councils*, vol. 2, ed. Norman Tanner (London and Washington, D.C.: Sheed and Ward and Georgetown University Press, 1990), 1076.

19. *She Who Is*, 164, n. 25.

20. Ibid., 176. Johnson told me in a letter that she will be more critical of von Balthasar in the book she is currently writing about Mary and the saints.

21. *She Who Is*, 107, 111.

22. The primary and secondary sources on von Balthasar are immense. The spirit of the critique I am formulating can best be gleaned from *Love Alone*, ed. and trans. Alexander Dru ([German orig. 1963] New York: Herder and Herder, 1969). Von Balthasar there criticizes what he terms the "anthropological" approach to theological method. I have found Edward T. Oakes, *Pattern of Redemption: The Theology of Hans Urs von Balthasar* (New York: Continuum, 1994) to be a most excellent introduction to von Balthasar's work.

23. I find, for example, Benedict Ashley's critique of Johnson to be cast in a somewhat von Balthasarian fashion, though he does not mention von Balthasar by name. See *Justice in the Church: Gender and Participation* (Washington, D.C.: Catholic University of America Press, 1996), 189-206. Ashley associates Johnson's methods with a Rahnerian approach, and he criticizes her for holding "women's flourishing" to be the ultimate criterion of truth. Ashley rejects also Johnson's radical egalitarianism, her stress on the unknowability of God, and what he takes to be her "docetic" Christology.

24. *She Who Is*, 167.

25. Ibid., 169.

26. Ibid., 145.

27. Ibid., 221.

28. "Does God Play Dice?" 17-18.

29. *She Who Is*, 5.

30. In a recent article, Goizueta acknowledges a possible parallel with von Balthasar's aesthetic approach, but he remains very cautious about von Balthasar's lack of a strong grounding in the option for the poor. See "U.S. Hispanic Popular Catholicism as Theopoetics," in *Hispanic/Latino Theology: Challenge and Promise*, eds. Ada María Isasi-Díaz and Fernando F. Segovia (Minneapolis: Fortress Press, 1996), 267, n. 21.

31. *Caminemos*, 84.

32. *Unity in the Church, or The Principle of Catholicism Presented in the Spirit of the Church Fathers of the First Three Centuries*, ed. and trans. Peter C. Erb (Washington, D.C.: Catholic University of America Press, 1996); the German original was published in Mainz in 1825. See also Dennis M. Doyle, "Möhler, Schleiermacher, and the Roots of Communion Ecclesiology," *Theological Studies* 57 (1996): 467-480.

33. *Caminemos*, 97.

34. Ibid., 65.

35. Ibid.

36. Ibid., 17.

37. Ibid., 91.

38. Ibid., 94.

39. Ibid., 83.

40. Ibid., 128.

41. "Current Trends in Catholic Theology and the Responsibility of the Christian," *Communio* (US) 7 (1980): 77-85.

42. Ibid., 85.

43. *Caminemos*, 161.

44. "Current Trends," 41.

45. Von Balthasar wrote that his own life work cannot be separated or considered apart from the work of von Speyr. See *Our Task: A Report and a Plan*, trans. John Saward ([German orig. 1994] San Francisco: Ignatius Press, 1994), 1.

46. Cited above in note 4. See also Dennis M. Doyle, "Communion Ecclesiology and the Silencing of Boff," *America* 167 (September 12, 1992): 139-143, which gives some analysis of the document.

47. *Some Aspects of the Church Understood as a Communion*, n. 9.

U. S. Hispanics Between the Borders of Catholicism and Protestantism

Jorge Luis Valdés
Doctoral Student in New Testament and Early Christianity
Loyola University Chicago

Hispanics in the United States of America constantly live *in between* borders, whether territorial, linguistic and cultural, or spiritual and faith oriented. The aim of this paper is to analyze critically the faith border, a border *in between* Roman Catholicism, which is part of the common background of all Hispanics, and Protestantism that is drawing many.

The approach this paper will follow is fourfold: First, we will analyze the *Hispanic reality* and look at the chaotic consequences among Hispanics when an immediate family member leaves the Catholic Church for a Protestant Church. Second, we will trace the *religious reality* surveying the Catholic and Protestant perspectives. We will look for clues as to what makes Catholics different from Protestants, and see if by understanding these differences, we are able to find what can unite us. Third, we will look at the *biblical reality* exegeting the Lord's Priestly Prayer in John 17, and see how an understanding of John 17 can provide Hispanics with a model for unity. Fourth, as a conclusion, we will present the *desired reality*. The ills that confront the Hispanic community are many, and can only be confronted as Hispanics stand in solidarity and togetherness in *familia* and *comunidad*, grounding our oneness with the Father and the Son in our common struggle. By identifying our common religious-cultural structure perhaps we can see that what separates us is minimal.

The Hispanic Reality

As a Cuban who immigrated to the United States at an early age, I struggled to find identity in an alien country which I now call home, yet will never be home. It took 30 years to realize why my parents never let go of the land which gave me birth, and now I yearn to discover. Roberto Goizueta writes,

> "*Caminemos con Jesús.*" One is the cry of the exile, forced into the solitude and loneliness of an alien country. The other is the call of the same person who, though still in exile, has discovered a new home. That home, however, is no longer simply a physical place, with its implied stability and security, but a community of persons who, as exiles themselves, are together "walking with Jesus."[1]

My parents survived their exodus by refusing to give up our Cuban heritage. *Nuestro español,*[2] and *nuestras fiestas*[3] gave them identity. My mother's faith, in a Jesus I did not know, and a Santa Barbara that heard her nightly cry, became the source of our strength, and our perseverance to survive.[4] My life has been one lived *in between* borders, a territorial and cultural border, but most important a faith border. A border between Roman Catholicism, which is a part of the common background of all Hispanics, and a Protestantism which introduced me to a Gospel that liberated me. It is this *in between* that this paper will examine.

Why is this *in between* so important to the Hispanic reality? The answer is very complex, and the reality very painful. Among Hispanics, when an immediate member or part of the family changes from the Catholic church to a Protestant church, the pain caused by this change is so severe that the consequences are chaotic. A convert no longer is an integral part of the family existence and *lucha*, but suddenly he or she is a traitor not only to the *fé*, but to the family's struggle for unity. The traumatic effects of leaving the Catholic Church in a Hispanic *familia* are lasting and at times beyond reconciliation.

In 1988 I was introduced to the Protestant faith, and the Gospel of Jesus Christ.[5] After three years of searching the Scriptures, I made a decision to become a "born again" Christian.[6] Immediately I wanted to share this experience with my family by bringing them to my new faith.[7] I wanted to introduce them to this Jesus, whom I now personally knew. Not only was my family not willing to convert, but my conversion was viewed as an unforgivable act of treason. My parents could forgive my "loose" past life, but this act of treason against everything they were, against everything that gave them life and sustained them, was not going to go unnoticed. To them Catholicism was not a religion; it was an identity. For the first time in my life my parents ceased to communicate with me. The greatest pain, in not talking with them, was not the immediate loss of family fellowship; to me it became the loss of my roots, my existence, and my identity as a *miembro de mi familia, de mi cultura*, as a part of my whole. It was not until I matured in my faith, and came to know a Christ who does not divide families, but unites them, a Jesus who is expressed and lived out in the faith and traditions of *mi familia*, that I was able to reconcile with my family, and introduce them to *nuestro Diosito*, who is lived and experienced differently, yet equally among our different *fes*.[8]

At this point it is crucial that we analyze the Hispanic religious history in order to address our present concerns.[9]

The Religious Reality

Part of every Hispanic's common background is the Roman Catholic Church, "if not personally, then at least in our ancestry."[10] According to Justo González most Hispanics that were born in the Church still belong to it, but others have converted to a Protestant denomination.

As a Protestant growing up in the United States, González reminds us that it is very difficult for Protestants to appreciate the changes that have occurred in the Roman Catholic Church during our lifetime, a change that should not surprise us. "We have always said and believed that unexpected things take place whenever Scripture is read anew and seriously. We are now seeing it happen, and we are discovering and having to confess that our prejudices did not agree with our theology."[11] González argues that we would not be so surprised had we realized that from the beginning the "apparent monolithic Catholic Church in Latin America had been two churches."[12]

Very few North Americans are aware that besides the "official" Roman Catholic Church, which was the force of the conquest, colonialism, and oppression in Latin America, there was another church which condemned and fought these forces. A church made up mostly of "Friars—Franciscans, Dominicans, Jesuits, and Mercedarians—who had taken vows of poverty and obedience and who therefore were able and ready to work in places and situations in which secular clergy would not work."[13] The vows of poverty of these friars allowed them the privilege of sharing in the suffering of the Indians. Through sharing in their suffering, these friars often became the defenders of the Indians.[14] Very few people even know the name of a Franciscan friar named Francisco Jiménez Cisneros, and his desire to care for the Indians.

Jiménez was called from solitude to enter into Isabella's court as her confessor, and eventually named Archbishop of Toledo. It was his desire that the Indians should be given liberty, ruled justly, and above all treated well so that those who were converted would not fall from the Holy Catholic faith. To accomplish this, he sent a number of friars, such as

Bartolomé de las Casas, from different monasteries to Hispaniola.

It is beyond the scope of this paper to treat all the issues related to Jiménez and his reforms among the Indians. It will suffice to say that when Las Casas returned to Spain to visit king Charles, after Ferdinand's death, in order to plea on behalf of the Indians, Jiménez promised Las Casas that he would look into the matter personally, and allowed Las Casas to proclaim his case to many high officials in Spain. Afterwards, he named twelve of the priors of Castille to look into building new villages—including homes, churches, schools, and hospitals—for the Indians. Jiménez felt that they should be taught agriculture and other trades to work on their own land, and not be forced to live outside their land. Finally, he appointed Las Casas as overseer of all the Indians.[15]

The name of Cardinal Jiménez and these friars often goes unmentioned; few even know of their existence. Yet they lived and fought for the reform of a church to which they gave their entire life, and for the people who made up that church. For these friars it was not the Crown or the elite who were the Holy Catholic church, it was the poor and downtrodden. It was the Indians for whose souls they cried. This was the other Catholic church, the church whose most fortunate saints have taken centuries to acknowledge, and others, not so fortunate, have gone forgotten.[16]

From the very beginning Spanish-American Catholicism has stood *in between*, in between the hierarchical church of the rich and powerful, and the more popular church of Las Casas and Jiménez.[17] Hispanics, whether Protestant or Catholic, have been shaped by this dual Catholicism, and it is the roots of the Catholicism of Las Casas and Jiménez that has not been recognized as the Hispanic Catholicism which prevails in our Hispanic communities today.

When looking at the Protestant Hispanic community, one must look at both Latin America and the United States. The

Protestant faith among Hispanics has its root in the missionary activities of James Thomson, a representative of the British and Foreign Bible Society.[18] Thompson introduced the common people to the freedom to read the Bible on their own. This revolutionary act not only allowed the common person to speak to God and to worship Him in their own manner, but it became a source of empowerment and liberation.[19]

Missionary activity was not the sole source for Protestantism in Latin America. Immigration from Europe, especially in the southern tip of the continent, was encouraged by the early leaders of Latin America. These immigrants demanded the religious freedom they had in their countries, and when it was given to them, it could not be denied to the natives. Another source of Protestantism grew from natives who had been exiled in the United States, and upon return to their native land brought the Protestantism they knew. This Protestantism that developed in Latin America had its origin among the poor.

The twentieth century saw new forms of Protestantism introduced into Latin America, first, fundamentalism—very rigid in structure and leadership; and second, Pentecostalism—a mixture of rigidity and flexibility, with emphasis on the power and freedom of the Spirit. These new forms of Protestantism had minimal effect on the basic ideology of Latin American Protestantism. The most noticeable change was in the devaluation of education, since the fundamentalist felt that secular education led to doubt the authority of Scripture.[20]

For centuries the Catholic church had taught that the laity was incapable of interpreting Scriptures;[21] consequently, Protestantism's greatest appeal to new converts is the source of power they find in the Scriptures; therefore, empowered with the knowledge of God's Word it becomes their duty and obligation to bring their brothers/sisters out of a religion which they perceive enslaves them, to a religion that empowers them.

Ever since Protestantism came on the scene the Hispanic community has lived in a constant religious turmoil. Catholics feel that Protestants are heretics and traitors to their traditional roots; on the other hand, Protestants feel that Catholics are anti-Scriptural heretics who worship idols; the tragedy behind all this is that Hispanics, Catholics and Protestants, are divided.[22]

Since Pope John XXIII and the Second Vatican Council, Roman Catholicism has gone through a tremendous transformation, "nothing short of miraculous."[23] Even conservative Protestants must admit that, based on their own theology, they must contend with what happens in a church that has begun to read the Scriptures, while demonstrating a spirit of submission to Jesus Christ, a church that has put added emphasis on the role of the laity at the local level, allowing Hispanics to have a greater voice in the church.

A great phenomenon is also occurring in the Hispanic Protestant churches as a result of not only the Hispanic's experiences of injustice and marginalization—which contradicted what they viewed as the Protestant ideology, but other events such as the civil rights movement—a struggle of Protestants against Protestants. Euro-American Protestantism did not show itself to be the force fighting for freedom and equality that Hispanics had been told it was. It seemed that the whites who were constantly quoting the Bible were not living what they quoted, while those who discounted the authority of Scripture, lived a life of love and justice. For J.L. González,

> This has made it difficult for many Hispanics to continue being fundamentalist in the traditional sense. The authority of Scripture is still held in high regard by that community. But there is also a growing awareness that there is a certain sort of fundamentalism that is grossly anti-biblical. For this reason, many Protestants are seeking ways of interpreting Scripture that, while respecting the authority of the Bible, are different from what we were taught. The net result is that we

find ourselves walking along the same path with Roman Catholics.[24]

The major influence in the Hispanic community today, both among Roman Catholics and Protestants, is the significance of Scriptures in the life of Hispanics. The reading and teaching of the Scriptures has empowered and liberated the Hispanic people. According to Manuel Ortíz, "the influence of the charismatic movement in Protestant mainline churches and in the Catholic church provides an avenue for fellowship and dialogue."[25] With this in mind let us now turn to the Word of God and what it teaches us about unity.

The Biblical Reality

But, not concerning these only do I make request, but also concerning the ones believing in me through their word, in order that they all may be one, just as you, Father, in me and I in you, *in order that* also they may be in us, *in order that* the world may believe that you sent me. And I have given to them the glory which you have given to me, *in order that* they may be one just as we are one; I in them and you in me, *in order that* they may be perfected into one, *in order that* the world may know that you sent me and loved them just as you loved me. (John 17:20–23)[26]

Throughout the New Testament, unity among Christians is thought of as extremely important. Nowhere is this more evident than in John 17, the climax of the Last Discourse, where Jesus lifts up his eyes to heaven, and in a majestic moment prays to the Father for oneness. It is this prayer that best emphasizes the overriding need to maintain unity among the Christian communities.[27] According to B.F. Westcott, "this chapter stands alone in the Gospels. It contains what may be most properly called 'the Lord's Prayer' the prayer which He Himself used as distinguished from that which He taught to His disciples."[28]

Gustavo Gutiérrez writes:

> Such are the commandment and prayer of the Lord: that we
> may be one as the Father and the Son are one with each other
> and in us, in a unity that we must live out while not with-
> drawing from a world in which the forces of evil tend to
> divide us (see John 17). This communion—common union—
> is at once a gift of God and a task set for us.[29]

John Paul II writes:

> The unity Jesus prayed for at the hour of his passion, "that
> they may be one" (Jn. 17:21), is at the very heart of Christ's
> mission. It belongs to the essence of the community of his dis-
> ciples. God wills the church, because God wills unity as an
> expression of the whole depth of God's love (agape).[30]

An exegesis of John 17:22–23 will show a oneness of believers modeled after a heavenly unity between the Father and the
Son. This unity is at the heart of Christ's mission, and in order
to bring this unity about, Jesus gives his disciples the glory that
he received from the Father, a glory found in humility and
lowly service, which in the end culminates in glorification. A
proper understanding of this prayer allows Hispanics, first, to
recognize that unity is a mandate from God, and once
Hispanics ground their own unity in the unity of the Father
and the Son, then, no matter what religious denomination we
are, we are one with each other. Second, an understanding of
John 17 allows Hispanics to see that there is glory in serving
others, Catholic or Protestant, and in this shared experience of
humility, service and struggle we can find unity.

In John 17:21–23 Jesus outlines the ultimate purpose of his
prayer. In doing so he establishes a series of striking parallels
between the Father's relationship to the Son, and the relationship desired for Jesus' followers. Raymond Brown
explains the significant grammatical parallelism found in the
six lines of verses 21–23.[31]

21a	ἵνα	(in order that)	They all may be one,
21b	καθὼς	(just as)	you, Father, in me and I in you,
21c	ἵνα	(in order that)	also they may be in us,
21d	ἵνα	(in order that)	the world may believe that you sent me.

22a And I have given to them the glory which you have given me

22b	ἵνα	(in order that)	they may be one
22c-23	καθὼς	(just as)	we are one; I in them and you in me,
23b	ἵνα	(in order that)	they may be perfected into one.
23c	ἵνα	(in order that)	the world may know that you sent me and loved them.

Each set of parallels contains one ἵνα clause, followed by a καθὼς clause and then two more ἵνα clauses. Brown believes that:

> the first and second *hina* clause in each involve the oneness of the believers, while the third involves the effect on the world. The second *hina* clause does not merely repeat the first but develops the notion of unity. The *kathos* clause in each block holds up for the believers the model of the unity of Jesus and the Father.[32]

Brown argues that in the καθὼς clauses, καθὼς has both a comparative and causative side. The comparative side is the model that the heavenly unity provides for believers. The causative side is that the unity between the Father and the Son becomes the basis of unity for all believers.[33]

The third ἵνα clauses in both set of parallels are the result of both the indwelling, and the unity established in the first and second ἵνα clauses. The heavenly unity of the Father and the Son provides us with a model of the type of unity that God wants for believers. This unity becomes the source for the believers' unity, with the expectation that as a consequence the world may believe that Jesus is the Son of God. It is important that we note that significance of verse 22a. In this verse the two verbs, δέδωκάς (*you have given me*), and δέδωκα (*I have given them*), are in the perfect tense.[34] The significance of the perfect tense in 22a is that Jesus continues to possess the glory the Father gave him, and in turn the disciples continue to possess the glory Jesus gave them. D. A. Carson defines the glory the Father gave the Son as, "the glory of the humility of the incarnation, culminating both in the glorification of the Son at the crucifixion and the glory of his resurrected and exalted state."[35] Jesus gives his disciples the glory that he received from the Father, in order that the indwelling of the Father and the Son can produce a unity of the believers with the Father and the Son. According to Leon Morris, "John writes of a glory that centers on lowly service. When anyone is entitled to an exalted position in ease and comfort and leaves that position in order to render lowly service to someone in need, then we have real glory."[36]

Walking with Jesus had been hard. The disciples were afflicted, despised, and rejected, but they had experienced that there was glory in serving orders, "and that experience was so that they may be one."[37]

From the above exegesis we deduce that the parallels found in John 17:22–23 show a oneness of believers modeled after the heavenly unity between the Father and the Son. This divine unity becomes the basis for the believer's unity, which in turn has an impact on the world.

The Father gave Jesus the glory of the humility of the incarnation, culminating in his glorification at the cross, and the glory of his resurrected and exalted state. The disciples experienced this glory when, like Jesus, they were afflicted, despised, and rejected, yet found glory in serving others.

This unity for which Jesus asked the Father in his prayer is a unity grounded in a common nature, rather than in an identity of minds or persons.[38] It is a unity that is exclusive, in that it is grounded in the unity that Christians share with the Father and Jesus, and inclusive, in that it is a unity that recognizes each other's diversity as a special gift that God has given us to share with others as a living Gospel.

When Hispanics share their rich culture, and participate in each other's struggle, they are sharing the gospel of a living Christ. Through our common religious-cultural structure, and our *lucha*, we are united with each other. But this unity is not perfected until it is grounded in the unity that Christians share with the Father and Jesus, recognizing that each other's diversity is a special gift from God, given to us to share with each other. Let us now look at the "desired reality," for unity among Hispanics.

Desired Reality

La lucha of the Hispanic communities is immense. Gang related killings are rampant, drug addiction and drug sales are epidemic, as are domestic violence and teen pregnancies. Ramírez is on target when he suggests that these ills can only be confronted when we as Hispanics stand in "solidarity and togetherness in *familia* and *comunidad*."[39]

En nuestra lucha we walk hand in hand with each other and Jesus. My brother's and sister's drug problem becomes mine, his and her hurt becomes mine. And as we *luchamos unidos*, we learn to correct the prejudices that have divided us. Denominational divisions are put aside, and when my brother or sister is oppressed it is not a Catholic or Protestant who is being hurt, it is a Hispanic. When we find no remedy for our illness, our shared tears unite us.

As we strive for unity among our rich and diverse Hispanic community we must be acutely aware of the diversity of our culture. We must stop trying to convince the "other"[40] to be like us. Instead we should share our treasures with our brothers and sisters, and allow them to take these treasures back to their denomination. Once we do this, our remaining differences can be identified and perhaps reconciled.[41] Let us love our brothers and sisters for the simple fact that we are different, yet the same. Let us go forward without imposing. Hispanics can only overcome the many challenges facing them today by being one. A oneness that respects each other's diversity, and demands nothing, yet at the same time gives all. A oneness with the Father and Jesus grounded in our common struggle, and expressed through our collective symbols. Elizondo correctly posits that,

> for a suffering and oppressed people, there is nothing more powerful than one's collective religious symbols. They are the roots of our existence and the source of our identity. They put us in contact with our ancestors and guarantee our life to future generations. They are the language of resistance and protest. In them and through them, no one of us is alone, for we are all in one and one in all.[42]

As we reminisce about the many struggles, pains, and hardships our ancestors endured, through this shared memory, we realize that they were able to persevere against all odds because of their unquestioned faith in their God who cared, when the world did not. Thanks to this faith we are alive today. Just like our ancestors, we are never alone, because *nuestro Jesús camina con nosotros*. Our suffering and victorious Jesus defeated death as our guarantee that God cares for us. When our ancestors were alone, our *madrecita santísima* was there with them, as she is with us today, encouraging us and listening when no one else will. She was with them, she is with us.

It is in our common religious-cultural structure and struggle that we can find the resources to help us unite. We find unity in a common language that shapes our world and grounds our identity. Isasi-Díaz correctly suggests,

Spanish has become "the incarnation and symbol" of our whole culture, making us feel that here in the U.S.A. we are one people, no matter what our country of origin is. The Spanish language identifies us by distinguishing us from the rest of society. It gives us a specificity that we need to be a certain kind of people within a culture not our own.[43]

Our rich language is gender inclusive: *nuestra comunidad Hispana, nuestra cultura, nuestra familia*. Our Hispanic community, our Hispanic culture, our family "are by no means exclusively masculine, indeed in Spanish they are feminine."[44] Whenever we desire to express our very personal feelings, we turn to Spanish. Amongst our friends we mostly speak in English, but when we have to search deep within ourselves to express those deeply rooted feelings, we are unable to express them in English, and suddenly we begin to speak, often times without noticing, in Spanish.[45] It is *nuestra lengua*, it was the only language *mi abuelita* spoke, unschooled as she was, when she shared her immense wisdom, night after night telling us *cuentos* about our ancestors. These were stories that fed us, when we went hungry daily; they were stories that gave us hope, when the future seemed hopeless. These stories shaped our feelings, and when we have to reach for these feelings, we must do so in Spanish, because it is in our *lengua* that they are stored. Our Spanish that will always unite us no matter where we are.

It is through our ancestors, through our rich and diverse religious-cultural expressions, and through our language that we have received *nuestra santa fe*, and as we struggle together, out of our *lucha* a new ecumenism is born, one not limited to issues of work and life, but also inclusive of what traditionally we have called *asuntos de fe y orden*. González suggests that, "indeed, it is our contention that there can be no division between life and work on the one hand and faith and order on the other, for as we work and live out the gospel we gain new insights into the meaning of our faith and the proper order for the church."[46] No matter how much the West desires to impose its post-Enlightenment ideologies on us, it will not work. We are communal people who find our identity in the religious-cultural expressions of our people. Destroy this expression and we cease to exist. According to Elizondo, "we can all enrich one another, but no one of us should seek to destroy or compete with the other."[47]

I often meditate on the story of Alex, a typical Hispanic living in Santa Barbara, California. Alex comes from a nominal Catholic family. He had a conversion experience, after a colleague witnessed to him at work. When he attempted to share his new faith with his family, he was immediately rejected, and labeled a traitor who had been brainwashed by *esos cristianos*. His family collapsed, while he was reassured that this was to be expected. After all, did not the Bible talk about Christ coming to turn a man against his family? Therefore, this family disaster was in fact scriptural. Alex went on to seminary and received his degree in Bible, yet something very interesting was happening. Alex felt that his new community was attempting to strip him of his identity, and no matter how much his new community told him that it was all right to be his own individual, it did not sit well with his Hispanic composition.[48] He missed his *familia*, his *fiestas*, and his *comunidad*. One day Alex called his priest, and asked if he could come back to the church, and have Bible studies. The priest agreed as long as Alex conducted the Bible studies. Now over 200 members of the congregation attend the studies regularly, including Alex's father, mother, and brothers, who through the Bible studies have dedicated their lives to serving Christ. They are no longer nominal Christians. Now they are devout Catholics, who have a deep love for the Scriptures, and for a Jesus that made whole their broken home. Not all families are as fortunate as Alex's, and the brokenness that permeates the Hispanic community cries for answers. It cries for a Jesus who heals and unites. It cries to *caminar con Jesús*.

Jon Nilson challenges us to ask each other: "What are you ready to surrender and suffer now for the sake of unity?"[49] As a *communidad de gran diversidad* let us search and realize that there is much we can abandon without sacrificing our identity, and when churches no longer insist that to be united "others" must accept their own particularities, "then the world—and even them—will find it easier to believe that Jesus comes from the one God and the Father of us all (John 17:20)."[50]

Notes

1. Roberto S. Goizueta, *Caminemos Con Jesús: Toward a Hispanic/Latino Theology of Accompaniment* (Maryknoll, NY: Orbis Books, 1995), 1. Goizueta has been able to put in writing what my heart feels and struggles to identify. For it is in finding this identity that healing begins.

2. José García Mazas, "Reflecting on Language," *Agenda* 10 (May-June 1980): 54. Professor García Mazas posits that "the millions of Hispanic who live in the United States must make a great effort to preserve and enrich their language, for language, and not race, gives us our Hispanic identity."

3. Virgilio Elizondo, *Galilean Journey: The Mexican-American Promise* (Maryknoll, NY: Orbis Books, 1983), 43. Elizondo speaks from within the Mexican-American context, yet his words are exemplary of all Hispanics. "Fiesta is the mystical celebration of a complex identity, the mystical affirmation that life is a gift and is worth living. In the fiesta the fatalistic/pessimistic realism and the adventuresome/optimistic idealism of the Mexican heritage are blended into the one celebration of the mystery of life . . . In the fiesta the Mexican-American rises above the quest for the logical meaning of life and celebrates the very contradictions that are of the essence of the mystery of human life."

4 Like Goizueta, I am also a Cuban-American. His reality is mine. His sentiments are mine, and yet our life has been very different. Ada María Isasi-Díaz, *Mujerista Theology* (Maryknoll, NY: Orbis Books, 1996), writes: "Every minute of the two weeks I was in Cuba I reminded myself I was only visiting . . . there I felt the same I feel in the United States: a foreigner. I am caught between two worlds, neither of which is fully mine, both of which are partially mine," 14.

5. Prior to becoming Protestant I was a nominal Catholic. I only attended church at Christmas, Easter and perhaps a Mass for someone who had died.

6. This is a phrase used by Protestants as an expression of a personal encounter with Christ. To be born again is to have made a personal choice to serve Christ. The most painful effect of this phrase is when Protestants use it to promulgate that Catholics are not Christians. Reflecting on that experience, today, I would not say I was born again, I would say, instead, that I made a commitment to serve Christ. The commitment my parents made for me when I was baptized as a child, I confirmed as an adult.

7. The most painful part of this experience for my family was that I not only abandoned the faith, but I now wanted them to abandon all they were. Only today do I realize what I was asking my parents to do, and it is with great compunction that I seek their forgiveness.

8. Justo L. Gonzáles, *Mañana: Christian Theology from a Hispanic Perspective* (Nashville: Abingdon Press, 1990). In the "Foreword," Virgilio Elizondo suggests that in the United States when an Anglo changes religion, he can do so without abandoning his cultural heritage, while among Hispanics "conversion demands a total break with one's culture. In the former (Anglos) one continues to be a member of one's people, while in the latter, one has to abandon and betray one's people to convert to the religion and the culture of the other," 15.

9. I am indebted to Justo L. González, "Hispanics in the New Reformation," in *Mestizo Christianity: Theology from the Latino Perspective*, ed. Arturo J. Bañuelas (Maryknoll, NY: Orbis Books, 1995), 236-260. Also see, *Mañana*, 55-73.

10. González, "Hispanics," 238.

11. Ibid., 239.

12. Ibid., 239.

13. Ibid., 240.

14. Bartolomé de Las Casas' writings about the abuse of the Indians have often been used by the English-speaking world to promulgate their anti-Spanish and anti-Catholic prejudices, yet these friars fought for the rights of the Indians, and cared deeply for their souls.

15. Rev. Dr. Von Hefele, *The Life of Cardinal Jiménez* (England: Catholic Publishing, 1860).

16. González, "Hispanics," 240. Many other names typified this "other" Catholic church: the Dominican Antonio Montesinos, first to protest the abuse of the Indians; St. Luis Beltran, the first of the Spanish missionaries to the New World, who constantly rebuked the Spaniards for living off the blood of the Indians; the Jesuit missionaries in Paraguay who organized the Indians into armies to defend the Indians

from the encroachment of slave hunters; the Dominican Gil González who, while living in Chile, convinced his fellow friars not to give absolution to those who abused the Indians, and many others too numerous to mention. González awakens us to the fact that because of their choice to identify with the poor and downtrodden history has forgotten these saints who in fact should be an inspiration to us today.

17. Ibid., 244.

18. Ibid., 249.

19. Ibid., 249.

20. Ibid., 249. It can be argued that the freedom Scriptures brought was now being taken away by denying education, the only vehicle of survival for the poor and downtrodden. Until recent times the one characteristic of all Latin American Protestantism has been its strong anti-Catholic resentment.

21. Without dismissing the belief that God reveals God-self in the Scriptures even to the most ignorant amongst us, one only needs to sit in a couple of different Hispanic congregations to see the mutilation of God's word at the hands of those who have not been trained to exegete Scriptures properly. It seems that today, among Hispanics in the United States, a person gets a few people willing to follow him or her and immediately opens a church in the midst of our neighborhoods. They have no formal affiliation, yet they call themselves charismatic or Pentecostal.

22. González, "Hispanics," 254. It is important to clarify that not all Catholics or Protestants feel the same, but a great number do.

23. Ibid., 254.

24. Ibid., 255.

25. Manuel Ortíz, *The Hispanic Challenge: Opportunities Confronting the Church* (Illinois: Inter Varsity Press, 1993), 96. In a study I conducted on religious practices in the federal prison system, it was interesting to note that Hispanic Catholics would not attend the Hispanic Protestant services, and Protestants would not attend Mass, yet when it came time to have Bible studies and pray, outside the chapel, Hispanics, Catholic and Protestant, came together. They would not attend each other's service or Mass, but they were comfortable, and thus encouraged each other, in their Bible studies. Yet, among Anglos, there never was a time when they would come together to worship or study the Word. Catholics congregated with Catholics, and Protestants with Protestants. It was evident that in reading the Scriptures and praying, Hispanics found identity in their shared struggle. This pattern is also evident outside of prisons.

26. The biblical quotations are my translations from the *The Greek New Testament*, Fourth edition, ed. Barbara Aland, et. al. (Münster/Westphalia: Deutsche Bibelgesellschaft, United Bible Societies, 1994).

27. It is beyond the scope of this paper to present all the ill that faced the Johannine community. It will suffice to say that the community was beset by danger from within as well as by the threat of persecution from without, which has been the subject of much of the Last Discourse. A case can be made that, even though almost 2000 years stand between the Johannine community and the Hispanic community, the dangers from within and the persecution from without are as real today as they were then.

28. Brooke Foss Westcott, *The Gospel According to St. John* ([1881] Michigan: Eerdmans, 1971), 236.

29. Gustavo Gutiérrez, *A Theology of Liberation* (Maryknoll, NY: Orbis Books, 1971), p.xlii.

30. John Paul II, "Ut Unum Sint, 9," in *The Encyclicals in Everyday Language*, ed. Joseph G. Donders (Maryknoll, NY: Orbis Books, 1996), 294.

31. For an extensive exegesis of this passage see Raymond E . Brown, *John*, Anchor Bible Dictionary 29a (Garden City: Doubleday, 1970), 769.

32. Ibid., 769. For the grammatical use of καθὼς, refer to Friedrich Blass and Albert Debrunner, *A Greek Grammar of the New Testament and other Early Christian Literature*, trans. Robert W. Funk (Chicago: University Press, 1961), 453.

33. Ibid., 769.

34. The perfect tense often points to action which happened in the past, but has a continuing impact or effect on state of being in the present.

35. D. A. Carson, *The Farewell Discourse and Final Prayer of Jesus* (Grand Rapids: Baker, 1980), 197.

36. Leon Morris, *Expository Reflections on the Gospel of John* (Grand Rapids: Baker, 1991), 596.

37. Ibid., 596. See Rudolf Bultmann, *The Gospel of John* (Philadelphia: Westminister, 1971), 514-515. For Rudolf Bultmann, the goal of glory is knowledge on part of the world, but "in addition to that the unity is described as the purpose and fulfillment of Jesus' work of revelation . . . Jesus' work finds its fulfillment in the existence of a unified community."

38. Merrill C. Tenney, *John the Gospel of Belief* (Grand Rapids: Eerdmans, 1989), 248-249. According to Tenney, we should make a clear distinc-

tion between four closely allied concepts: unanimity—absolute agreement within a given group of people; uniformity—complete similarity of organization; union—that which implies political affiliation without having to include individual agreement; and unity—oneness of inner heart or purpose, through a common interest or a common life. "Within the church of historic Christianity, there has been wide divergences of opinion and ritual. Unity, however, prevails wherever there is a deep and genuine experience of Christ; for the fellowship of the new birth transcends all historical and denominational boundaries."

39. Ricardo Ramírez, C.S.B., "Together in Pilgrimage Toward the Third Millennium," *Ecumenical Trends*, vol. 24 no. 6 (1995): 12.

40. I use the word "other" to refer to our Hispanic brother and sister who belongs to another religious denomination different from ours.

41. Oftentimes it seems that Christians, Hispanics as well as Anglos, spend more effort in bringing others to their denomination, instead of bringing them to Christ. See Elizondo, "Foreword," in González, *Mañana*, 14.

42. Ibid., 16. Elizondo expresses how the Christian experience of our ancestors was as real and genuine as that of European or U.S.Christianity. Yet, fundamentalists, Protestants, and mainline U.S. Catholics have continuously attempted to destroy the cultural-religious ethos of the Hispanic people. "They have been quick (and often mistaken) to point out the defects of the religions of other peoples but remain totally blind to the idols they accept and venerate, without even recognizing them as such within the mainline culture of the United States."

43. Ada María Isasi-Díaz, *En La Lucha/In the Struggle: Elaborating a Mujerista Theology* (Minneapolis: Fortress Press, 1993), 52-53.

44. Goizueta, *Caminemos*, 13.

45. Ibid., 53. Goizueta relates how he felt when, in graduate school, he was told that Spanish was not the equivalent of French and German: "what was rejected was not simply my ability to use some linguistic tool of expression—i.e., some mere technical communication 'skill.' I experienced that rejection, instead, as a denigration of my self and, therefore, of my family, my community, my culture, and my entire history as a Latino. These, among whom have been accomplished writers, lawyers, doctors, college professors, engineers, etc., were simply dismissed as intellectually inadequate. What was dismissed, then, was much more than just my language and more, even, than just my individual self."

46. González, "Hispanics," 255.

47. Elizondo, "Foreword," 19.

48. Isasi-Díaz, *En La Lucha*, 171. Isasi-Díaz notes that in Spanish the word *individuo*, carries a negative connotation: "Commonly, when one says *ese individuo* (that individual), one is talking about someone who for one reason or other is outside the Latino community."

49. Jon Nilson, *Nothing Beyond the Necessary: Roman Catholicism and the Ecumenical Future* (New York: Paulist Press, 1995), 66.

50. Ibid., 75.

Ecumenical Ethics: Authoritative Catholic Teaching Confronts the Principles of Vatican II

Tom Poundstone
Assistant Professor of Religious Studies
Saint Mary's College of California

My goal in this paper is straightforward: to explore the implications for Roman Catholic moral theology of Vatican II's declaration that God's Spirit is at work in other Christian churches. As we continue to reflect on expanding the borders, I will try to ask what effect such an acknowledgment of the expanded domain of activity for God's Spirit should have on authoritative Catholic teaching.

This paper will be divided into three sections. In the first part I will elaborate on the scope of this paper, consider how disagreements among Christian churches should be characterized, and supply a concrete example of churches in conflict. The second part will be a brief historical interlude in which I sketch the status of ecumenical ethics going into Vatican II and then note what happened at the council. In this section I will use the position paper prepared by the minority on the Papal Birth Control Commission as a foil. In the final section I will consider five implications of the principles of Vatican II for Roman Catholic moral theology. The focus will not be on what ecumenical ethics says about others, but how ecumenical ethics will change the landscape of Catholic ethics.

Characterizing the Conflict

First, the title of this paper refers to "Authoritative Catholic Teaching." By that I have in mind the Roman Catholic Church's teaching on sexual and medical ethics, not its teaching on social ethics. It has become quite common to contrast the methodologies used in these different fields.[1] While the Catholic church's social ethics tends to be inductive in its method, historically conscious in its worldview, and tentative in its conclusions, the church's sexual and medical teaching tends to be deductive in its method, classicist in its worldview, and absolute in its conclusions. Quite naturally, it is the sexual and medical teaching which poses the significant challenge for ecumenism. In the areas of social ethics, a great degree of coordinated ministry has already begun.

Second, the title also refers to "Ecumenical Ethics." There is no shortage of literature on ecumenism, but very little of it has to do with disagreements on concrete moral issues.[2] Most ecumenical dialogues such as ARCIC—the Anglican-Roman Catholic International Commission—have been focused on matters of doctrine, worship, and church polity.[3] Only in 1994, 25 years after ARCIC was established in 1969, did ARCIC release its first joint statement dealing specifically with morality. This statement, "Life in Christ: Morals, Communion, and the Church,"[4] appears to be the first and perhaps the only international, bilateral dialogue to have taken up this topic. Consistent with my first point that the focus of discussion should be on the sexual and medical questions, the document singles out four areas of moral dispute: marriage after divorce, contraception, abortion, and homosexuality. This paucity of formal dialogue on moral disagreements is surprising. For those of us who believe that the principle of mediation is one of the central planks of Roman Catholic moral theology,[5] authentic Christian unity will be as much a matter of life as of faith. Indeed, I maintain that our most committed profession of faith in God is made, not in words, but in the way we live our lives.

Third, how one characterizes the disagreements between denominations is significant. Typically, the ecumenically sensitive try to say that the disagreements are on the level of practical judgments rather than fundamental values.[6] That is perhaps too optimistic and also perhaps too trivializing of the consequences of disagreement. Consider the pain caused by the disputes on marriage after divorce, contraception, abortion, and homosexuality. True, the fundamental values might be shared, but between fundamental values and practical conclusions there are several intermediary steps. It is in those intermediary steps that the Roman Catholic Church and the Anglican Communion tend to rely on very different underlying anthropologies and very different methods for analyzing acts. For example, one of the factors which makes *Humanae Vitae*[7] so difficult for other denominations to accept is not simply its conclusions but that its conclusions are rooted in a physicalist anthropology which they find unconvincing. In *Humanae Vitae*, biological structures and rhythms are given priority over the human person considered in totality.

Fourth, my particular interest in this topic was inspired by the embryo experimentation debate in Great Britain. On April 23, 1990, the day the British House of Commons was to vote on its human embryo experimentation bill, *The Times* of London carried conflicting editorials by John Habgood, the Anglican Archbishop of York, and Cardinal Basil Hume, the Roman Catholic Archbishop of Westminster. Cardinal Hume, who opposed all such experimentation, characterized the vote as a decision between absolute moral principles and utilitarian expedience.[8] Archbishop Habgood, who supported the bill, did not see this as a matter of basic principles, he thought this topic allowed for large areas of disagreement, and he thought that Hume's particular stance was biologically, theologically, and philosophically unsustainable.[9] After the bill was passed, Cardinal Hume wrote that, as a society, Britain had "abandoned fundamental aspects of Christian morality" and "dispensed with the traditional Christian vision of the sanctity of human life."[10] In contrast, Archbishop Habgood did not think that disagreement between Christians was a cause for a scandal. He saw it as a dispute between different judgments on how best to respect human life.[11]

Though Hume is the Roman Catholic and Habgood the Anglican, it is in Habgood's rhetoric that we hear strong echoes of both Vatican II's *Gaudium et Spes* and the recent pastoral letters of the United States Catholic bishops which hold that circumstances can be interpreted differently by people of good will. Like Habgood, both expected a certain diversity of views among Christians on complex questions even though all hold the same universal moral principles.[12]

At the same time, Cardinal Hume's remarks in this dispute echoed the tone of Pope Pius XI in the 1930 encyclical *Casti Connubii*.[13] Since the tone and details of this exchange are significant for ecumenical ethics, a brief review of the historical evolution of the Anglican position on birth control might be helpful. In 1908 and again in 1920, the Lambeth Conference of the bishops of the Anglican Communion issued solemn warnings against "unnatural means for the avoidance of conception."[14] In 1930 the Conference, by a vote of 193 to 67, conceded that there were some limited circumstances in which the use of contraceptives could be legitimate.[15] In 1958 the Conference unanimously approved a report which laid full responsibility for the use of contraception on the consciences of parents.[16]

In 1930, the same year that the Lambeth Conference opened the door slightly to the acceptance of contraception, Pius XI responded in the encyclical *Casti Connubii* by effectively describing the Anglican bishops as leading their flocks into "poisoned pastures"[17] and giving a teaching which would lead to "moral ruin."[18] Quite similarly, in 1990 Cardinal Hume implicitly described the Archbishop of York as having "abandoned fundamental aspects of Christian morality" and having "dispensed with the traditional Christian vision of the sanctity of human life."

The Status of Ecumenical Ethics Going into Vatican II
It should be no surprise to say that in the centuries following the Reformation up until Vatican II, the hierarchical magisterium of the Roman Catholic Church tended to see the Catholic church as the only true church. As a natural result, Catholics had a privileged access to the truth, and little credence was formally given to the experience of those outside the church. This sentiment was expressed in Pius XI's encyclical of 1928, *Mortalium Animos*,[19] which saw no role for Catholicism in the nascent ecumenical movement. This idea of the one true church was so entrenched that even a year after the Second Vatican Council was over, we still see it expressed in the position paper prepared by the minority on the Papal Birth Control Commission. It was inconceivable to this minority that the Holy Spirit might have protected the Anglican Communion from an error which Roman Catholicism was not spared. The disagreement in conclusions was so striking that the question was obvious: In 1930, was the Holy Spirit moving in the halls of the Vatican or Lambeth? One of the minority's strongest arguments against a change in church teaching was precisely that implication. The position paper states,

> If contraception were declared not intrinsically evil, in honesty it would have to be acknowledged that the Holy Spirit in 1930, in 1951 and 1958 assisted Protestant churches, and that for half a century Pius XI, Pius XII and a great part of the Catholic hierarchy did not protect [us] against a very serious error, one most pernicious to souls; for it would thus be suggested that they condemned most imprudently, under the

pain of eternal punishment, thousands upon thousands of human acts which are now approved. Indeed, [were we to change our teaching,] it must be neither denied nor ignored that these acts would be approved for the same fundamental reasons which Protestantism alleged and which [we] condemned or at least did not recognize. Therefore one must very cautiously inquire whether the change which is proposed would not bring along with it a definitive depreciation of the teaching and the moral direction of the hierarchy of the church and whether several very grave doubts would not be opened up about the very history of Christianity.[20]

Vatican II irrevocably rejected any presumption that the Roman Catholic Church is the sole locus of activity for God's Spirit. In doing so, it put a clear end to the hostility towards ecumenism enshrined in *Mortalium Animos*. As none less than Pope John Paul II writes in his 1995 encyclical on ecumenism, "At the Second Vatican Council, the Catholic Church committed herself irrevocably to following the path of the ecumenical venture, thus heeding the Spirit of the Lord."[21]

Clearly John Paul II is correct in both acknowledging and embracing ecumenism as a central component of Vatican II. However, what is the foundation for this irrevocable ecumenism? It is not simply the Lord's prayer that we all be one. I maintain it is more fundamentally rooted in the claim that the Spirit is working in other denominations and faiths. Vatican II's *Gaudium et Spes* and *Unitatis Redintegratio* (Decree on Ecumenism) encouraged Catholics to see that God's spirit and saving will is at work beyond the boundaries of the Roman Catholic Church, even beyond the bounds of Christianity and Judaism. Hence John XXIII's *Pacem in Terris* is the first of the encyclicals addressed to "all people of good will."[22] Similarly *Gaudium et Spes* is addressed, not simply to the sons and daughters of the church, and not simply to those who invoke the name of Christ, but to all of humanity.[23] Along with this switch,

Gaudium et Spes, with its emphasis on the signs of the times, spoke of the importance of listening to life and learning from experience.

To connect these two points of the working of the Spirit and the signs of the times, the renewal of Catholicism at Vatican II calls us to acknowledge that the experience of people of good will, both non-Catholic Christians and non-Christians, is an inspired source which the Catholic Church should consider in its attempt to understand what the demands of respectful living in our day and age entail.[24] If that is not the case, what then are we to make of the following statement from Vatican II?

> In fidelity to conscience, Christians are joined together with the rest of men and women in the search for truth and for the genuine solution to the numerous problems which arise in the life of individuals and from social relationships.[25]

The statement would appear to be saying that we are all engaged in a common search. As such, we are obliged to respect the integrity and competence of committed men and women. Thus, if we are to remain open to this fundamental declaration of Vatican II, if we are to be a church attentive to the promptings of God's Spirit, we must listen to what Schillebeeckx calls "foreign prophets" coming from outside our own ranks.[26]

We must also frankly acknowledge that Vatican II admitted the possibility of the Roman Catholic Church being in error. Not only did the church explicitly acknowledge that there might be deficiencies in the formulation of doctrine,[27] clearly the church's teaching on issues such as ecumenism and religious freedom coming out of the council bore little relation to the church's official teaching when the council began.[28] Similarly, the very theologians who were placed under severe restrictions with regard to their ability to teach and publish—John Courtney Murray, Henri de Lubac, and Yves Congar, to name a few—were among the principal architects of the council.

Now, even though the council seems willing to explicitly admit deficiencies and implicitly acknowledge error and the legitimacy of dissent, the position paper written by those in the minority on the Papal Birth Control Commission could not imagine how error on the matter of birth control might be possible. Instead, it argued as follows:

> [The teaching] is true because the Catholic church, instituted by Christ to show men a secure way to eternal life, could not have so wrongly erred during all those centuries of its history. The church cannot substantially err in teaching doctrine which is most serious in its import for faith and morals, throughout all centuries or even one century if [the teaching] has been constantly and forcefully proposed as necessarily to be followed in order to obtain eternal salvation. The church could not have erred through so many centuries, even through one century, by imposing under serious obligation very grave burdens in the name of Jesus Christ if Jesus Christ did not actually impose these burdens . . . If the church could err in such a way, the authority of the ordinary magisterium in moral matters would be thrown into question. The faithful could not put their trust in the magisterium's presentation of moral teaching, especially in sexual matters.[29]

How Ecumenical Ethics Will Change
Roman Catholic Moral Theology
1) Authoritative Catholic Teaching Does Not Necessarily Equal
the Definitive Christian Position

If, as Vatican II recognized, God's Spirit is at work in other Christian churches, then post-Vatican II Roman Catholic ethics must have an ecumenical dimension to it. This means that, while the hierarchical magisterium may speak of authoritative Catholic teaching on a topic, it is another step altogether to declare that such teaching is the final and definitive Christian position on the subject. What we can say is that, to the best of our lights, and in our trust in the Spirit's guidance, this is where we now are. Far from being the whole truth, our authoritative teaching is not the final word, but the best expression of the truth as we can understand it at the present moment. We remain committed to continue dialogue. We continue as a learning and listening church.

2) A Shift in the Balances

Gula in his *Reason Informed by Faith* tries to set up a seesaw balance between two extremes he says we want to avoid in our response to authoritative church teaching. On the left side, we want to avoid regarding the church's teaching as only as good as the arguments supporting it. On the right side, we do not want to treat church teaching as though its authority were totally independent of supporting arguments. Ecumenical ethics would clearly shift the balance more to the left.[30]

While ecumenical ethics will put more stress on supporting argument, appeals to authority will no longer have the same weight. In effect, that will give the arguments of dissenting theologians another day in court. Attempts to silence dissenting theologians in the Catholic Church will prove futile since similar questions will now be directed to the church by theologians from other denominations. Neither will non-Catholic theologians show deference to statements such as *Humani Generis'* declaration that when the pope deliberately states an opinion on a controverted matter, it can no longer be held as a matter of free debate among theologians.[31] Theologians from other denominations will not consider the matter closed to debate; instead, they will ask for better arguments. Such unilateral papal declarations will no longer be discussion stoppers.

Almost by default, this will also shift the balance in the debate on how to best translate *obsequium religiosum* as it appears in *Lumen Gentium*, n. 25.[32] Simple translations like "submission" will be outweighed by the more nuanced translations such as Francis Sullivan's "make an honest and sustained effort to overcome any contrary opinion,"[33] and Richard McCormick's "make a docile personal attempt to assimilate."[34]

Similarly, the balances will shift in the age-old debate as to the role of the theologian in the church. Rather than playing the role of apologists called upon to give a defense for magisterial teaching, moral theologians will be called to be more like scientists in an open-ended pursuit of the truth. Ethics, especially ecumenical ethics, is dependent on honest probing questions, not apology. This will no doubt lead to situations of dissent, but as Bernard Häring has said, dissent can be a prophetic ministry within the church. Without dissent there would be an ossification of doctrines. "Common dedication to truth," Häring writes, "is possible only if there is freedom of inquiry and freedom to speak out even in dissent from official documents."[35] Dissent is not the end but the beginning of a search for a deeper, more adequate response.

3) Increased Consultation

With ecumenical ethics there will be a much greater emphasis on consultation, especially broad consultation. The curia has often demonstrated a tendency to consult only like-minded theologians. The respect which a teaching deserves will be in direct proportion to this breadth of consultation. To the extent that the Vatican fails to do this, the presumption of truth is weakened and the very teaching office is rendered less credible.

We do claim that the church is guided by the Holy Spirit. However, that does not exempt the church from the human task of thoroughly and adequately studying the question. As Richard Gula has written,

[T]he guidance of the Holy Spirit does not exempt the magisterium from the human process of gathering data, consulting, reflecting on the data, making a proposal, entertaining counter proposals, doing more research, and so on . . . [A] teaching is only as strong as the thoroughness of the homework which produced it and the cogency of the arguments which support it.[36]

The model for consultation should be what the United
States Catholic bishops did in the writing of the peace and
economic pastorals in the 1980s.[37] The Vatican is in an even
more ideal situation to seize upon the church's global
resources for consultation. We are no longer a Roman,
European, or even a Western church. We should demonstrate
that.

4) Contraception and Humanae Vitae

If and when a truly ecumenical ethics takes hold, the issue of
contraception will return to being a moral question rather
than an authority question. The current acrimony in the
debate is fueled by the implicit challenge that any question
about the truth of *Humanae Vitae* presents to the authority of
the hierarchical magisterium. As soon as we can move away
from what David F. Kelly has termed "ecclesiastical positivism,"[38] the natural law argument in *Humanae Vitae* will be
able to enter the debate on its own merits.

5) The Basic Vision of the Church

When we speak of the belief that Christ will not abandon the
church to error, the question is, who is it that constitutes the
church? Many implicitly equate the church with the hierarchical magisterium. Others understand Christ's church as
larger than any existing group or communion, including the
Catholic church. It is that latter perspective which calls for
the hierarchical magisterium to consult much more broadly,
for it is the broader church, and not simply the hierarchical
magisterium which is protected from error. This calls for a
revitalization of the idea of the *sensus fidelium* and a much
greater emphasis on experience, especially the experience of
married couples as an authentic source of theology. As a
comparison between the drafting and reception of *Humanae
Vitae* and the pastoral letters of the U.S. Catholic bishops
shows, an ethics which respects and values the experience of
the faithful calls for a method which discovers the truth with

the faithful rather than one which declares a teaching and expects the faithful to embrace it.

Conclusion

The age of truly ecumenical ethics is not yet here. To contribute effectively to its arrival and its success, we must first probe deeply into what we believe and why we believe it. As we read in 1 Peter 3:15–16, we must, with gentleness, be able to give reason for this hope which resides in us. This greater knowledge of our own tradition in its strengths and weakness can do nothing but good. Second, as Dan Finn has written about the ethics of communication, we must seek to describe the other's position in a way the other would endorse. In our dialogue, we must strive to find arguments that are persuasive, not simply to those in our own group, but also to those in the groups we critique.[39]

In *Gaudium et Spes*, the council fathers wrote that, even among those who hold the same universal moral principles, a diversity of sincerely held views should be expected on complex questions.[40] Though such diversity might be a cause of scandal for the weak, it could also be a valuable stage along the road toward better understanding and a fuller, deeper appreciation of the truth. One thing which we must be cautious about is thinking that the goal of dialogue is the type of consensus in which one or all participants in the dialogue must dilute or abandon certain views. Instead, each group must feel free to maintain its own distinctive beliefs including the blunt judgment that other Christians are in dangerous error. The result of dialogue might be an increasing measure of agreement among the dialogical partners, but that agreement should come voluntarily and not from a pressure to conform or compromise. In short, there is room for blunt criticism in dialogue. This is especially so on matters of justice. For example, we don't have to split the difference on apartheid with the white church in South Africa.

If we are to remain open to the declaration of Vatican II

that God's Spirit is at work in other Christian churches, if we are to be a church attentive to the promptings of God's Spirit, we must listen to what Schillebeeckx calls "foreign prophets" coming from outside our own ranks.

Notes

1. See Charles E. Curran, "Catholic Social and Sexual Teaching: A Methodological Comparison," *Theology Today* 44 (January 1988): 425-440. See also Richard M. Gula, *Reason Informed by Faith* (Mahwah, NJ: Paulist Press, 1989), 30-38, 237-240.

2. There is little need to review the voluminous material on ecumenism here, little of which touches upon matters of ethics directly. In the last few years there has been an increased interest in ecumenical ethics, though much of the discussion has remained on the level of theory rather than focusing on concrete issues of disagreement. Two ethicists have approached the topic in book-length form: James Gustafson, *Protestant and Roman Catholic Ethics: Prospects for Rapprochement* (Chicago: University of Chicago Press, 1978), and Charles E. Curran, *The Church and Morality: An Ecumenical and Catholic Approach* (Minneapolis: Fortress Press, 1994). There have also been a three notable collections of dialogues between ecclesial traditions on moral matters: Oswald Bayer, et. al., *Zwei Kirchen-eine Moral?* (Regensberg: Putset, 1986); Oswald Bayer and Allan Suggate, eds., *Worship and Ethics: Lutherans and Anglicans in Dialogue* (New York: Walter de Gruyter, 1996); and Michael Cromartie, ed., *A Preserving Grace: Protestants, Catholics, and Natural Law* (Grand Rapids, Michigan: Eerdmans, 1997). Pope John Paul II's moral encyclicals have also elicited two collections of Protestant responses: O. Abel, et. al., *Paroles de Pape, Paroles Protestantes* (Paris: Les Bergers et Les Mages, 1995) and Reinhard Hütter and Theodor Dieter, *Ecumenical Ventures in Ethics: Protestants Engage Pope John Paul II's Moral Encyclicals* (Grand Rapids, MI: Eerdmans, 1998).

3. For example, the first major document which ARCIC released in 1971 was on the Eucharist. Subsequently, among others, ARCIC released a document on ministry and ordination in 1973, a document on authority in the church in 1977, and a document on salvation in 1987. For a complete collection of the ARCIC documents, see *Common Witness to the Gospel: Documents on Anglican-Roman Catholic Relations 1983-1995*, ed. Jeffrey Gros, et. al. (Washington, DC: United States Catholic Conference, 1997).

4. "Life in Christ: Morals, Communion, and the Church" can be found

in both *Common Witness to the Gospel* and in the Pontifical Council for Promoting Christian Unity's *Information Service* 85 (1994): 54-70.

5. Richard P. McBrien lists mediation as one of the three principles by which he distinguishes Catholicism from other Christian churches. See his *Catholicism*, new edition (San Francisco: HarperSanFrancisico, 1994) 11-12. This idea is also expressed in Karl Rahner's "Reflections on the Unity of Love of Neighbor and the Love of God," *Theological Investigations*, vol. 6 (New York: Crossroad, 1982), 231-249. The two most frequently cited scriptural warrants for this principle are 1 John 4:20–21 and the great judgment scene in Matthew 25:31–46.

6. See "Life in Christ," n. 83-84.

7. Paul VI, *Humanae Vitae* (1968), in *The Papal Encyclicals. 1740-1981*, vol. 5, ed. Claudia Carlen (Wilmington, NC: McGrath, 1981).

8. Basil Hume and the Archbishops of England and Wales, "Moral Criteria on Embryo Research," *The Times*, April 23, 1990, 13.

9. John Habgood, "When Genesis Is in Conflict," *The Times*, April 23, 1990, 12.

10. Basil Hume, "Parliamentary Debate on Human Life," *Briefing* 20 (May 4, 1990): 165.

11. It should be noted that Cardinal Hume and the other Roman Catholic archbishops in England and Wales were staunchly unified in their opposition to the bill. However, in the House of Lords, of the six Anglican bishops who appear to have voted, four were opposed to all experimentation while only one joined Archbishop Habgood in support of it. Interestingly, one of the leading Roman Catholic moral theologians in Great Britain, John Mahoney, agreed with the stand taken by Archbishop Habgood.

12. See *Gaudium et Spes* (Pastoral Constitution on the Church in the Modern World), n. 43, in *Vatican Council II: The Basic Sixteen Documents. Constitutions, Decrees, Declarations*, A Completely Revised Translation in Inclusive Language, ed. Austin Flannery, O.P. (Northport, NY: Costello Publishing, 1996), and National Conference of Catholic Bishops, *The Challenge of Peace: God's Promise and Our Response* (Washington, DC: United States Catholic Conference, 1983), n. 11.

13. Pius XI, *Casti Connubii*, in *The Papal Encyclicals*, vol. 3. This point was brought to my attention by Kevin T. Kelly in his *New Directions in Moral Theology* (London: Geoffrey Chapman, 1992), 10.

14. *Resolutions of the Twelve Lambeth Conferences, 1867-1988*, ed. Roger Coleman (Toronto: Anglican Book Center, 1992).

15. *Lambeth Conference*, 1930, Declaration 15. The vote count is cited in

William H. Shannon's *The Lively Debate: Response to 'Humanae Vitae'* (New York: Sheed and Ward, 1970), 10.

16. The changes in official church teaching on the issue of contraception are outlined in Norman St. John-Stevas, *Life, Death, and the Law* (Bloomington, IN: Indiana University Press, 1961), 71-105, especially 71-82.

17. Pius XI, *Casti Connubii*, n. 3.

18. Ibid., n. 56.

19. Pius XI, *Mortalium Animos* (1928), in *The Papal Encyclicals*, vol. 4.

20. "The State of the Question: The Doctrine of the Church and Its Authority (*Status Quaestionis: Doctrina Ecclesiae Ejusque Auctoritas*)," in *The Birth Control Debate*, ed. Robert G. Hoyt (Kansas City, MO: National Catholic Reporter, 1968), 53. The primary author of the paper was John Ford, S.J., of the Catholic University of America. It was also signed by Marcelino Zalba, S.J., Stanislas de Lestapis, S.J., and Jan Visser, C.S.R. The media immediately began to call this document the "minority report." More accurately, it is a position paper prepared for the commission by a small group of theologians who opposed the overall commission's description of the church's teaching as being in evolution.

21. John Paul II, *Ut Unum Sint*, n. 3, in *Origins* 25 (June 8, 1995).

22. John XXIII, *Pacem in Terris* (1963), in *The Papal Encyclicals*, vol. 5.

23. *Gaudium et Spes*, n. 2.

24. This idea of experience as a fundamental source for developing our moral knowledge was further affirmed by Cardinal Hume at the 1983 Synod on the Family in Rome. He spoke, "The prophetic mission of . . . husbands and wives is based upon their experience as married persons and on an understanding of the sacrament of marriage of which they can speak with their own authority. This experience and this understanding constitute, I would suggest, an authentic source of theology from which we, the pastors, and indeed the whole Church can draw." Cited in K.T. Kelly, *New Directions*, 66.

25. *Gaudium et Spes*, n. 16.

26. Edward Schillebeeckx, *God, the Future of Man* (New York: Sheed and Ward, 1968), 163.

27. *Unitatis Redintegratio* (Decree on Ecumenism), n. 6, in *Vatican Council II*.

28. For an article listing some changes in church teaching, see James Burtchaell, "Too Bad to Be True," *The Tablet* (April 8, 1989): 388-390. Letters to the editor in subsequent issues catalogued more changes. In Hoyt, 181-184, John T. Noonan provides a concise list of statements of

earlier popes that have since been rejected by the church.

29. "The State of the Question," 37-38.

30. Gula, 156.

31. Pius XII, *Humani Generis* (1950), n. 20, in *The Papal Encyclicals*, vol. 4. It is worth noting that this statement from *Humani Generis* was cited in article 30 of the initial schema on the church discussed at Vatican II. The schema as a whole was rejected, and that passage did not resurface in later drafts. The non-ratification of this papal assertion by the council fathers points to a more fundamental problem. The one time in modern history that the bishops have had a chance to voice their opinions on curially produced documents, they flatly rejected all but one of the preparatory schema. Now that the council is over, however, it is the same curia which continues to produce authoritative teaching with no opportunity for the bishops as a whole to review the teaching in advance.

32. *Lumen Gentium* (Dogmatic Constitution on the Church), in *Vatican Council II.*

33. Francis A. Sullivan, *Magisterium: Teaching Authority in the Catholic Church* (Mahwah, NJ: Paulist Press, 1983), 164.

34. Richard A. McCormick, *The Critical Calling: Reflections on Moral Dilemmas Since Vatican II* (Washington, D.C.: Georgetown University Press, 1989), 41.

35. Bernard Häring, *Free and Faithful in Christ*, vol. 1 (New York: Seabury, 1978), 280-281.

36. Gula, 154.

37. National Conference of Catholic Bishops, *The Challenge of Peace* (1983), and *Economic Justice for All* (Washington, DC: United States Catholic Conference, 1986).

38. David F. Kelly, *The Emergence of Roman Catholic Medical Ethics in North America* (New York: Edwin Mellen, 1979), 109, 231.

39. See my report of a talk given by Daniel Rush Finn in "Catholic Social Teaching: Reformists and Radicals in Theological Economic Ethics," *The Catholic Theological Society of America Proceedings* 51 (1996), 257.

40. *Gaudium et Spes*, n. 43.

Part III
THE BORDER
BETWEEN THEOLOGY
AND SOCIETY

Theology from the Margins: A Caribbean Response A People of God in the Caribbean

Carmelo Alvarez
Visiting Professor of Church History and Theology
Director of Cross-Cultural Studies
Christian Theological Seminary

When I started to think about this important theme, two important concerns came to mind. Are we talking about a marginal theology that is just for the people of the Caribbean as they practice their faith and reflect theologically? Is it a theology done by a marginalized people from the underside of history? It is my understanding that our theology is the expression of, the aspiration toward, and the search and struggle for emancipation in the midst of a history of oppression and with a future of hope. Our Christian experience offers the rich heritage of a people of God that has accepted and continues to witness to the Christian faith and its transforming power in the context of Caribbean society.

The People of God in the Caribbean experience faith as a constant process of search for and affirmation of human dignity. To marginalized people, having human dignity affirmed means moving beyond a colonial heritage toward a new humanity. In trying to be faithful to its identity and mission, the church has offered a community of solidarity, sometimes as an invisible community of spiritual resistance, sometimes as a visible community of active accompaniment to the people of God. The church confesses Jesus Christ, a marginalized Jew, who, as God incarnate, identified with the oppressed and took upon himself the realities of pain and suffering in the conviction that through his resurrection a new way would open to liberate the people and offer them the new values and promises of God's reign.

The church has provided both a meaningful spiritual community of celebration in liturgy and a relevant community of service in mission. The Holy Spirit is present in the church, the presence of the living God, as promised by Christ, as comforter and liberator. The Caribbean people strive to break the chains of colonialism—marginalization, fragmentation, and division—moving actively in hope to reconstruct anew both church and society to the glory of God and for the freedom of the people. A "god" who was absent and marginalized (many times silenced) in a colonial structure is now revealed in this search for freedom and in the fullness of God's promise of redemption and liberation.

During my years as Regional Secretary in the Caribbean (1984-1986) for the Latin American Council of Churches I became very aware and conscientized about the complexities, riches, and beauties of this marvelous region. Having been born in Puerto Rico, which is part of the microcosm of the Caribbean, I realized the increasing importance of the region and the marginal role that it played in international affairs (although mentioned only in connection with a tragedy or political tension or crisis!).

For many people in the world, and particularly for North Americans and Europeans, the Caribbean has the reputation of being an exotic, mysterious, almost magical paradise—a tourist attraction with beautiful beaches and attractive women! This view of the Caribbean cannot be allowed to hide the fact that ours is really a region, a colonized and dominated land that is in constant turmoil. It is also a land of colonial and genocidal experiments. Spain and Great Britain began the Caribbean onslaught early in the sixteenth century with colonial expansion and various instruments and mentalities of conquest and domination. Columbus and Drake contributed to the destruction of Caribbean land and society, further imposing Europe's presence.

A Marginalized People: Making History

I also learned, during my years with the Latin American Council of Churches, that there is a great potential for resistance, for affirmation of life, for celebration and hope, and for a contagious joy in these islands! As Philip Potter, Methodist pastor and theologian from Dominica and former General Secretary of the World Council of Churches, clearly stated:

> I happen to come from an area where probably the earliest intensive and somewhat violent meeting of cultures took place. And I contain in my own self many cultures, from Mongolian (which Caribs were) all the way to Africa, with Europe in between, I contain within me oppressed and oppressors, white and black and yellow. Therefore, *this dialogue of cultures has being going on inside me all my life*. It has not been difficult for me to be conscious of both the tensions and the marvelous privilege of sharing in so much of humanity.[1]

It is in the context of these "tensions and the marvelous privilege of sharing" that I also find my Caribbean identity and struggle. As a Puerto Rican, I understood our pilgrimage as one of a multifaceted struggle to exit and to reclaim our space and place within the Caribbean community, sharing some of the common heritage of colonial domination and affirming the values and blessings of our common dignity and humanity that have been so neglected for more than five centuries.[2] *Ours is a history lived from the margins, as marginalized people, looking for a new world order with new relationships in equality and respect.* We were marginalized. We did not have the option of choosing our destiny, our place in history, and space in society.

It is very important to emphasize that the issue of marginality has at least two dimensions. The Caribbean region was part of the European expansion of the sixteenth century that included Africa and Asia. The Caribbean was an obstacle on the way to the Orient, but it was incorporated within the colonial system and became part of a *world system* that started in the sixteenth century and that today is expressed in terms of a *globalizing process* of Western hegemony and market economy. Another important dimension of marginalization is the existence of people from the underside of history reclaiming their right to be visible in history and assuming their destiny as *makers of history*. Winston D. Persaud, a Lutheran theologian from Guyana, expressed this dimension very clearly: "The marginalized make history when they refuse to accept their own and others' condition of powerlessness, alienation, and oppression as normative and unalterable."[3] God in Jesus Christ gives life through the resurrection and offers a freedom to change structures and systems in order to change a fatalistic and tragic vision of history into a positive attitude toward the future. According to Persaud, the "history of the marginalized is, therefore, history that critiques and undermines the dominant ideological notion of history."[4]

For people who are marginalized or oppressed, it is fundamental to see God's liberating force in their history. As Persaud states,

> Their experience of anguish, pain, and suffering are authentic signals of the presence of God in weakness and shame. God will not let them be pushed out to the periphery. To hear them is to recognize them as *makers of history, not theirs only, but human history which is shaped, energized, judged, and redeemed by the divine initiative.*[5]

The marginalized people of the Caribbean can, then, see history as the place to create new life, promote justice, see themselves as persons, affirm others and be in solidarity with others, and be open to a future of hope in newness of life. For us as colonized and marginalized people, this emphasis on being *makers of history* is crucial because our own existence and meaning as persons have been neglected. We need an empowering, divine force to declare that free from all bondage our hidden stories are known and our humanity accepted and embraced in the sight of God and the rest of humanity.[6]

A poem by Aurora Levins Morales describes this paradoxical existence of the marginalized people:

I am a child of the Americas,
a light-skinned mestiza of the Caribbean,
a child of many diaspora, born into this continent at a crossroads.

I am a U.S. Puerto Rican Jew,
a product of the ghettos of New York I have never known.
An immigrant and the daughter and granddaughter of immigrants.
I speak English with passion: It's the tool of my consciousness,
a flashing knife blade of crystal, my tool, my craft.

I am Caribeña, island grown, Spanish is in my flesh,
ripples from my tongue, lodges in my hips:
the language of garlic and mangoes,
the singing in my poetry, the flying gestures of my hands.
I am of Latinoamérica, rooted in the history of my continent:
I speak from my body.

I am not african. Africa is in me, but I cannot return.
I am not taína. Taíno is in me, but there is no way back.
I am european. Europe lives in me, but I have no home there.

I am new. History made me. My first language was spanglish.
I was born at the crossroads
and I am whole.[7]

This poem summarizes the fundamental ethos and genesis of Caribbean people. We are a mixture of races, colors,
ethnic groups, the product of colonialism, experiencing a
spiritual pilgrimage in search of a Caribbean identity, at the
crossroads, with much anger and anxiety, but always affirming, being joyful, proud, and grateful.

Our colonial past is part of a legacy, but it is not necessarily part of our present quest. There is a culture of resistance
in the Caribbean that is trying to reconstruct societies, digni-
fy lives, affirm human values, and make people feel proud
and whole in the midst of oppression and marginalization.
In this context we need to understand and develop an ecumenical theology of solidarity, originating from the margins
and created by marginalized people, that reclaims a protag-
onist role in history and society and dares to envision a
future of hope, trusting in God's promise. In other words, as
Sergio Arce and Dora Valentín assert:

> The history of the Caribbean Basin since Columbus's arrival
> is the history of the struggles of empires against our people
> in order to conquer our lands. However, it is also the story of
> the struggles of empires among themselves, in order to take
> over the land conquered by the other. Last, but not least, it is
> the history of our people to free themselves from any imperi-
> alistic master.[8]

Dr. Kortright Davis, an Anglican priest from Antigua, and
one of the leading theologians of the Caribbean, expresses a
similar view quite clearly:

> Although the Caribbean can boast of a history which pre-
> dates the exploits of Christopher Columbus in the late 15th
> century, the historical antecedents for the contemporary situ-
> ation lie in the period of European mercantile expansion and

the colonial societies which were created by Europe for its own economic advantage. The historical developments from the conquest and exploitation, through economic and industrial prosperity (based on slavery, indentured labour and colonial domination), provide the real context for an understanding of the place of religion in Caribbean history and the significance of ecumenical endeavours by Christian churches.[9]

Both our colonial heritage (marginalization and fragmentation introduced from the outside) and our cultural resistance (emancipation and unity from within) provide the framework for an ongoing struggle toward the identity of the people in the Caribbean.

Caribbean history is plagued with inconsistencies and contradictions. Early in the conquest the region was a laboratory for all kinds of colonial experiments. The *encomiendas*, a system introduced by the Spaniards for the first time in the Caribbean, was used as socioeconomic religious instrument of exploitation and oppression. In theory, the colonizers were to teach the Indians the Christian faith and provide for the sharing of Christian values and way of life. This trusteeship (*encomienda*) required that those Indians who were entrusted to the colonizers for labor be evangelized. The system was good in theory but very oppressive in practice. The other experiment was the *Requerimiento*, a document based on theological principles that was read by as a requirement to the Indian chiefs. Through this document the conquerors stated that Christ was now Lord over the whole world and invited them to accept and submit themselves to the authority of the Pope and to the Spanish crown.[10]

The conquest and colonization in the Caribbean was established as an ideological-religious structure of domination. Spain tried to justify its colonization of and political right to the Caribbean through their Christian belief. From the very beginning the emphasis was on a "Christian civilization" that was expanding and extending the blessings of the Christian faith to these infidels and barbarians who were living outside of the church and the faith. The presence of the crown and the papacy were to be the visible institutions of Christendom. The cross and the sword were the instruments that symbolized the visible marriage of these politico-religious institutions in what has been called "A Violent Evangelism."[11]

A Marginalized People: Colonialism and Fragmentation

By the late fifteenth century the Caribbean Sea was already a region populated by a diversity of people and ethnic groups. The coming of the Spaniards and the British introduced new factors of confrontation and conflict and initiated a clash between two systems and ways of life. The colonizers and the soon to be colonized started a complex process of the formation of new racial, social, ethnic, and economic entities. What we consider today as the Caribbean is the by-product of a colonial enterprise in which slavery and plantation economy, as well as race and class within Creole culture and institutions, forged a Caribbean identity. We cannot understand the contemporary situation in the Caribbean unless we recognize these deep historical roots.[12]

This wide ranging diversity has elevated fragmentation as another fundamental issue. The Caribbean has oscillated between homogeneity and integration, and diversity and fragmentation. For five hundred years the region as a whole has experienced the ambivalence of trying to empower independence and nationalism in order to be liberated from the colonial powers while trying to promote regional integration in order to protect its integrity and sovereignty.[13] Most of these projects have failed; ironically, only some of the ecumenical efforts succeeded.

William G. Demas of Trinidad, and a leading voice on issues of development and economic integration, emphasizes what he calls "extreme fragmentation" in the

Caribbean. Emerging from the colonial experience, the region needs not only economic development but also a sense of collective identity in community as one people. Unity as an effective tool for economic cooperation, political integration, real independence, enabling us to relate with our Latin American neighbors and the rest of the world as equal partners, is crucial for Caribbean integration. In his view,

> If we had effective integration in the Caribbean, I repeat, our power in relation to the outside world, and hence our ability to change our state of dependence, in order to have genuine development and to have genuine identity, would increase tremendously. This means that we have to understand the vital, urgent need for total integration of the Caribbean.[14]

The Caribbean region became a mosaic of colorful contrasts, combinations, and shades. The history of the Caribbean is a complex texture with many layers. Its mosaic of languages includes new formations of Creole (French and English) and new combinations of European languages in Papiamento. For more than five hundred years the people of the Caribbean have lived, struggled, constructed, survived, dreamed, and created a new cultural form. The Caribbean consists of various national entities with regional commonalities, a common colonial history of domination, a common culture of resistance.[15]

These societies have recreated and transformed the initial colonial fabric into a new social and anthropological texture. One of the most important components of this culture is the faith of a people expressed in a popular religiosity that is as complex and diverse as colonial domination itself. The fact is that on each Caribbean island, religion plays a dominant role. The Caribbean is one of the most religious regions of the world, taking into consideration the number of territories and national entities and the population as a whole. The number of distinctive religious movements in the Caribbean is impressive. Neither syncretism nor accommodation in the analysis can exhaust or explain the intricacies and dimensions of this religious factor. One of the issues that the churches need to face in the Caribbean is the role of non-Christian religions: How can the church develop the necessary interreligious dialogue and broaden its scope of ecumenical commitments both in terms of doctrine and mission?[16] I have visited most of the territories of the Caribbean, including the Caribbean coast of Central America, Guyana, Surinam, and Cayenne. It was in 1982, during the twentieth anniversary celebration of the independence of Trinidad and Tobago from Great Britain that I really began to discern some of the racial, ethnic, and religious diversities of the Caribbean. We visited an Anglican cathedral, a Roman Catholic convent, a Muslim mosque, a Jewish synagogue, and Pentecostal churches, in addition to universities and government buildings and museums. Our hosts were intentional about giving us a complete tour of the main island, Trinidad, including a day in the beach! On a Saturday night we were official guests in the mayor's office and were taken to the main plaza for an evening concert. The well-trained steel band solemnly began with European classical composers such as Mozart and Beethoven and then progressed to calypso and reggae.

During those days I had the chance to sit and talk with people of Chinese, Indonesian, Afro-Caribbean, Spanish, Philippine, and Korean descent and to visit the home of a Trinidadian pastor married to a Canadian Caucasian missionary, ending on their porch conversing with their son born in Trinidad. This diversity is the primary essence of the Caribbean microcosm. It is at the crossroads of that diversity that we need to understand and reclaim the Caribbean.

A People's Search for Freedom:
Emancipation and Unity

The struggle for freedom in the Caribbean is the saga of colonized, acculturated people, racially mixed, oppressed and marginalized but always affirming their dignity. This cry for freedom is deeply rooted in the region's history of enslavement and exploitation. That is why to understand the cry for justice in the Caribbean we need to see the interconnection of social, economic, cultural, religious, and anthropological elements in the formation of Caribbean society and life.

For us the quest for freedom has a dimension of deep spirituality in which both freedom and hope are intertwined. As Noel Leo Erskine suggests:

> So, in the quest for a theology of freedom it becomes appropriate to ask about hope's relationship to freedom. The crucial question here is, Does hope set people free? This question is central for Christian history because, if hope does not mean struggle for freedom in history, then it is the opium of the oppressed. For Christian theology to talk about hope without relating it to the struggle of the oppressed for freedom in history is for it tacitly to sanction the structures of oppression, which deprive the oppressed of their dignity. To hope, then, is not merely to plan the future. Hope is more than the anticipation of freedom. It gives both form and content to human freedom.[17]

This struggle to be free is the key to the contemporary struggle of Caribbean people. Erskine offers an insightful analysis that helps in understanding why we need to "decolonize theology." For centuries we have lived a colonial theology, but now we need a theology to liberate us from the methodology, ideology, and perspective of a dominant theology and to further our quest toward freedom.

One recent approach to theology is expounded in the book *Emancipation Still Comin': Explorations in Caribbean Emancipatory Theology* by Kortright Davis. Davis sees Emancipation as the "major thrust of Caribbean existence."[18] He explores the complexities of Caribbean history with its slavery, colonialism, neocolonialism, and structures of dependence, and seeks to affirm and reclaim an emancipatory experience of freedom in the midst of many contradictions and obstacles, as well as of celebration, hope and the liberating news of the Gospel. Davis analyzes the Caribbean reality as a scenario in which the people struggle to reclaim their dignity as they trust in the God that emancipates. "When God emancipates, the strength, the dignity, the promise, and the beauty of the Caribbean right hand become the most powerful sign of human freedom."[19] One of the main creative features of Davis' methodology is to emphasize more the emancipation principle than the liberation concept so predominant in liberation theologies. He sees that emancipation is more accurate due to the history of slavery, the role of cultural life and religion in the deep experiences of the Caribbean people. In that way emancipatory theology is closer to the cries and aspirations, as well as concrete liturgical and missiological perspective in the Caribbean.[20]

The late Idris Hamid, considered by many to be "the founder of Caribbean liberation theology," was a key figure in providing the space and opportunity to gather important pastors and theologians from all Caribbean sectors for dialogue. His books, *In Search of New Perspectives*,[21] *Troubling Waters*,[22] and *Out of the Depths*[23] are major seminal collective efforts, intended to provoke dialogue. "We simply recognize that the 'waters are troubled' and perceive this to be a divine troubling. We are simply trying to encourage response to it by our own humble response."[24] In his second important collection of essays, Hamid insists on the dialogical character of the theological endeavor in the Caribbean and the historico-missiological challenge that lies ahead in the formulation of any Caribbean theology. "It is our conviction that the guidelines for any new missiology will arise *out of the depths* of the historical and spiritual experience of the peoples of this region."[25]

All these perspectives have one element in common: they take seriously the deep spiritual roots of Caribbean people, defining methodologically the locus of any Caribbean theology as the search for freedom, liberation, emancipation, and unity that is articulated in an ecumenical theology. Davis

points out that ecumenism in the Caribbean touches many
levels of this search for unity and integration:

> There is a natural ecumenism of concern in the Caribbean; it
> touches the political ethos, the social morals, the economic
> development of the region, and the crises that generally affect
> the well-being of our people . . . Radical integration at the
> religious level in the Caribbean can usher in a deeper level of
> integration at the political and social levels.[26]

That ecumenical experience touches the deep spirituality
of Caribbean people, a Jamaican hymn expresses this conviction in a calypso tune:

Let us talents and tongues employ.
Reaching out with a shout of joy; bread is broken, the wine is
     poured,
Christ is spoken and seen and heard.

Chorus:
Jesus lives again, earth can breathe again,
pass the Word around: loaves abound!
Christ is able to make us one.
At the table he sets the tone, teaching people to live to bless,
love in word and in deed express.

Jesus calls us in, sends us out
bearing fruit in a world of doubt, gives us love to tell,
bread to share. God (Immanuel) every where![27]

A People in Mission and Unity:
Toward an Ecumenical Solidarity

The Caribbean region has been struggling and hoping for a
long time. Ours is an ongoing process of hope against hope.
One of the key issues is how to respond responsibly to this
crucial moment. Some of the challenges are very clear and in
desperate need of concrete response.

One of the most creative projects in the Caribbean, and

certainly the most ecumenical, is the Caribbean Conference of Churches. It started as an effort to respond to some of the emerging issues in the region, particularly development and justice.

In 1957 the International Missionary Council held a consultation in Puerto Rico, trying to organize a joint action with the Caribbean churches. The consultation established Christian Action for Development (CADEC), the precursor of the Caribbean Conference of Churches. CADEC established programs for leadership training and youth and initiated development projects. In 1971, CADEC convened a group of leaders representing the major denominations of the Eastern Caribbean. This consultation decided to promote the founding of a Council or Conference of Churches. The Caribbean Conference of Churches was founded in Kingston, Jamaica, in 1973, under the theme: "The Right Hand of God," with the participation of eighteen denominations, including the Antilles Episcopal Conference of the Roman Catholic Church. The Conference decided that human liberation, social justice, and dignity would be among the priorities of its programmatic and cooperative actions.

The Caribbean Conference of Churches assembled for the second time in Guyana in 1977, with the theme "Workers Together with Christ." During this assembly the main topics were promotion of human rights, full human development, and Caribbean unity. The third assembly was held in Curaçao in 1981: "Thine is the Kingdom the Power and the Glory," responded to a World Council of Churches emphasis during its Commission of World Mission and Evangelism Conference in Melbourne, Australia (1981).

The fourth assembly, gathered in Barbados in 1986, focused on "Jesus Christ, Hope and Peace." Great emphasis was placed on the root causes of oppression in the Caribbean, the role of the churches in slave emancipation, and the need to combine a prophetic-pastoral role in times of crisis. The fifth assembly was held in Trinidad and Tobago in

1991 and the theme was "Participants in God's World: Preserve-Renew-Recreate," which stressed the importance of nation-building, denouncing the corruption, discrimination, and violence in the region and, most important, the destruction of nature, the depletion of natural resources.[28]

In August 1985 a Mandate was approved by the Caribbean Conference of Churches, with the consensus of the churches and other non-religious organizations in the Caribbean. The four issues underlined by the Mandate were:

1. An ecumenism in the region to promote Caribbean integration.

2. The call to social change as an integral, holistic concept of transformation and development.

3. Solidarity with the poor as a concrete manifestation of the communion of the Holy Spirit.[29]

Looking toward the future I want to enumerate some of the pressing issues that need some urgent action:

1. We need to continue our decolonization process. There is no way to avoid this issue in a region in which many countries still have colonial status (i.e., Martinique, Puerto Rico). We must reclaim a real sovereignty for all countries and real democracy within national boundaries.

2. The issue of identity must be addressed as a collective effort, affirming whom we are as a people and defending our integrity when cultural invasion and market economy expansion tend to recolonize our population.

3. We must advance the process of integration that is so vital to confronting any external or internal enemy. The late Eric Williams has written: "The whole history of the Caribbean so far, can be viewed as a conspiracy to block the emergence of a Caribbean identity in politics, in institutions,

in culture and in value."[30] I will add the religious element to this consideration of integration, as expressed in both diversity and unity, through an accumulated ecumenical experience that has more positive than negative historical lessons.

4. In order to fight underdevelopment and exploitation we need to reconsider the issues of fragmentation and economic injustice and to promote the economic growth along with cultural values, human dignity, and the quality of life.[31]

5. Another very important dimension of ecumenical solidarity that must be addressed is religious plurality. Today, more than ever, religious diversity and religious fragmentation are present all over the region. We need a solid and deep analysis of the missiological and theological implications of interreligious dialogue. The churches need to take seriously this challenge in a region that every day is more religious, more sectarian, and having the potential to canalize all the religious forces as positive liberating force toward Caribbean emancipation.[32] For Christian believers it means reclaiming once more the liberating force of the Gospel in the hope and trust that the God who made us free in Jesus Christ is revealing to all people in the Caribbean God's enduring love and presence.

A People of Survival: The Cuban Example

Since visiting Cuba for the first time in the late 1970s, I have been there more than twenty times. But beginning with January of 1984, my first visit as Caribbean Regional Secretary of the Latin American Council of Churches, those churches have made a unique impact on my life and ministry. I conducted a series of Bible studies on reconciliation. Early in the morning we gathered for worship and Bible study and then did voluntary work in the cane sugar fields. Doing manual labor in the fields alongside the workers was an impressive testimony of the Cuban Church as an agent of reconciliation in society and among ourselves!

I visited Cuba again in January 1997. This latest experience has yielded several vivid impressions concerning Cuba and its people.

Cuba is a country in transition and in deep crisis. No one, including government officials, dares to deny this fact in Cuba today. The economic situation is critical. A country that in the past produced a basic daily diet for its eleven million inhabitants today has people in the streets, begging and homeless—not as a great a number as in other Latin American and Caribbean countries, but for Cuba enough to indicate a serious situation.

Cuba is surviving with an economy plagued by limited natural resources and by lack of diversity in the national production (cane, sugar, coffee, bananas, tobacco, some citrus). The victim of an economic blockade orchestrated by the United States, Cuba is struggling to maintain its levels of education, health, housing, employment security, and the supply of its people's basic needs. Some of my closest friends (four medical doctors who are members of the Christian Pentecostal Church of Cuba) commented with a sense of nostalgia and desperation: "You can have a major surgery, but you can die of a simple infection, due to the lack of antibiotics." Some of the most basic medications, which in the United States and Europe are sold over the counter, are scarce or nonexistent in Cuba. In many hospitals penicillin and other antibiotics need to be reserved only for emergencies, particularly for children.

Cuba, which was able to maintain stability and social equality for three decades, is facing serious instability today. The quality of life which it maintained earlier is now fast deteriorating. The majority of the population lives in anxiety, desperation, and frustration. A deep anger, close to bitterness, is felt when church leaders try to explain or make some sense of this national crisis.

One of my most rewarding experiences is to see how the Cuban society is coping with the crisis. We know that people are very creative in times of crisis; in Cuba to be creative is the rule rather than the exception. In Cuba people have transformed anger into joy and bitterness into optimism. A sense of national pride and profound consciousness of nationality (*"cubanía"*) in a culture of preservation is noticeable. Young people, who are at times weary of a situation that sees no end near, still expressed the message of a generation that will not give up seeking human dignity and justice. Many young leaders in the churches are involved in economic production, educational programs, national health plans and cultural activities. Many are even studying theology on weekends!

It seems to me that Christians in Cuba understand the reconciling, transforming power of the Gospel and will dare to give a witness to that end. They are the Caribbean people of God creating new society in the midst of crisis.

Conclusion

We have come a long way in the Caribbean. As colonized people, we have increasingly raised our consciousness of our potential and capacity to affirm who we are. "Who we are" means that as a people we continue our quest toward integration and unity. Ecumenical solidarity in the Caribbean means that we embrace each other in a real *koinonía* and open our arms to embrace brothers and sisters from all over the world. Caribbean people unite their voices to those of the marginalized people of the world to form a great chain of solidarity and hope. All of us belong together to a great choir of human solidarity.

A Cuban chorus, composed by the Christian Pentecostal Church of Cuba in Camagüey challenges us:

> Sent out in Jesus' name,
> our hands are ready now to make the earth
> the place in which the kingdom comes.
> The angels cannot change a world of hurt and pain
> into a world of love, of justice and of peace.
> The task is ours to do, to set it really free.
> O, help us to obey, and carry out your will.[33]

Notes

1. Thomas Wieser, ed., *Whither Ecumenism? A Dialogue In The Transit Lounge Of The Ecumenical Movement* (Geneva: World Council of Churches Publications, 1986), 1. My emphasis.

2. I wrote an autobiographical essay dealing with these issues for a faculty retreat of Christian Theological Seminary, September 1996: "My Spiritual Heritage: Culture and Mission in Crisis."

3. Winston D. Persaud, "The Marginalized: Makers of History," *Currents in Theology and Mission* 14 (October, 1987): 354-356.

4. Ibid., 357.

5. Ibid., 358. My emphasis.

6. Ibid., 359-360. Two important contemporary discussions on marginality are: Virgilio Elizondo, *Galilean Journey: The Mexican American Promise* (Maryknoll, NY: Orbis Books, 1983), a groundbreaking theological reflection on the *mestizaje* of Mexican American people in U.S. history, as an attempt of marginalized people to affirm the incarnation and reclaim, from the margins, a place in the center. Jung Young Lee, *Marginality: The Key to Multicultural Theology* (Minneapolis: Fortress Press, 1995), emphasizes, from a Korean American perspective, seeing Jesus Christ as a creative paradigm to go beyond existing structures of marginalization, toward a new humanity of inclusiveness and mutual acceptance in which all peoples and races are central.

7. Aurora Levins Morales, "Child of the Americas," in *Barriers and Borderlands: Cultures of Latinos and Latinas in the United States*, ed. Dennis Lynn Daly Heyck (New York, London: Routledge, 1994), 447.

8. Sergio Arce and Dora Valentín, "The Caribbean: An Overview," in *The Caribbean: Culture of Resistance, Spirit of Hope*, ed. Oscar Bolioli (New York: Friendship Press, 1993), 2.

9. Kortright Davis, "Caribbean," in *Dictionary of the Ecumenical Movement*, eds. Nicholas Lossky, José Míguez Bonino and John S. Pobee (Geneva, Grand Rapids: World Council of Churches Publications, 1991), 124.

10. Justo L. González, "The Christ of Colonialism," *Church and Society* 1 (January-February, 1992): 21-23.

11. An excellent discussion of these issues is expanded in Luis Rivera Pagán, *A Violent Evangelism* (Louisville: Westminster John Knox Press, 1992) and Armando Lampe, *História do Cristianismo no Caribe* (Petrópolis-São Paulo: Comisión de Estudio de la Iglesia en Latinoamérica & VOZES, 1995).

12. Gordon K. Lewis, *Main Currents in Caribbean Thought* (Baltimore-

London: The John Hopkins University Press, 1983), 10-28.

13. Franklin W. Knight, *The Caribbean: The Genesis of a Fragmented Nationalism*, second edition (New York: Oxford University Press, 1990), 66-87.

14. William G. Demas, *West Indian Nationhood and Caribbean Integration* (Bridgetown: Caribbean Conference of Churches Publishing House, 1974), 8.

15. Eric Williams, *From Columbus to Castro: The History of the Caribbean 1492-1969* (New York: Vintage Books, 1970).

16. See an excellent approach to these issues in Gerard-Pierre Charles, *El Pensamiento Socio-político Moderno en el Caribe* (México: Fondo de Cultura Económica, 1985), 11-35; Franklin W. Knight, *The Caribbean: The Genesis of a Fragmented Nationalism*, second edition (New York: Oxford University Press, 1990), 3-87, 159-192. On religious syncretism and beliefs see, *At the Crossroads: African Religion and Christianity*, ed. Burton Sankeralli (St. James: Caribbean Council of Churches Publishing House, 1995).

17. Noel Leo Erskine, *Decolonizing Theology: A Caribbean Perspective* (Maryknoll, NY: Orbis Books, 1981), 119.

18. Kortright Davis, *Emancipation Still Comin': Explorations in Caribbean Emancipatory Theology* (Maryknoll, NY: Orbis Books, 1990), ix.

19. Ibid., 144.

20. Ibid., 1-11, 68-87.

21. Idris Hamid, ed. (Bridgetown: Caribbean Ecumenical Consultation for Development, 1971).

22. Idris Hamid, ed. (San Fernando: Rahaman Printery Ltd., 1973).

23. Idris Hamid, ed. (San Fernando: Ramahan Printery Ltd., 1977), IX.

24. Hamid, ed. *Troubling of the Waters*, 10.

25. Hamid, ed. *Out of the Depths*, ix.

26. Davis, *Emancipation Still Comin'*, 65-66.

27. "Let Us Talents and Tongues Employ," in *Chalice Hymnal*, words by Fred Kaan, music from Jamaican folk melody, adapt. Doreen Potter (St. Louis: Chalice Press, 1995), 422.

28. Robert W. M. Cuthbert, *Ecumenism And Development: A Socio-historical Analysis of the Caribbean Conference of Churches* (Bridgetown: Caribbean Conference of Churches, 1986), 1- 27, 41-92.

29. Adolfo Ham, "Caribbean Ecumenism and Emancipation Theology," in *The Caribbean: Culture of Resistance, Spirit of Hope*, ed.

Oscar Bolioli (New York: Friendship Press, 1993), 104-112.

30. Williams, 503.

31. Adolfo Ham, "Caribbean Theology: The Challenge of the 21st. Century," *Ministerial Formation* 63 (October, 1993): 1-7; Roy Neehall, "No Turning Back: Caribbean Ecumenism," in *Voices of Unity*, ed. Ans J. Van der Bent (Geneva: World Council of Churches, 1981), 57-69.

32. Armando Lampe, *Descubrir a Dios en el Caribe* (San José, Costa Rica: Departamento Ecuménico de Investigaciones, 1991), 27-30.

33. "Sent out in Jesus' Name," in *Cáliz de Bendiciones*, adap. and trad. [1988] Jorge Maldonado, arreg. [1996] Carmen Peña (St. Louis: Christian Board of Publication, 1996), 307.

Liberation Theology:
Looking Back to Blondel
and Social Catholicism

Peter Bernardi
Assistant Professor of Religious Studies
Loyola University of New Orleans

Last year (1996) marked the twenty-fifth anniversary of the publication of Gustavo Gutiérrez's *Teología de la Liberación*. The 1997 College Theology Society convocation theme: "Theology: Expanding the Borders" makes it especially appropriate to mention Gutiérrez's volume and its attempt at revisioning the church's role in the Latin American context. The "liberationist" model of salvation seeks to more fully integrate into the Christian conception of the process of salvation human efforts aimed at building a just society. Underlying the liberationist model is a renewed understanding of the nature-grace relationship in this century to which Maurice Blondel made a significant contribution. Gutiérrez explicitly mentions Blondel twice in his *Theology of Liberation*. In the opening chapter, the Peruvian theologian cites Blondel's influence on theology understood as "critical reflection on praxis." Blondel's philosophy "reinforces the importance of human action as the point of departure for all reflection."[1] In the fourth chapter dealing with the "crisis of the distinction of planes model," Gutiérrez refers to Blondel's characterization of the existential human condition as "transnatural."[2] This term was coined by Blondel to designate the orientation of the human spirit—in its concrete historical condition—to the supernatural. Blondel's influence was significant for the retrieval of a unitary understanding of human destiny, over against a dualism that prevailed in modern scholasticism which did so much damage in Catholic thinking and praxis.

What I propose to do in my paper is to elaborate on Gutiérrez's appreciation of Blondel by recalling a sociopolitical controversy that engaged the philosopher of Aix in the years shortly before the outbreak of the First World War. This controversy opposed Maurice Blondel (1861-1949) to a fledgling Jesuit philosopher, Pedro Descoqs (1877-1946). Blondel defended the efforts of those he termed "social Catholics" who sought to renew society from within by working collaboratively for social justice. In contrast, Descoqs defended the program of the "national security" party of his day, Action Française. In *The Church and the National Security State*, José Comblin makes explicit reference to Action Française and its harnessing of the church to its own purposes as a "good precedent for reflection on the present problem of the church and the ideology of national security" in Latin America.[3] Blondel's defense of the social Catholics coupled with his critique of Catholic collaboration with Action Française still have something to teach us. At the core of his dispute with Descoqs were different conceptions of the role of the church in society, rooted in differing views of the nature-grace relationship, and ultimately, in different conceptions of salvation. In this paper I intend to review Blondel's diagnosis of these conflicting mentalities. Time does not permit a thorough exposition of the controversial exchange between Blondel and Descoqs.[4] Perhaps a review of Blondel's analysis will serve to illuminate certain tensions that have arisen in some Latin American countries concerning the church's role in society.

My paper will unfold in three parts: first, a description and contextualization of the dispute that involved Blondel and the social Catholics, on the one hand, and Catholic sympathizers of the proto-fascist political movement of Action Française, on the other; second, an exposition of three theses and three corresponding antitheses formulated by Blondel to diagnose the roots of the conflicting mentalities; third, an evaluation and suggestions of some contemporary applications. I have concentrated on Blondel's side of the argument and will only briefly sketch Descoqs' perspective.

The Dispute and its Context

In the heat of the Modernist crisis, Maurice Blondel was called on to defend the social Catholics of the *Semaine sociale* movement from the accusation of "social modernism." The *Semaines sociales* (literally, "social weeks") were a sort of peripatetic university that sought to spread Catholic social teaching among a varied groups of academics, workers, students, and clergy in annual week-long summer conferences. They promoted a progressive interpretation of the church's social teaching by advocating, for example, independent labor unions and stressing the social function of property. Their critics accused them of undermining natural law principles by teaching "an egalitarianism incompatible with any hierarchy and any idea of authority and subordination."[5] For Blondel, this invitation also afforded an opportunity to defend his own "philosophy of action" from the attacks of some of the same critics.

Between October 1909 and December 1910, Blondel published a series of articles in his journal *les Annales de philosophie chretienne* [*APC*] that defended the *Semaine sociale* Catholics against their detractors. This series is variously referred to as the "Testis" series—the pseudonym he used— or the "La *Semaine sociale* de Bordeaux" articles or "Social Catholicism and Monophorism."[6] While composing this series, Blondel coined the term "monophorism" to designate any one-sided understanding of the nature-supernature relationship.[7] He charged that the critics of the "social Catholics" held an extrinsicist and authoritarian type of monophorism. After initially delineating the mentality of the social Catholics, Blondel turned his attention to a diagnosis of this monophorist mentality to illuminate the roots of the conflict.

In the course of defending the social Catholics, Blondel sharply criticized Pedro Descoqs' qualified defense of French Catholic collaboration with atheist Charles Maurras and his neo-monarchist movement Action Française.[8] Following the enactment of the anti-clerical Third Republic's Law of Separation (1905) which sundered the historic tie between church and State, Maurras' program received significant ecclesiastical support. He promised to restore the fortunes of the institutional Roman Catholic Church in France. Maurras' anti-liberal, anti-revolutionary ideology struck a sympathetic cord with many Catholics including Pope Pius X, Jacques Maritain, and Cardinal Louis Billot, perhaps the most eminent Roman theologian of the era.

Blondel viewed Descoqs' indulgent stance towards Maurras and Action Française as an egregious instance of the extrinsicist "monophorist" mentality. Descoqs was a keen admirer of Maurras' social program with its stress on discipline, order, and authority as characteristics of a healthy society. Though Maurras rejected both classical metaphysics and the Christian supernatural, Descoqs did not regard his Comtean inspired positivism as inimical to the church's goals in the social-political order. Catholics and Maurrassians could collaborate on a sociopolitical agenda, with Maurras' assurance that the traditional rights of the church would be respected. Blondel, for his part, viewed this alliance as a great scandal and considered the mentality that justified it as "fatal to the Christian spirit." Blondel contrasted the approach of the social Catholics of the *Semaines sociales* and the *Sillon* who "attempt[ed] a cure of our contemporary society by way of education, of penetration and of methodical reconstitution" with their monophorist critics who, protesting at once against all the evil that is being done and against everything that is being tried to improve this evil by conciliation or collaboration, think that it can only be healed by authority, rely mainly on takeovers by force and deathblows, and do not shrink from any surgical intervention, even caesarean.[9]

Both the social Catholics and the Catholic Maurrassians agreed that society need to be re-Christianized—but their strategies for bringing about this end were very different. Two different understandings of the social role of the church were in play.

Blondel's Diagnosis

In the second and third "Testis" installments, Blondel gave his analysis of the conflicting mentalities that opposed the social Catholics to their critics. Blondel illuminated the underlying causes of this opposition by identifying three fundamental orientations which undergirded the practice of the social Catholics:

The first concerns the whole process of our knowledge, the value and function of our ideas, their relationship with the actions from which they proceed and to which they tend. The second problem concerns the very nature of reality, the relations among the different orders that constitute the harmony of the world. The third concerns the very unity of our destiny, the relationship between the natural and supernatural orders, and, therefore, also the whole attitude of the person, the citizen, the philosopher, the theologian, in their reciprocal duties.[10]

Concisely put, the three basic orientations implicated in their practice concerned the relation of our thoughts to reality (i.e., epistemology), the relationships among the different orders of reality (i.e., ontology), and the nature-supernature relationship (i.e., theology). Blondel ascribed three theses (*a, b, c*) to the *Semaine sociale* Catholics that stem from these fundamental orientations. Then he set out parallel but contrasting theses (*a'*, *b'*, *c'*) which he imputed to the extrinsicist monophorists. These two sets of interconnected theses ground two antagonistic systems in which "the initial thesis (*a* or *a'*) philosophically commanded the following (theses), while the final thesis (*c* or *c'*) theologically commanded the preceding (theses)."[11] Blondel was convinced that only an analysis of these fundamental positions could illuminate the underlying disagreements in which he asserted the "Christian spirit" itself was at stake.

The first thesis concerns "the problem of knowledge and the relations of thought with action."[12] This thesis is the philosophical crux of the other two.

> Actions are not simply the putting into practice of logically defined ideas and of geometrically shaped theories; and everything is not decided in the domain of abstractions, as if human beings were only pure intellects, as if concepts were the adequate substitute of things and the sole motivation of the will, as if we governed ourselves by them and them alone. In individual and social practice, there is always something more and different than in the speculative systems which appear to inspire it. That is why the ideas which determine actions do not prevent actions from prompting new ideas which, even setting out from inexact and mutilating theses, can become liberating and healing. The life of human beings and of peoples obeys a more complex logic than that of abstract thought; what one does is often better or worse than what one thinks.[13]

The second thesis formulated the particular ontology that corresponded to "this dynamic philosophy of thought and action." This conception of being recognizes the "solidarity and continuity" among its different orders "without failing to recognize the distinction of beings and the hierarchy of different orders."[14] According to Blondel, the social Catholics are committed to viewing reality as an interconnected whole in which no order of being is absolutely enclosed in itself. In

contrast with every "exclusive ideology" which compart-
mentalizes the world in accord with its mental habit of "iso-
lating ideas like intellectual atoms and logical blocks," the
social Catholics view reality as a continuum where "there is
action from the top down and from the bottom up."

> ... the lower degrees, without ceasing to be lower and pow-
> erless to provoke any ascent by themselves, are nevertheless
> steps, that is to say, stepping stones and as it were spring-
> boards. The higher degrees [or levels] are really the final
> cause of this world, which is not a simple patchwork of jux-
> taposed episodes, but an order in which the unity of the
> divine design circulates. "Reality is a continuum," like the
> circulatory system in which the heart would not be able to
> send out the life-giving blood if it did not call for and receive
> the blood to which it gives life. There is no level which does
> not include a place for a staircase or the movement of an ele-
> vator. By the condescension and action of the higher level, the
> lower level is as it were giving birth to a higher cooperation.
> Material things become the support of economic phenomena;
> economic facts, even those which appear to relate to entirely
> physical needs, are already pregnant with moral and social
> relationships. One cannot legitimately and with impunity
> enclose oneself in any one order; there is action from the top
> down and from the bottom up.[15]

This philosophy of the interconnectedness of the various
levels of reality counters classical economics and philosophical rationalism which effect a "murderous vivisection" on
the unity of the human being and the world.[16] In a negative
allusion to the influential social doctrine of Auguste Comte,
Blondel declared "deceptive and myopic, that social physics
which desires to suffice for scientifically regulating public
and private interests from a positivist point of view."[17]

The third fundamental orientation that distinguishes the
social Catholics from their critics is their understanding of
the nature-supernature relationship. Blondel declared this
thesis to be "the most delicate of the disputed points, that

which dominates the entire debate."[18] While insisting that the supernatural order is "entirely gratuitous and absolutely transcendent," Blondel contended that this order is not only "superimposed," but it is also "supposed and presupposed" by the natural order. Carefully adding that the supernatural order "is never able to be *naturalized*," he continued:

[The supernatural order] is destined to penetrate and to assume [the natural order] in itself without becoming confused with it. And at the same time that it is proposed from on high by revelation, the Incarnation and the Redemption, which substantially constitute it and which are not simply facts to observe and mysteries to believe but reach souls invisibly by the effulgence of the grace of which they are the source, act upon all human beings so to speak from below to enable them to break out of all the enclosures in which they would like to confine themselves, to raise them above themselves, to burst every merely natural equilibrium, to put them on a level, and require them to be in accord, with the plan of providence.[19]

The social Catholics adhered to a philosophical anthropology that dealt with the human person in his actual, concrete historical conditions and not some hypothetical state of "pure nature."

. . . they never forget that one cannot think or act anywhere as if we do not all have a supernatural destiny. Because, since it concerns the human being such as he is, *in concreto*, in his living and total reality, not in a simple state of hypothetical nature, nothing is truly complete [*boucle*], even in the sheerly natural order.[20]

This open-ended anthropology recognizes that human striving can never be satisfactorily explained or fulfilled in sheerly positivist terms. The social Catholics look to specifically "Christian solutions" to socioeconomic problems because, contrary to the prevalent economic liberalism and sociological positivism, they recognize that a self-contained socioeconomic order is an abstraction that falsifies the actual supernatural destiny of the concrete person.[21]

Blondel termed this ensemble of philosophical and theological positions "integral realism."[22] In marked contrast are the theses (*a'*, *b'*, *c'*) held by their critics "formed in the science of the manuals and a militant politics."[23] In brief order, he outlined them:

> *a'*) The concept [*l'idée*], enclosing the essence of reality in its precise outline, single-handedly captures reality: *indivisibilium apprehensio*. It is both exterior to and formally identical to the object which it eminently possesses. . .
>
> *b'*) By reason itself of the precise, sufficient character of the concepts which express the essence and so to speak the solidity of things, the orders [*genres*] remain separated in reality as in thought. Each order is constituted apart, in its place, in the stability of its own being. . .
>
> *c'*) The supernatural order is a gratuitous superimposition by purely extrinsic command which relates to a purely passive obediential potency, without the external gift being able or having to entail the help of an interior contribution . . . [specifically supernatural truths] are only supernatural in the measure that they are defined, named, and expressly imposed by way of authority.[24]

Those who pride themselves on being "intransigents, in the role of public prosecutors" maintain these positions "as the necessary condition of orthodoxy and of salvation."[25] Blondel averred that all discussion and cooperation were useless unless one got beyond the surface misunderstandings to analyze the fundamental conflicts.[26] Between the mentality of the social Catholics and that of their critics there is "a duel unto death."[27] To think that these mentalities could work together, even in a common civic and social project, "would be like harnessing two horses, one at the front, the other at the back, of the same cart, and inciting them to pull with all their might."[28] Only a depth analysis that considers the underlying theses that ground these mentalities will get at the real sources of the conflict between Maurras' positivism and the social Catholics who are accused of naturalism or fideism.[29] Blondel sought to clear the way so that a probing investigation could determine where "philosophic truth" and the "Christian spirit" are to be found.[30]

In the sixth "Testis" installment, Blondel explicitly targeted Descoqs' apology for an alliance between Catholics and Action Française. Having pointed to the fatal separation between theory and practice of Descoqs' position, Blondel put forward a more sinister explanation to account for the attraction of intransigent Catholics to a political alliance with pagans:

> It is their *a-Christianity* and even *anti-Christianity* that you love and assist in them, and, dare I say, that which is systematically irreligious. That is the terrible observation that we are going to make.[31]

Blondel maintained that Catholic monophorists and Maurrassian positivists shared a common conception of authority that suppressed "interiority" [*le fait intérieur*]. For both types of authoritarians, "the enemy is the liberty of souls and the initiative of spirit."[32]

Blondel charged that the Catholic Maurrassians turned Catholicism into a "war machine, an instrument of earthly reign" under cover of admiring a notion of "order" which suppresses "the spontaneous movement of souls."[33] Blondel repeatedly and emphatically stressed the "fundamental error" which poisoned both the Maurrassians and their monophorist apologists: "the failure to recognize the inner working of the divine gift, the doubly religious spontaneity of souls which are under the action of both grace and liberty."[34] In contrast with this authoritarianism which suppressed all spontaneity of spirit is Blondel's philosophy of action which delineated a phenomenology of human aspiration constantly impelled to pass beyond its particular realizations.

With scathing irony, Blondel denounced Maurras' profoundly anti-spiritual view of the Catholic church. Having slanderously praised Catholicism for having replaced the Christ of history and of conscience with an "orthopedic apparatus" which transformed the church into a useful "straitjacket" to control "humanity run amok" [*l'humanité en folie*], Maurras uprooted "the principle of every spiritual need, of all aspiration towards the infinite."[35] "By a supreme crime against the Spirit," Maurras extolled the church for "having known how to organize the idea of God by removing from deism its own venom, by having exorcised the phantom of the infinite...of having proposed the only idea of God now permissible in a well-civilized state."[36]

An Assessment and Some Applications

The differing types of Catholic sociopolitical engagement defended by Descoqs and Blondel were expressive of two fundamentally different conceptions of the Christian renewal of society. The methods and goals of Action Française, on the one hand, and of the social Catholics of the *Semaines sociales*, on the other, exemplified contrasting strategies for combating the secular liberalism, individualism, and naturalism that had been steadily gaining ground in the modern era. In effect, the fundamental question which Descoqs and Blondel disagreed on was *how best to realize the public mission of the church*. Their dispute can be viewed as "the watershed which divided the world of Pio Nono, Veuillot and the Temporal Power from the present" age that commenced with Vatican II.[37]

At stake in the dispute was the very understanding of the dynamics of salvation and the understanding of grace integral to the process of salvation. On the one hand, the practitioners of each approach to the Christian renewal of society viewed themselves as "integral" Catholics. Both approaches were anti-liberal, that is, they refused the privatization of Christian faith. On the other hand, they attached different meanings to their differing conceptions of what ought to be done in the sociopolitical order. These different meanings correlate with the way salvation is envisioned and grace is understood. Descoqs affirmed the principles of tradition, authority, hierarchy, order, and discipline. He held that these principles were essential to the health of the temporal order and that they secured the necessary conditions for the church's saving work. Thus the Jesuit had responded to Blondel's attack that "*in theory*, it may be permissible for Catholics to ally themselves with a man who has nothing more at heart than to bring about the triumph of the Church, if not in souls, at least in society."[38] Yet, the distinct impression is given that the temporal order is important only as a locus for the evangelization of souls. Descoqs wrote: "A prevailing social order and, consequently, the facility assured to individuals to accomplish their essential duties as human beings and as members of society, has always seemed to the true apostle a sovereignly efficacious condition *to hasten the establishment of the Kingdom of Christ in souls.*" God's saving grace "only begins to appear, in any event only develops and only fully manifests its effects, where the cultural terrain has been prepared, where the natural obstacles have been set aside."[39] Descoqs envisioned the church fulfilling its supernatural mission after Maurras had implemented his positivist agenda for society. The preparation of the "cultural terrain" seems to have been valued in purely extrinsic terms vis-à-vis the church's mission. But is that all that the church asks for of society, viz., a context of order and discipline in which she can minister to "souls"? Descoqs viewed the task of bringing order to society as an important arranging of the "stage" for the work of salvation rather than as an intrinsic dimension of the task of evangelization.[40]

Blondel granted the importance of social structures for Christian life, but he favored the approach of the social Catholics of the *Semaines sociales* who sought "to infuse a

Christian sap in the legislation and institutions."[41] These Catholic "integralists" viewed the work of building a just society as something more than securing the peaceful conditions in which the church could carry out its mission. In Blondel's conception of the dynamic interconnectedness of reality, efforts to establish justice were closely connected with God's saving grace. Christian salvation was about more than "mastering souls."[42] However, this view of the matter was very controversial because it shifted attention to efforts to pass "social justice" legislation. During the pontificate of Pius X, the Vatican regarded these efforts with a wary eye, convinced that only acts of charity had true salvific import. In this view, efforts to pass legislation to secure justice for the workers might actually be a hindrance to salvation because it would impose as an obligation what could only be meritorious if done freely, out of a spirit of charity!

   If Descoqs' conception of the mediation of salvation was vulnerable to criticism, Blondel's position was also vulnerable. The philosopher of Aix claimed the label of "integrally Christian" for the social Catholics of the *Semaines sociales* and of the *Sillon*. By this he meant that these Catholics sought a closer relationship between their faith and their sociopolitical stances in contrast with the extrinsic monophorists that he criticized. However, Blondel was accused of confusing the natural and supernatural orders. The Jesuit argued that Blondel's position resulted in a dangerous "integralism" that removed from the temporal order its proper and wholly diverse teleology.[43] The "exigence" for the supernatural that Blondel's philosophy of action claimed to establish had the result, whether intended by Blondel or not, of suggesting that solutions to the problems of the sociopolitical and economic orders can be "deduced" from the truths of Christian revelation per se. In such a view, it appears that natural law reasoning no longer has validity. Indeed, there is no "nature" per se to reflect upon. In the strong sense of the expression, there would exist only Christian economics, Christian politics, and Christian sociology. Only Christian faith could guarantee the validity and certainty of conceptions pertaining even to the temporal order.[44]

There are some contemporary parallels that surprisingly mirror central facets of the exchange between Blondel and Descoqs. Latin American liberation theology has put into relief conflicting conceptions of the church's role at work among Catholics and the proliferating fundamentalist sects. On the one hand, liberation theology is oriented to the pursuit of *freedom and justice* in society; on the other hand, *intégriste* groups promote *order* in society. Consider the contrast between the ecclesial witness of Archbishop Oscar Romero with the current Opus Dei archbishop who has no difficulty accepting office within El Salvador's armed services. Or compare the behavior of the Argentinian bishops during the "Dirty War" with the behavior of Chilean Cardinal Raúl Silva Henríquez and the Vicariate of Solidarity under the regime of General Pinochet. In the 1970s, José Comblin remarked that Maurras' approach to social order "is the practice of today's Latin American military governments and [is] deeply imbedded in their ideology."[45] In Latin America, the principal integralist movement (besides Opus Dei) is "Tradition, Family, Property" which has supported the dictatorships in Brazil and Chile. John Coleman remarks that the journals and social stance of this movement "would seem to agree with Msgr. Benigni's sour judgment: 'History is one long desperate retching and the only thing humanity is fit for is the Inquisition.'"[46] Perhaps Blondel's original critique of the Catholic alliance with Maurras is still serviceable as a diagnosis of this mentality.

Most Christians accept that their faith requires involvement in the sociopolitical order. However, rarely, if ever, does unanimity exist about the precise fashion in which that involvement should be expressed. Sincere people will come to different prudential judgments about the best course of action to take in given circumstances. There will never be total agreement among Christians over what political course of action will best realize gospel values. This being said, the investigation of the dispute between Blondel and Descoqs highlights the pitfalls of theological ideology, viz., the tempting *connubium* of a particular time-bound theology with a specific sociopolitical approach that imperiously claims "scientific" and/or theological validity for its conclusions. The particular sort of *intégrisme* expressed by the intermarriage of the nationalist ideology of Action Française with the anti-liberal, French Catholic traditionalism is a prominent example of theological ideology on the political "right."

A contemporary instance of a questionable coupling of Christian faith with a specific socioeconomic arrangement is the neo-conservative attitude to the liberal free market economy. Michael Novak's effusive praise of liberal capitalism suggests that this particular set of political and economic arrangements accords with the requirements of the gospel. In the wake of the collapse of Russian communism, which many have hailed as a victory for free market capitalism, the tendency to view the structures of liberal capitalism as theologically sanctioned especially needs to be called into question.[47] Social sciences like economics and politics contribute to the persuasiveness of such an ideology by co-opting theological notions, thus creating the impression of unassailable legitimacy.

On the other hand, since Vatican II the church also has experienced examples of theological ideology on the "left" that seems to mirror the history of Action Française and its Catholic adherents on the political right. Some contemporary Christians have viewed the coupling of their faith with the imperious claims of social science, in this case Marxist social theory, as a legitimate marriage.[48] However, the dynamism of faith challenges both its inadequate theological expressions and any regnant social scientific theory. The gospel resists being harnessed to and, as a result, often reduced to, any particular social theory or system. Blondel's critique of Maurrassian positivism remains instructive.

Blondel's diagnosis of the conflicting mentalities among French Catholics points to the close correlation between political options and theologies of nature and grace. Differences of view concerning the relationship between church and society are fundamentally tied to different understandings of the nature-grace relationship. The practical pertinence of the theology of the nature-grace relationship is evident in Blondel's critique of extrinsicist monophorism. A consideration of the dispute between Blondel and Descoqs serves to illuminate several contemporary disputes concerning the church's role in society.

Notes

1. Gustavo Gutiérrez, *A Theology of Liberation*, rev. with a new introduction, trans. and ed. Sister Caridad Inda and John Eagleson (Maryknoll, NY: Orbis Books, 1988), 7-8.

2. Ibid., 44.

3. (Maryknoll, NY: Orbis Books, 1979), 85. Comblin spent many years in Brazil under the military dictatorship that came into power in 1964.

4. For a full exposition, see Peter J. Bernardi, *Theology and Politics: The Dispute between Maurice Blondel and Pedro Descoqs, S.J.* (Ann Arbor, MI: UMI, 1997).

5. "C'est au nom de la Fraternité chrétienne qu'il professe un égalitarisme incompatible avec toute hiérarchie et toute idée d'autorité et de subordination," Julian Fontaine, *Le Modernisme sociologique: Decadence ou Regeneration?* (Paris: Lethielleux, 1909), v.

6. *APC* 159 (Oct. 1909): 5-21 [*CSM*, 1-17]; (Nov.): 163-184 [*CSM*, 17-38]; (Dec.): 245-278 [*CSM*, 39-72]; (Jan. 1910): 372-392 [*CSM*, 72-92]; (Feb.): 449-471 [*CSM*, 92-114]; (March): 561-592 [*CSM*, 114-145]; 160 (May): 127-162 [*CSM*, 145-180]. In 1910, Blondel reissued the entire "Testis" series in a monograph with the epexegetical title: *Catholicisme social et monophorisme: Controverses sur les methodes et les doctrines* [henceforth, *CSM*] (Paris: Bloud, 1910), 252 pp. I will use the pagination of the *CSM* reprint for purposes of citation and reference. Both the *APC* and the *CSM* texts are difficult to find. Only a few hundred copies of the *CSM* were printed, and then for private circulation and not for public sale. The *APC* had a limited subscription and ceased publishing in the spring of 1913. The "Testis" articles have never been translated or edited. The translations here are largely my own.

7. Blondel created the term "monophorism" from two Greek words: "*monos*" meaning "sole" or "only" and "*phoros*" meaning "that which is brought in" or "payment." See *CSM*, 64-5. Blondel indicted both a monophorism of sheer immanence which undermined the transcendent reality of revelation and grace as well as an extrinsicist monophorism which reduced the human recipients to sheer passivity before the imposition of revelation and grace by authority.

8. See Pedro Descoqs, "A travers l'oeuvre de M. Ch. Maurras: Essai critique," *Études* 120 (July 20): 153-186; (August 5): 330-346; (September 5): 593-641; 121 (December 5): 602-628; (December 20), 773-786.

9. "Nous aurons d'ailleurs, en finissant, à apprécier cette expression que nous employons ici dans son sens courant et le plus large. Nous profiterons en effet de ce que, dès les premières années, les *Semaines sociales* ont attiré des concours très divers, collaborateurs de *la Reforme sociale*, membres de *la Jeunesse catholique*, *Sillonistes*, etc., pour examiner, au double point de vue philosophique et chrétien et en ce qu'elle a déjà de plus organique, l'attitude de tous ces hommes de foi, de science et d'action qui tentent une cure de notre société contemporaine par voie d'éducation, de pénétration et de reconstitution méthodique, en opposition avec l'attitude de leurs censeurs qui, protestant à la fois contre tout ce qui se fait de mal et contre tout ce qui s'essaie pour améliorer ce mal par de conciliantes initiatives ou d'apaisantes collaborations, n'admettent de guérison que par voie d'autorité, ne comptent guère que sur les coups de force ou de grâce, et ne reculeraient devant aucune opération chirurgicale, fût-elle césarienne" (*CSM*, 1, n.1). *La Reforme sociale* was the review of the disciples of Le Play. *La Jeunesse catholique* refers to the movement founded by Albert de Mun. The *Sillonistes* were followers of Marc Sangnier.

10. "Par un premier effort, nous allons dégager, de la *pratique* même des *Semaines sociales*, les éléments *théoriques* qu'elle implique: nous verrons, peut-être à la surprise de quelques-uns de ceux qui agissent sans analyser les principes de leur action, que se trouvent enveloppées dans le débat trois grandes questions spéculatives, des questions telles qu'il ne saurait y en avoir de plus importantes, telles qu'à partir d'elles la moindre déviation peut en effet entra(ner) d'infinies conséquences. La première concerne tout le processus de notre connaissance, la valeur et la fonction de nos idées, leur rapport avec les actions d'où elles procèdent et où elles tendent. Le second problème concerne la nature même de la réalité, la relation des divers ordres qui composent l'harmonie du monde. Le troisième concerne l'unité même de notre destinée, le rapport de l'ordre naturel avec l'ordre surnaturel, par conséquent aussi toute l'attitude de l'homme, du citoyen, du philosophe, du théologien dans leurs devoirs réciproques" (Ibid., 20-21).

11. "Les thèses que nous avons opposées par couples se groupent naturellement en deux systèmes liés; et chacun de ces systèmes (comme il serait aisé de le montrer) est tel que la thèse initiale (*a* ou *a'*) commande philosophiquement les suivantes, tandis que la thèse finale (*c* ou *c'*) commande théologiquement les précédentes" (Ibid., 39).

12. "C'est d'abord du problème de la connaissance et des rapports de la pensée avec l'action, que la pratique même des *Semaines sociales* suppose que la solution s'est élargie et enrichie" (Ibid., 26).

13. "Les actions ne sont pas simplement la mise en pratique d'idées logiquement définies et de théories aux contours géométriques; et tout ne se tranche pas dans le domaine des abstractions, comme si les hommes n'étaient que de purs intellects, comme si les concepts étaient le substitut adéquat des choses et le seul ressort de la volonté, comme si nous nous gouvernions par eux et pour eux seuls. Dans la pratique individuelle ou sociale il y a toujours plus et autre chose que dans les systèmes spéculatifs qui paraissent l'inspirer. C'est pour cela que les idées qui déterminent les actions n'empêchent pas les actions de susciter des idées nouvelles qui, même à partir de thèses inexactes et mutilantes, peuvent devenir libératrices et réparatrices. La vie des hommes et des peuples obéit à une logique plus complexe que celle de la pensée abstraite: ce qu'on fait vaut souvent ou pis mieux que ce qu'on pense" (Ibid., 26-7). See also p. 32.

14. "A cette philosophie dynamiste de la pensée et de l'action répond une conception de la réalité qui, sans méconnaître la distinction des êtres et la hiérarchie des ordres différents qui composent l'harmonieuse unité du monde, établit entre eux une solidarité et une continuité de fait. . ." (Ibid., 30).

15. "La vérité contraire (to the "notionalism" of exclusivist ideologies), à laquelle d'instinct ou de propos delibéré s'attachent les Catholiques sociaux, c'est que, pour distinguer les choses, il n'est pas besoin de les désunir; c'est que les degrés inférieurs, sans cesser d'être inférieurs et d'être impuissants à provoquer aucune ascension par eux-mêmes, sont cependant des degrés, c'est-à-dire des points d'appui et comme des tremplins; c'est que les degrés supérieurs sont réellement la cause finale de ce monde, lequel ne forme pas une marquetterie d'épisodes juxtaposés, mais un ordre où circule l'unité du dessein divin; c'est que 'la réalité est un continu,' comme le torrent circulatoire dans lequel le coeur ne pourrait lancer le sang vivifiant s'il n'appelait et ne recevait le sang à vivifier; c'est qu'il n'y a point d'étage où ne soit ménagée la place de l'escalier ou le passage de l'ascenseur; c'est que, par la condescendance et l'action du supérieur, l'inférieur est comme en gestation d'une coopération plus haute. Les choses matérielles deviennent le support de phénomènes économiques; les faits économiques, même

ceux qui paraissent se rapporter à des besoins encore tout physiques, sont déjà gros de rapports moraux et sociaux. Impossible de se murer impunément et légitimement en un ordre: il y a action de haut en bas, action de bas en haut" (Ibid., 30-31). See also Ibid., 33.

16. "... et si, de fait, nous ne formons, corps et âme, qu'un tout naturel, l'unité du composé humain comme l'unité du monde ne comporte point les vivisections meurtrières où se complurent l'économie classique et le rationalisme philosophique" (Ibid., 31).

17. "... trompeuse et de courte vue, cette physique sociale qui veut suffire à régler scientifiquement les intérêts publics et privés au point de vue positiviste, sans plus..." (Ibid.). Auguste Comte (1798-1857) was the founder of "positivism," an anti-metaphysical social philosophy that metamorphosed into a "religion of humanity." It would be hard to underestimate his intellectual sway in *fin de siècle* France. For example, his notion of "subjective synthesis" played a crucial role in Charles Maurras' philosophy of nationalism. In 1904, Comte's remains were solemnly interred in the Pantheon.

18. "Et c'est ici que nous touchons au plus délicat des points litigieux, à celui qui domine tout le débat" (Ibid., 31).

19. "L'ordre surnaturel est tout gratuit et absolument transcendant; mais il n'est pas seulement superposé, il est supposé et préposé à l'ordre naturel, étant tel qu'il ne saurait jamais être *naturalisé*; il est destiné à le compénétrer et à l'assumer en lui sans se confondre avec lui. Et, en même temps que par la Révélation il vient se proposer d'en haut, l'Incarnation et le Rédemption qui le constituent substantiellement et qui ne sont pas seulement des faits à voir et des mystères à croire, mais qui atteignent invisiblement les âmes par le rayonnement de grâce dont elles sont la source, actionnent tous les hommes pour ainsi dire d'en bas, afin de leur faire franchir toutes les enceintes où ils voudraient se murer, afin de les soulever au-dessus d'eux-mêmes, afin de rompre tout équilibre purement naturel, afin de les mettre à même et en demeure de correspondre au plan providentiel" (Ibid., 33).

20. "... ils n'oublient jamais qu'on ne peut penser et agir nulle part comme si nous n'avions pas tous, de fait et obligatoirement, une destinée surnaturelle. Car, puisqu'il s'agit de l'homme tel qu'il est, *in concreto*, dans sa réalité vivante et totale, non dans un simple état de nature hypothétique, rien ne boucle vraiment, même dans l'ordre simplement naturel" (Ibid., 32).

21. "On admet encore volontiers que les problèmes économiques se relient inévitablement aux problèmes moraux, et que les éléments humains s'insèrent au mécanisme des forces brutales: mais que de ces

questions mêmes surgissent les problèmes religieux, *et qu'à ces questions il ne soit donné de réponses adéquates que les solutions chrétiennes*, c'est ce que beaucoup trouvent trop édifiant pour n'être pas très scandaleux" (Ibid., 31-32; my emphasis added).

22. "Voici donc, en trois mots, les positions philosophiques et théologiques qu'implique le *réalisme intégral* de nos catholiques sociaux" (Ibid.).

23. "*Énoncé des thèses philosophiques et théologiques qui sont l'origine des malentendus et le principe des oppositions irréductibles que rencontrent les catholiques sociaux* . . . tels qu'ils se rencontrent en beaucoup d'esprits formés à une science de manuels ou à une politique militante" (Ibid., 34).

24. "*a'*) L'idée, enfermant dans son contour défini l'essentiel de la réalité, est par elle-même captatrice d'être: *indivisibilium apprehensio*. Elle est extérieure et elle est formellement identique à l'objet qu'elle possède éminemment. . .

"*b'*) En raison même du caractère défini, suffisant, des idées qui expriment l'essentiel et pour ainsi dire le solide des choses, les genres, dans la réalité comme dans la pensée, demeurent séparés; chaque ordre est constitué en soi, à sa place, dans la stabilité de son être propre. . .

"*c'*) L'ordre surnaturel est une superposition gratuite par dictamen purement extrinsèque est qui s'adresse à une puissance obédientielle toute passive, sans que le don extérieur puisse ou doive comporter le concours d'un apport intérieur . . . elles [vérités spécifiquement surnaturelles] ne sont elles que dans la mesure où elles sont définies, dénommés, imposées expressément par voie d'autorité" (Ibid., 34-35).

25. "Débarrassés des distinctions qui, dans les écoles, peuvent encore les limiter ou des hypothèses qui, dans la pratique, peuvent parfois les corriger, telles sont les thèses cohérentes—très cohérentes et très simples—que des hommes de plume, de combat, d'action théorique (ils sont légion) mettent leur gloire d'intransigeants, dans un rôle d'accusateurs public, à maintenir comme la condition *sine qua non* de l'orthodoxie et du salut" (Ibid., 36).

26. "Comment, de ce point de vue, toute discussion est inutile et toute coopération impossible, aussi longtemps que l'on ne sort pas de malentendus pour aborder les conflits de fond" (Ibid.).

27. "Entre les deux conceptions en présence c'est donc un duel à mort qui ne peut s'éviter, parce que les uns voient un mal certain et pire, là où les autres voient un mieux et un véhicule possible du bien" (Ibid.).

28. "Vainement prêchera-t-on l'union et encore l'union, sur le terrain de l'action (je parle, non de l'action religieuse, mais de l'action civique

et sociale et de ce droit naturel dont on rappelle si fort la valeur propre): c'est comme si l'on attelait deux chevaux, l'un à avant, l'autre à l'arrière d'une même voiture, et qu'on les stimulât à tirer de toutes leurs forces" (Ibid., 37).

29. "S'il fallait croire (selon *b*') que l'ordre naturel n'a de solidité qu'en se suffisant au sens positiviste d'un Maurras, ou si vraiment le surnaturel ne conservait son caractère spécifique qu'en étant expressément et nommément proposé du dehors, il serait en effet périlleux, il serait subversif même, et pour l'ordre humain et pour l'ordre chrétien, de prétendre qu'ils se compénètrent, que l'un ne s'achève pas sans l'autre, que l'autre ne se fait pleinement reconnaître et accepter que par le concours de deux dons, intérieur et extérieur; et on devrait proscrire une confusion ruineuse, qui nous ferait osciller du naturalisme au fidéisme. Mais les Catholiques sociaux n'ont rien dit et ils n'ont rien eu à redouter de semblable, parce que leur doctrine (*b* et *c*) n'a pas à méconnaître les distinctions spéculatives et abstraites, au moment où elle considère l'union concrète ou les solidarités pratiques. Les uns sont dans le réel, les autres, dans le notionnel. Et ce notionnel, vrai en un sens, devient faux et tyrannique, dès qu'il prétend s'appliquer, s'imposer, se substituer même au réel, comme si ce réel n'était qu'une épure de logique. . ." (Ibid., 37-38).

30. ". . . c'est que nous voulions justifier l'onéreuse nécessité d'aborder maintenant les litiges de fond, de reprendre l'offensive, et, cherchant où est la vérité philosophique, où est l'esprit chrétien, de dire aux accusateurs des Catholique sociaux, avec une franchise qu'excusera la gravité du débat et le sentiment d'un devoir à remplir: 'Prenez garde; si vous les incriminez à tort dans une question de si décisive importance, c'est que peut-être vous-mêmes dénaturez la doctrine et manquez à l'esprit'" (Ibid., 38).

31. ". . . ce que vous aimez, ce que vous aidez en eux, c'est ce qu'ils ont d'*a-chrétien* et même d'*anti-chrétien*, que dis-je, c'est ce qu'ils ont de systématiquement irreligieux? Et telle est la terrible constatation que nous allons faire" (Ibid., 139).

32. ". . . l'ennemi c'est la liberté des âmes et l'iniative de l'esprit, comme ce qui importe c'est l'ordre dans la discipline passive qui matérialise jusqu'aux vertus morales en les mesurant à l'utilité sociale, comme rien ne s'impose que du dehors par contrainte logique et physique, c'est donc désormais la lettre qui vivifie et l'esprit qui tue" (Ibid., 137-38).

33. "Et par la façon même dont théoriquement vous prétendez permettre de telles coopérations, vous aboutissez, parce que vous y tendiez préalablement, à ne voir, à ne montrer dans le catholicisme qu'une machine de guerre, qu'un instrument de règne terrestre, et, sous

couleur d'y admirer la merveille de *l'ordre, ORDO*, à en faire votre *ordre* à vous, *JUSSUS*, l'ordre, d'après la thèse monophoriste, ne pouvant résulter que d'un commandement ou d'une consigne passivement obéie, et, en l'absence de tout don immanent, de toute règle intérieure, le mouvement spontané des âmes ne pouvant être que caprice et arbitraire" (Ibid., 124).

34. ". . . tout cela part de l'erreur fondamentale qui consiste à méconnaître l'apport intime du don divin, las pontanéité doublement religieuse des âmes sous l'action de la grâce et de la liberté; et tout cela répond à un idéal matériel, à un besoin d'ordre et de commandement" (Ibid., 144).

35. "Après qu'on a jeté au catholicisme la sanglante injure de le louer pour avoir substitué au Christ de l'histoire et de la conscience un appareil orthopédique et pour avoir fait de l'Église la camisole de force de l'humanité en folie, il restait à extirper, jusqu'à sa racine la plus profonde, le principe même de tout besoin spirituel, de toute aspiration vers l'infini, de toute la religion véritable" (Ibid.).

36. "Et, par un crime suprême contre l'Esprit, on admirera donc, on remerciera l'Eglise d'avoir su organiser l'idée de Dieu en ôtant au déisme le venin qui lui est propre, d'avoir exorcisé le fantôme de l'infini, 'l'infini, son absurde, forme honteuse, obscène chaos'; d'avoir ainsi 'proposé la seule idée de Dieu tolérable aujourd'hui dans un État bien policé'" (Ibid., 140-41).

37. Alexander Dru, "From the *Action Française* to the Second Vatican Council: Blondel's *La Semaine sociale* de Bordeaux," *Downside Review* 81 (1963): 226. See also Joseph Komonchak, "Theology and Culture at Mid-century: the Example of Henri de Lubac," *Theological Studies* 51 (1990): 595-602.

38. "Nous avions écrit *qu'en théorie* il pouvait être loisible aux catholiques de faire alliance avec un homme qui 'n'a rien de plus à coeur que de faire triompher l'Église, sinon dans les âmes, du moins dans la société'" ("Monophorisme et Action française," *APC* 160 [June 1910]: 247).

39. Ibid., 248 (my emphasis added).

40. The relationship between evangelization and human efforts to ameliorate society has been the subject of important treatments during and after Vatican II. *Gaudium et Spes* stated: "Earthly progress must be carefully distinguished from the growth of Christ's kingdom. Nevertheless, to the extent that the former can contribute to the better ordering of human society, it is of vital concern to the kingdom of God" (para. 39). The 1971 Synod document "Justice in the World" stated:

"Action on behalf of justice and participation in the transformation of the world fully appear to us as a constitutive dimension of the preaching of the Gospel . . ." (para. 6). "The 1974 Synod in its working paper spoke only of an 'intrinsic connection' between evangelization and human promotion," Avery Dulles, *The Reshaping of Catholicism* (San Francisco: Harper and Row, 1988), 259, n. 8. See Charles M. Murphy's detailed review of the discussion concerning the precise nature of this relationship in his article "Action for Justice as Constitutive of the Preaching of the Gospel: What did the 1971 Synod Mean?," *Theological Studies* 44 (1983): 298-311.

41. "Mais tout autre chose est de maintenir, de procurer, de promouvoir 'cet ordre régnant dans la société' comme 'une condition souverainement efficace' de l'instauration dans les âmes du royaume du Christ, en travaillant, comme les catholiques sociaux, à infuser dans la législation et les institutions une sève chrétienne, un ordre catholique où tout procèderait des vérités religieuses et métaphysiques et naturelles, tout autre chose est de prétendre imposer un ordre originellement issu d'une conception positiviste, obtenu par la force, et dans lequel après coup l'Église viendrait travailler" (*CSM*, 244-5, n. 2).

42. ". . . ce qui apparaît comme la raison formelle de l'alliance, c'est le dessein de procéder du dehors au dedans; de traiter les hommes et les sociétés de haut en bas; c'est l'espoir de mâter les âmes, pendant que d'autres mâteront les corps et les intelligences et gagneront peut-être à cette besogne d'avoir part au 'bénéfice' sans être 'contraints' ni trop inquiétés pour leur athéisme" (Ibid.).

43. For a concise statement of Descoqs' position, see the "excursus" in his *Praelectiones theologiae naturalis: cours de theodicee*, vol. 2, *De Dei cognoscibilitate* (Paris: Beauchesne, 1935), 292-297.

44. It is not without interest that John Milbank's *Theology and Social Theory: Beyond Secular Reason* (Oxford: Blackwell, 1990), which touts Blondel's philosophy as indicating the way "beyond secular reason," has been the object of a similar critique. See, for example, Gregory Baum's discussion "For and Against John Milbank," in *Essays in Critical Theology* (Kansas City, MO: Sheed & Ward, 1994), 52-76.

45. *The Church and the National Security State*, 92.

46. "Catholic Integralism as a Fundamentalism," in *Fundamentalism in Comparative Perspective*, ed. Lawrence Kaplan (Massachusetts: University of Massachusetts Press, 1992), 77.

47. See David Schindler's critique of the theology of the neo-conservatives in "The Church's 'Worldly' Mission: Neoconservatism and American Culture," *Communio* 18 (Fall, 1991): 365-97. There is also a

follow-up discussion on pp. 425-472. Schindler's perspective manifests a blondelian stamp.

48. For an example of this coupling, see Clodovis Boff, *Theology and Praxis*, trans. Robert Barr (Maryknoll, NY: Orbis Books, 1987).

Perspectives on Undocumented Workers: Catholic Social Teaching and the United Farm Workers

Jennifer Reed-Bouley
Assistant Professor of Religious Studies
Lewis University

The United Farm Workers (UFW), the union founded by Cesar Chávez in 1962, consistently encounters severe obstacles to improving the wages and working conditions of domestic agricultural laborers. A primary impediment is employers' practice of breaking domestic workers' strikes by hiring undocumented workers. This paper compares two sources on treatment of undocumented workers: Catholic social teaching's principles and norms, and the United Farm Workers' policy from 1967 to 1974.[1] The comparison seeks to determine the wisdom that ecclesial social teaching and the UFW's practical experience could offer one another regarding treatment of undocumented workers.

Catholic Social Teaching on Economic Immigration as a Human Right

Catholic social teaching regularly exhibits concern for immigrants. Prior to 1952, Catholic bishops issued many letters, radio addresses, and other instructions about migrants. However, the unprecedented number of migrants and refugees caused by World War II required an international rather than a local response. The increased number of migrants prompted Pope Pius XII to issue in 1952 the apostolic constitution *Exsul Familia*, known as the Church's "Magna Charta for Migrants."[2] Pope Pius XII recognized that the right to emigrate (i.e., to leave one's country) lacks practical meaningfulness if there is no corresponding right to immigrate into another country. He understood both emigration and immigration as natural rights of the human person.

Although Pope John XXIII does not devote all of his 1963 encyclical *Pacem in Terris* to immigration, he does place the natural right to immigrate within the broader context of human rights. According to *Pacem in Terris*, membership in the human family holds primacy over national citizenship. Human personhood confers the right to enter another country "when there are just reasons in favour of it" and despite deprivation of citizenship in a particular country.[3] Pope John specifies that a person may immigrate to "a country in which he hopes to be able to provide more fittingly for himself and his dependents," thus indicating that economic factors may justify immigration.[4] Likewise, *Gaudium et Spes* (1965) affirms that immigration is a "personal right," which "is not to be impugned."[5] In their 1969 "Instruction on the Pastoral Care of People Who Migrate," the Sacred Congregation for Bishops similarly identifies immigration as a right of the human person.[6]

Catholic social teaching limits the right to immigrate for economic reasons to specific cases. The documents caution that those who enjoy comfortable conditions but seek greater economic opportunity in a new land do not have a right to immigrate. Rather, the right to immigrate applies to those who face desperate economic situations in their homelands with little or no prospect of improvement. Economic immigrants leave situations of "sheer destitution" and "poverty" in order to survive.[7]

Catholic social teaching acknowledges two moral claims at stake regarding economic immigration: a person's right to immigrate and a nation's right to control its borders as an expression of sovereignty. The documents insist that the first constitutes a stronger moral claim.[8] In *Exsul Familia*, Pius XII cites his 1948 "Letter to the American Bishops," which admonishes them that

> the sovereignty of the State, although it must be respected, cannot be exaggerated to the point that access to this land is, for inadequate [sic] or unjustified reasons, denied to needy and decent people from other nations . . .[9]

According to ecclesial teaching on immigration, if the common good would be harmed, the usual subordination of national sovereignty to the right to immigrate does not pertain.[10] Pope Pius XII affirms that needy people should have access to land in other, less densely populated nations pending consideration of the common good.[11] He expects generosity and even sacrifice on the part of the country receiving immigrants. He does not specify, however, in what particular situations the public wealth would be harmed gravely enough to warrant exclusion of new immigrants.

The Sacred Congregation for Bishops specifies that a country may restrict or reject immigrants "where grave requirements of the common good, considered objectively, demand it."[12] Determination of the common good, according to Catholic social teaching, requires appraising not only the receiving country's needs but also the immigrants' situation. Although nationality divides residents of the receiving country from would-be immigrants, their membership in the human family overcomes this division from a moral perspective. Drew Christiansen correctly concludes that "the practical import of Catholic teaching [is] that the United States and other nations ought to permit virtually open borders for all those who have serious reason to abandon their ancestral homeland and seek a new life elsewhere."[13] The exception occurs when immigrants would cause the receiving country's economic situation to become worse than the sending country's situation. The needs of all persons involved—the citizens of the receiving and sending countries, and the would-be immigrants—must be assessed, and the plan which best facilitates everyone's good should be adopted. Mexican nationals who immigrated to the U.S.A. from 1967-1974 in order to perform agricultural labor clearly meet Catholic social teaching's definition of economic immigrants: they fled a situation of poverty rather than relative comfort. The Mexican economy's incapacity to provide adequate employment and sufficient compensation for workers to survive impelled workers to immigrate. Mexican nationals' willingness to accept deplorable living and working conditions in the United States indicates they did not leave a situation of relative financial security in order to seek increased economic opportunity. Rather, the poverty they faced in the U.S.A. was less severe than that in Mexico. According to Catholic social teaching, they have a natural right to immigrate for economic reasons.

Catholic Social Teaching's Norms Regarding Obligations to Economic Immigrants

In addition to its provision of instructions regarding the right to immigrate, Catholic social teaching also supplies guidelines for hospitable reception of immigrants by Christians in host countries. Ecclesial teaching specifies that Christians must match an attitude of welcome with concrete actions. These actions would promote national recognition of immigrants' rights, as well as improve immigrants' experience of worship, work, housing, education, and membership in associations. Catholic social teaching's recognition that immigrants are extremely vulnerable grounds this view.

Whereas earlier social teaching focuses primarily (although not exclusively) on the spiritual needs of immigrants, both conciliar and postconciliar teaching explicitly attend both to immigrants' spiritual and material needs.

Gaudium et Spes exhorts Christians to perceive immigrants and foreign laborers as neighbors and to respond generously to their needs.[14] This admonition is apt, because natives tend to view immigrants as inferiors and economic competitors rather than neighbors. *Gaudium et Spes* specifies the implications of viewing immigrants as neighbors by urging countries to recognize the economic contributions of migrant workers. It recognizes that immigrants are easily instrumentalized and warns countries to avoid "all discrimination with respect to wages and working conditions . . ."[15] The document recommends that local people help to mitigate all of the ways in which migrants experience vulnerability—from working conditions and wages to housing and social life. This demands overcoming excessive nationalism.

In various documents, Pope Paul VI discusses host countries' obligations to immigrant laborers. He urges each nation to fashion a charter protecting migrant laborers' rights. In *Octogesima Adveniens* (1971), he stipulates that the charter would "assure them a right to emigrate, favour their integration, facilitate their professional advancement and give them access to decent housing where, if such is the case, their families can join them."[16] In his 1973 address to the European Congress on the Pastoral Care of Migrants, he specifies that the charter "would guarantee the rights of migrants to respect for their own personality, job security, vocational training, family life, suitable schooling for their children, social insurance, and freedom of speech and association."[17] Both lists express Pope Paul VI's recognition of the myriad ways in which migrant laborers experience deprivation and manipulation in host countries, as well as his insistence that countries have an obligation to protect the human rights of migrant workers.

Like Pope Paul VI, the Sacred Congregation for Bishops comprehensively addresses the needs of immigrants. Furthermore, it offers recommendations to Catholic unions regarding immigrant workers: "Catholic associations should expend great effort on the immigrant people who need housing, work, education and the necessities of life."[18] It also urges existing unions to extend membership to immigrants and assist them in developing their professional skills.

This brief perusal of Catholic social teaching identifies the following guidelines regarding immigration: 1) Economic immigrants possess a human right to work in the United States unless their entrance would harm the common good (understood broadly); 2) Christians have a moral obligation to transcend nationalism in seeking the common good; and 3) Christians, including those organized in associations and unions, have a duty to extend hospitality to immigrants. The next section juxtaposes ecclesial teaching with the UFW's actions in order to determine how the two sources might inform one another.

The Effects of Undocumented Immigrants on Unionization: An Historical Overview

A brief historical review of the relationship between immigration and farm labor organizing in the Southwestern United States provides a critical context for understanding the UFW's policy toward undocumented immigrants from 1967-1974. Southwestern agricultural employers' access to immigrants has historically posed severe obstacles to organization of domestic farm laborers. Importation of foreign laborers yields financial advantages to agricultural employers. Because immigrants typically are poorer than domestic workers and can be deported if they demand higher wages or better working conditions, they are more vulnerable, reliable, and docile than domestic workers during the short harvest season. Immigrant workers are less likely than domestic workers to resist long working hours, low wages, arduous labor, and short and uncertain terms of employment.[19] Much farm work requires little training, so new workers easily adapt.

From 1942-1964, the Bracero Program legalized importation of Mexican workers into the agricultural labor force.[20] The United States and Mexican governments engaged in this cooperative venture, in which the U.S. government guaranteed transportation and a wage rate to Mexican employees. Braceros had no power to bargain with employers. If they objected to their working conditions, they were deported at the federal government's (not employers') expense. Furthermore, growers created a labor surplus by recruiting more braceros than they actually needed, thus further decreasing each bracero's control over working conditions.[21]

The growers' practice of importing a large number of Mexican workers rendered the organizational efforts of domestic workers unsuccessful. Although the Bracero Program most obviously represents agribusiness' exploitation of domestic and Mexican workers, general employment of Mexican and other foreign-born workers has historically destabilized the agricultural labor force. Scholars document domestic workers' attempts to form labor unions in the Southwest from as early as the 1880s.[22] Some of their strikes succeeded in attaining moderate improvements in wages and/or working conditions for the season in which they struck, but agribusiness often broke their strikes by importing laborers. At the point at which one ethnic group became sufficiently unified and experienced to demand improvements, growers imported another ethnic group in order to foster competition among workers of various nationalities. Ethnic divisions lowered wage scales and encouraged workers to comply with formidable working conditions. Agribusiness succeeded not only in breaking individual strikes but in destroying farm labor organizations. No farm labor organization matured into an institution that continued to exert pressure beyond initial strike efforts, because workers lacked the (geographic and financial) stability necessary to support a union. All farm labor associations prior to Chávez's movement failed to sustain improvements of laborers' situation.

Employers responded to the United Farm Workers' strikes just as they did to previous strikes: they immediately attempted to destabilize the labor force. Growers' recruiting and hiring of undocumented immigrants posed severe obstacles for the United Farm Workers. Growers claimed that no strikes existed; they pointed to the (undocumented) workers in the fields as proof of their claim. Because the new workers harvested their crops, the strike caused growers little financial harm. The strike, therefore, did not influence growers to recognize the union and negotiate contracts. In addition to prolonging the length of the strike, the presence of undocumented immigrants decreased wages and worsened working conditions, even at farms not targeted by the UFW for the strike. This harmed striking UFW members who had little or no savings.

The historical background on growers' importation of strikebreakers to crush strikes and unions indicates that the UFW was rightly concerned about growers' penchant for hiring undocumented workers as strikebreakers. Employers' hiring of undocumented workers could not only frustrate and ruin the strike but eventually destroy the union. The union judged that it would not achieve success unless growers took the following actions: acknowledged the existence of the strike; recognized the union as the legitimate representative of the striking workers; and negotiated with the union. In the union's view, these goals could not be met while growers hired undocumented immigrants. The union, therefore, resolved to address directly growers' hiring of undocumented immigrants. The union had three options: 1) It could strive to remove undocumented immigrants from fields in which the union had established a strike; 2) It could attempt to remove undocumented immigrants from fields in which the union had established a strike, as well as from fields where they were not striking; 3) It could organize undocumented immigrants and help them become legal residents of the United States, thereby removing the financial incentive for employers to hire undocumented rather than documented workers. From 1966-1974, the union primarily chose the second policy.

The United Farm Workers' Policy
Toward Undocumented Workers

In trying to stop growers from breaking strikes by hiring undocumented workers, the UFW endeavored to prevent undocumented immigrants from entering the U.S. and to deport undocumented immigrants already established in the U.S.A. The union implemented these strategies through various tactics. First, the UFW tried to persuade government leaders responsible for enforcing U.S. immigration law to fulfill their objectives more responsibly. Cesar Chávez met with directors of the Immigration and Naturalization Service (INS) and Labor Secretaries several times, and UFW members picketed their offices. The UFW claimed that the INS inadequately identified and deported undocumented workers.

The UFW also sought to change laws governing employment of green-card workers. In 1969 Congressional testimony, the UFW requested that Congress either enforce regulations prohibiting green-card workers from being employed as strikebreakers or require them to maintain permanent residences in the United States.[23] Furthermore, the UFW sought legislation outlawing employment of persons lacking permanent U.S. addresses during strikes.

Government officials failed to prevent undocumented immigrants from entering the United States and working as strikebreakers. Chávez contended that if the U.S. government refused to enforce immigration laws, and growers continued to hire undocumented workers, the union would be destroyed. Chávez's explanation of the campaign to a volunteer who disagreed with the policy illustrates his perception that the 1974 situation constituted a crisis:

> We have the choice to be for the illegals and against our own workers, or be for our workers and be against the illegals. It's one of those cases where we don't have the luxury to be for all workers . . . So the whole life of the Union depends on stopping this attack which is being masterminded by the growers, the Immigration Service and the Government.[24]

In response to the perceived threat, the UFW undertook more direct action to deport undocumented workers in 1974 through its "illegals campaign." In the campaign, the UFW pursued more systematically its goal of preventing undocumented immigrants from entering and deporting those already established in the U.S.A.

The UFW furthered its goal of exposing the government's failure to enforce immigration laws by urging UFW supporters to write their congressional representatives. The union requested letters from seventy-five Fresno, California community groups as well as many religious supporters, boycott assistants, and sympathetic dioceses throughout the country.[25] In these letters, supporters were to urge their representatives to pressure Attorney General Saxbe to ensure that the Border Patrol and INS would effectively perform their jobs. By requesting that their supporters write these letters, the UFW simultaneously informed them about the government's failure to enforce the law and attempted to influence government officials.

Beginning in June 1974, the UFW reported to the U.S. Border Patrol undocumented workers and farms that used illegal laborers. The union also reported nearly two hundred persons who illegally harbored (or provided shelter for) undocumented workers. The UFW claimed the Border Patrol, however, did not arrest any harborers.[26] The union's efforts proved futile.

Furthermore, the UFW secured undocumented workers' signed declarations describing their exploitation by labor contractors and growers. The UFW collected other declarations proving that some growers deducted Social Security from undocumented workers' compensation. Because the undocumented workers possessed no Social Security numbers and could never collect Social Security benefits, the UFW deduced that growers would keep this money rather than deliver it to the Social Security Administration.[27] The UFW contended that growers and labor contractors benefitted from hiring undocumented workers not only because undocumented workers provided inexpensive labor and growers stole their Social Security payments, but also because growers charged workers exorbitant rates for room, board, and transportation.

Despite the UFW's efforts, the Border Patrol did not intervene to deport undocumented workers established in the United States. Furthermore, growers continued to import workers from Mexico. In response, the UFW established in 1974 its so-called "wet-line" along twenty-four miles of the Arizona-Mexico border. In effect, the UFW became a self-appointed border patrol. Patrollers attempted to prevent undocumented immigrants from crossing the border. Although the UFW had previously criticized the INS, here the UFW effectively aided it in preventing immigration.

The UFW also attempted to mobilize the general public against undocumented immigrants by distributing 10,000 leaflets in Fresno, California shopping centers regarding the ways in which undocumented immigrants harmed the union and community.[28] The UFW's community health clinic also organized house meetings "in areas with high concentrations of illegal aliens to discuss what local residents could do about the problem" and to organize them against importation of undocumented workers.

By October 1974, the UFW recognized that its policy toward undocumented workers was ineffectual. A report to the UFW executive board concluded that the union had failed in its efforts to prevent Mexican nationals from entering the U.S.A. and to aid the INS in deporting undocumented persons. Growers continued to employ undocumented workers despite the UFW's efforts, and the UFW alienated potential allies who opposed its treatment toward undocumented workers.[29] The UFW determined to change its strategy.

Conclusion

What can be learned from the disparity between Catholic social teaching on immigration and the UFW's treatment of immigrants? Catholic social teaching can be used as a corrective or resource to critique growers' and the UFW's treatment of undocumented workers. According to Catholic social teaching, persons' rights must be respected regardless of their national origins. This demands similar treatment of documented and undocumented persons. The UFW did not direct its campaign toward removing all strikebreakers from strike zones but focused instead on undocumented workers and green-card workers. The UFW's practices from 1967-1974 contradict Catholic social teaching's principles and norms regarding treatment of undocumented workers.

By late 1974 the UFW recognized that although its policy may have been necessary, targeting undocumented workers diminished worker solidarity by pitting documented and undocumented workers against one another. Although ecclesial teaching did not serve as the impetus for the UFW's change in policy, the union's policy after 1974 accorded with Catholic social teaching. The union currently opposes immigration restrictions such as California's Proposition 187 and does not inquire about workers' immigration status. Given the current atmosphere of nativism in the U.S.A., the UFW's 1974 admission of its tactical mistake could prove instructive for other unions' treatment of immigrants. Unions currently face obstacles to organizing not only from immigrants to the U.S.A. but from increasingly mobile capital. Companies can easily outsource or move entire plants to countries where labor is cheaper. U.S. unions have generally attempted to preserve their own wage rates but have resisted joining with workers from other countries. The case study of the UFW indicates that organizing across borders, though difficult, may be in the long-range interest of all workers.

The UFW's experience from 1967-1974 can also serve as a resource for further development of Catholic social teaching on immigration. Cognizant of the history of agricultural labor organizing, the union deemed it impossible to successfully agitate for higher wages and better working conditions while employers easily hired undocumented workers. Catholic social teaching on immigration falls short when the rights to organize and to a just wage conflict with the right to immigrate. Catholic social teaching does not provide instruction for action when this conflict of rights exists. Here the UFW's experience indicates a weakness in ecclesial social teaching.

Although the UFW was unaware of Catholic social teaching on immigration, many Catholic supporters of the union were familiar with the teaching. Catholic priests, bishops, and others who aided the union from 1967-1974 did not critique the UFW's policy toward undocumented workers. The UFW's most comprehensive and deliberate actions to remove undocumented workers, the "illegals campaign," occurred at the same time that the U.S. Bishops' Ad Hoc Committee on Farm Labor was most directly involved with the union. There is no evidence that the members of this committee attempted to influence the UFW's policy. This indicates that although ecclesial teaching on immigration expresses laudable goals, even those closely associated with it did not apply it. They did not translate Catholic social teaching's principles and norms into action. This may indicate that the teaching is inaccessible or that Catholic supporters recognized the conflict of rights the UFW faced. In either case, the UFW's experience offers wisdom for further development of ecclesial teaching on immigration.

Notes

1. Mexican nationals who immigrate to the United States without legal authorization and then find employment shall be referred to here as "undocumented workers" rather than "illegal aliens." Proponents of deportation, including the United Farm Workers from 1967-1974, use the terms "illegal alien" or "illegals." The term "undocumented" is preferred here because it implies that Mexican nationals may have a right to immigrate despite U.S. (United States) laws to the contrary. I thank Michael J. Schuck, Ph.D., Roberto S. Goizueta, Ph.D., and Alex Mikulich, M.Div. for their comments on an earlier draft of this paper.

2. Pope Pius XII, *Exsul Familia: The Church's Magna Charta for Migrants*, ed. Giulivo Tessarolo (Staten Island, NY: St. Charles Seminary, 1962), 25-60.

3. Pope John XXIII, *Pacem in Terris*, 25, 105. The numbers following encyclical titles refer to the paragraph numbers in *Proclaiming Justice and Peace*, eds. Michael Walsh and Brian Davies (Mystic, CT: Twenty-Third Publications, 1991).

4. Ibid., 106.

5. *Gaudium et Spes*, 65. References to conciliar documents are from *The Documents of Vatican II*, ed. Walter M. Abbott (New York: Guild Press, 1966).

6. Sacred Congregation for Bishops, "Instruction on the Pastoral Care of People Who Migrate," *Catholic Mind* 70/1238 (December, 1969): 37-58.

7. National Catholic Welfare Conference Administrative Board in the Name of the Bishops of the United States, "World Refugee Year and Migration," in *Pastoral Letters of the United States Catholic Bishops*, vol. 2, 1941-1961, ed. Hugh Nolan (Washington, D.C.: National Conference of Catholic Bishops/United States Catholic Conference, 1984), 226; Sacred Congregation for Bishops, paragraph 7.

8. On the primacy of the right to immigrate over the right of states to control borders, see Allan Figueroa Deck, S.J., "A Christian Perspective on the Reality of Illegal Immigration," *Social Thought* 4 (Fall, 1978): 45; and Drew Christiansen, S.J., "Sacrament of Unity: Ethical Issues in Pastoral Care of Migrants and Refugees," in *Today's Immigrants and Refugees: A Christian Understanding*, ed. Office of Pastoral Care of Migrants and Refugees, National Conference of Catholic Bishops (Washington, D.C.: United States Catholic Conference, 1988), 88-89.

9. Pope Pius XII, 51.

10. Christiansen, 88. Luis Tampe, S.J., also concludes that, according to

Catholic social teaching, if "the original situation of the state welcoming foreigners is so harsh as to be even worse than the condition of those trying to come in, then that government can, while following the precepts of the church concerning immigration, morally restrict or even block the attempts of newcomers from entering its territory." Luis Tampe. S.J., "A *Loophole* in the Social Teaching on Immigration of the Catholic Church" (Unpublished Master's Thesis: Loyola University Chicago, 1994), 12.

11. Pope Pius XII, 51.

12. Sacred Congregation for Bishops, 7.

13. Christiansen, 90.

14. *Gaudium et Spes*, 27.

15. *Gaudium et Spes*, 66. See also Pope Paul VI, *Octogesima Adveniens*, 17.

16. Pope Paul VI, 17.

17. Pope Paul VI, "Migrant Workers and the Local Churches," *The Pope Speaks* 18/3 (1973): 206.

18. Sacred Congregation for Bishops, 61.

19. J. Craig Jenkins, "The Demand for Immigrant Workers: Labor Scarcity or Social Control?" *International Migration Review* 12/4 (Winter 1975): 525.

20. With the increase in the domestic labor pool caused by the end of World War II, the U.S. government engaged in "Operation Wetback." From 1952 to 1955 the U.S. deported almost two million braceros to Mexico. When Mexican laborers were again needed after 1955, the U.S. restored the Bracero Program.

21. Jenkins, 526.

22. Donovan O. Roberts reviews the history of California farm labor organizing in "Theory and Practice in the Life and Thought of Cesar E. Chávez: Implications for a Social Ethic" (Ph.D. diss.: Boston University Graduate School, 1978), 72-175.

23. Dolores Huerta, Testimony before Senate Subcommittee on Labor of the Committee on Labor and Public Welfare, 91st cong., 1st sess., 16 April 1969, 14; Jerry Cohen, ibid., 18-19.

24. Cesar Chávez, Keene, CA, to Paul Pumphrey, Apopka, FL, 27 June 1974, UFW Information and Research Collection, Archives of Labor and Urban Affairs, Wayne State University, Detroit, Michigan (hereafter Archives), box 39, folder 6.

25. Liza Hirsch and Wendy Batson, "Illegals Campaign: Report to the Executive Board," 12 October 1974, UFW Vice President Pete Velasco, Archives, box 7, folder 15.

26. Ibid.

27. Demetrio Díaz, Affidavit, Maricopa County, AZ, July 1974, UFW Information and Research Collection, Archives, box 38, folder 32.

28. Hirsch and Batson. See Steven Johnson, "Fresno County Illegals Campaign, [June] 1974-Oct. 12," UFW Vice President Pete Velasco, Archives, box 7, folder 15.

29. Ibid.

Why Send in the Troops? Christian Ethics and Humanitarian Intervention

J. Milburn Thompson
Professor of Religious Studies
Saint Joseph College, West Hartford

One of the most vexing questions for foreign policy in the post-Cold War world is whether and when military intervention on behalf of human rights might be ethically justified. Can one or more states send their troops across the border into another state to protect citizens from their own government or from each other? This essay will address this question from the perspective of Christian ethics. It will argue that humanitarian intervention can sometimes be justified, and that for some interventions to be truly humanitarian, they must go beyond *rescue* to include *nation-building*.

Humanitarian intervention can be defined as "the forceful, direct intervention by one or more states or international organizations in the internal affairs of other states for essentially humanitarian purposes."[1]

There is nothing new about intervention, but the post-Cold War context poses the question in a fresh way. Both superpowers indulged in interventions during the Cold War—in Korea, Vietnam, Afghanistan, Africa, Central America, and the Caribbean, for example—but for reasons of power politics and national self-interest. In terms of justice, democracy, and peace, most of the Cold War interventions, in hindsight, turned out badly.

Today, tensions such as ethnic conflict (Bosnia, Rwanda, Sri Lanka), chaos and anarchy in states where the government appears to have failed (Somalia, Liberia), the proliferation of weapons of mass destruction (North Korea, Iraq, Iran), and gross violations of human rights (Haiti, Myanmar) raise the question of intervention on behalf of human life and human rights, rather than for purposes of national self-interest. In an interdependent world made transparent by the global reach of the media, can massive or pervasive human suffering justify or even obligate other states to intervene in the internal affairs of a country?

This question has caused some interesting switches in ethical and political positions among pundits and scholars of international relations.[2] Some who were "doves" during the Cold War, that is, who were vocal critics of United States (U.S.) intervention, now advocate humanitarian intervention (such as Thomas Fox, editor of *The National Catholic Reporter*, and Michael Walzer); some Cold War "hawks" have now taken a much more isolationist position (such as political commentator Charles Krauthammer); and sometimes Cold War adversaries now find themselves taking the same position regarding a particular intervention (*New York Times* political columnists William Safire and Anthony Lewis both supported intervention in Bosnia). It is difficult to articulate a principled and coherent rationale regarding humanitarian intervention.

Arguments Against Intervention

The principles of the *sovereignty* of states and, therefore, of *nonintervention* in the internal affairs of a sovereign state stand against the right or the duty to intervene on behalf of human rights. Sovereignty and nonintervention have imposed some semblance of order upon an international system with no central government.[3] Sovereign states resent interference in their internal affairs. (How would North Americans have reacted if China or France had sent troops to protect civil rights protesters on their march from Selma to Montgomery in 1965?)

A second reason against intervention is the tendency of states to rationalize national self-interest under a cloak of humanitarian rhetoric.[4] Colonial powers always thought of themselves as benevolent, bringing a "higher civilization" to primitive peoples, while taking their land, wealth, and resources. Although the United Nations authorized the U.S.-led intervention in Haiti in 1994, the Organization of American States did not approve because of well-founded suspicions of previous U.S. interventions in Latin America.[5]

A third set of concerns about intervention has to do with the difficulty of developing a policy that is clear and consistent, rather than capricious and selective. What violations of human rights would justify intervention? Who would authorize it? What would be the feasible goals of humanitarian intervention? Would short-term actions create worse long-term problems?[6] Why, for example, did the United States of America push for a response to Iraq's invasion of Kuwait in 1991, but delay for three years before leading an armed intervention on behalf of a democratically elected president who was overthrown in Haiti? Why was there no response from the world community to genocide in Rwanda in 1994? When idealism motivates foreign policy, it results in inconsistency because of the overwhelming human need in the world that deserves some response. Since not every violation of human rights can be addressed, a humanitarian foreign policy is easily charged with hypocrisy.[7]

A realist (or *realpolitik*) theory of international relations, therefore rejects idealistic or humanitarian reasons for military intervention. Only national security or important national interests can justify sending in the troops. In the post-Cold War world, seldom do violations of human rights and egregious human suffering pose direct threats to U.S. national security or to important U.S. interests.[8] Thus, the United States of America should generally resist the temptation to intervene.

Realists raise a fifth set of concerns about humanitarian intervention—its effectiveness and feasibility. Even with the best of intentions, critics contend that humanitarian intervention seldom works. The deeply rooted political and economic problems posed by failed states or longstanding repression and poverty (as in Somalia, Liberia, or Haiti) may be impervious to military solutions. Outside parties may be able to do little to resolve such conflicts; sometimes they aggravate the situation (as in Lebanon in 1983). Ethnic conflict, in particular (such as Bosnia or Rwanda), is motivated by historical animosities and passions that are not very amenable to political solutions. Moreover, nationalism tends to inspire deeper determination than does altruism. So the hate-filled locals bide their time until the foreign troops get tired and go home, or try a few suicide bombings or ambushes to see how many body bags it will take for the folks back home to insist that their sons and daughters be re-called.[9]

To be prudent, the benefits of an intervention should outweigh the costs. This can be a difficult calculation because both benefits and costs can be somewhat illusory. If the intervention will not work, then of course it will be difficult to justify. Yet the success of an intervention might be very difficult to document in that a catastrophe may have been prevented. Perhaps more than 500,000 people were slaughtered in the genocide in Rwanda in 1994. In hindsight, it can be said that quick and decisive action by the world community may have saved half a million lives, but had such intervention happened, few would believe that such an atrocity had been prevented, and troops might now be mired down in what may appear to be an intractable situation. Lives saved are speculative and statistical.[10]

Costs can also be difficult to predict or to measure. Who

would have thought that there would be so few allied casualties in Desert Storm? Casualties and financial costs eventually can be toted, but how can factors such as the future risk of terrorism, an increase in anti-Americanism, or the diminishment of American credibility be measured?[11] Realists also point out that interventions always have unintended consequences, and they are almost always bad.[12]

Although compassion may often stimulate the impulse to intervene, it may not be feasible to follow that desire to right every wrong. For example, while advocates of human rights may be shocked by China's crushing of nonviolent protestors at Tiananmen Square in 1989, few people would think sending in the Marines a proportionate response. Indeed, even token economic sanctions against the world's largest market have proven impossible to sustain. Similarly, to send ground troops against the Serbs in Sarajevo or Bosnia before a truce was arranged would most likely have begun an uphill battle against a well-armed and passionate opponent. Unless direct national interests are at stake neither leaders nor popular opinion are likely to have the stomach for such a fight.[13] These pragmatic and utilitarian concerns can provide powerful arguments against intervention in nearly every case. Thus, humanitarian intervention is often thought not militarily or politically feasible or effective.

The Case for Humanitarian Intervention

Arrayed against these reasons for nonintervention are the horrors of genocide in Rwanda, ethnic cleansing in Bosnia, famine caused by the collapse of the state in Somalia, repression by military rulers in Haiti, and pogroms against the Kurds in Iraq and Turkey. Such human suffering cries out to the conscience of the international community.[14]

Christian ethics can be helpful in working through this foreign policy dilemma. First of all, Christian ethics would contend that the sovereignty of the state is a real, but relative value. State sovereignty is conditioned from below by human rights and from above by the international common good. Thus, when states grievously abuse the human rights of their citizens, they cannot use sovereignty to silence the concern of others.[15] Neither sovereignty nor nonintervention are absolute principles, although both carry real moral weight. The challenge, then, is to develop clear criteria for justified military intervention into the internal affairs of states.

The Christian tradition offers two perspectives on war and military intervention—nonviolence (or pacifism), and just war—although it has long been dominated by the just-war position.[16]

Christians and others who adhere to nonviolence have been perplexed by the question of military intervention for humanitarian purposes. Pacifists oppose warfare in principle. During the Cold War, with every conflict a possible spark for a nuclear holocaust and with power politics the primary purpose of military interventions, Christian pacifists passionately resisted the U.S. military excursions abroad. But humanitarian interventions in the post-Cold War world often are motivated by efforts to remedy injustice and alleviate human suffering. When these cherished values are genuinely the purpose of intervention, and when the violence of the armed intervention is expected to be minimal, can a pacifist condone it?

Some pacifists have been able to justify humanitarian interventions, such as those in Somalia, Haiti, and Bosnia, under the rubric of police actions rather than warfare. Most pacifists are not opposed to all uses of force (although some are), and see the threat of force, or the limited use of force in these cases as justified by the greater human good that can be accomplished. It is analogous to the force used by the police to protect the community from violent criminals.[17] Although it is true that there is a real difference between humanitarian armed intervention and aggressive warfare, the willingness to use violence will continue to trouble pacifists. Once violence is justified, it seems that one has inevitably crossed the line into just-war thinking. The criteria developed by the just-war tradition can offer a framework for justifying humanitarian intervention which responds to the arguments marshaled against it.

The transition from nonviolence to justified force yields the first point in a revised ethic of intervention: military intervention should be a *last resort*. The just-war tradition has always maintained that war is evil, a rule-governed exception to the presumption in favor of peace. Preventative efforts and nonviolent remedies should be applied before force is justified.[18] Economic sanctions can be effective and should be considered, although these too are fraught with ethical problems. The economic sanctions applied against Haiti, for example, seemed to cause the most suffering among poor children, while the wealthy ruling elite escaped their sting. The last resort criterion also gives the necessary weight to the principles of sovereignty and nonintervention. "Because of the diversity of states and the dangers of rationalization, the wisdom of Westphalia [regarding respect for the sovereignty of states] should be heeded. Intervention may be necessary, but it should not be made easy."[19] The burden of proof should always rest on those who are in favor of military intervention.

It is the *just-cause* criterion that makes humanitarian intervention tempting. Everyone agrees that genocide merits an exception to the nonintervention principle, but how serious and egregious must a violation against human rights be in order to justify intervention? This judgment no doubt looks different from the perspective of the victims than from that of the offenders, or of the potential intervenors. The famine in Somalia, ethnic cleansing in Bosnia, the slaughter of Kurds in Iraq, and the military repression in Haiti all appear to be just causes for intervention. Just cause, however, is a necessary, but not a sufficient, criterion for intervention.[20]

The just-war tradition has insisted that military engagement be *proportionate*, that the benefits of the intervention outweigh the costs. Such a prudential calculation has always been a matter of perspective and judgment. It has been pointed out above that evaluating the often illusory consequences of humanitarian intervention is especially complex and difficult and that critics of humanitarian intervention are skeptical that it can be effective or the lesser evil. Realists, however, bring a more constricted perspective to bear on this cost/benefit calculation than that of the just-war tradition. Realists believe that foreign policy should focus narrowly on national security and national self-interest. The just-war tradition, as interpreted in the Christian tradition, is concerned more broadly about justice and the common good. Humanitarian concerns have a legitimate place at the table in a just-war perspective.

Moreover, in a broad sense, humanitarian concerns can be in the national interest. Uncivilized behavior tends to spread. "Pay the moral price of silence and callousness, and you will soon have to pay the political price of turmoil and lawlessness nearer home."[21] While it is true that this understanding of global justice as a legitimate national interest is based in history and philosophy (and theology), the noninterventionists' belief that intervention is ineffective has the same basis. The costs that noninterventionists wish to include, such as the possibility of anti-U.S. Americanism (no good deed goes unpunished) or the diminishment of the U.S.A.'s credibility, are equally indirect and unquantifiable as the benefits of preventing genocide or standing against ethnic cleansing.

The just-war criteria of *right intention* and *the probability of success* are also important as parts of a framework of ethical analysis regarding humanitarian intervention. These criteria, along with proportionality, focus attention on clearly defining the political goals of the intervention, and on the feasibility of effective intervention.

There is no such thing as an apolitical military intervention, and it is a dangerous delusion to pretend that political goals can be avoided while only humanitarian aid is offered. It is also cruel to bring a people back from the brink of death, through famine aid, for example, only to have them continue to suffer from government oppression or social chaos. Thus, it may be that for intervention to be truly humanitarian and just, in many cases it will need to go beyond mere aid or even peacekeeping, and engage in nation-building, that is, in reforming or creating the social and political structures necessary for honoring human rights.[22] This means some sort of ongoing assistance in reorganizing government, disarming military or paramilitary forces, establishing safe enclaves, re-establishing civic peace, supporting negotiated settlements of grievances, punishing the perpetrators of genocide or ethnic cleansing, instituting a judicial system, training and equipping an impartial police force, and so on.[23]

Such goals may require a lengthy commitment of personnel and resources. And such an expanded agenda opens the intervenors to the charge of a sort of colonial control over other nations or even of naked imperialism. Yet, to exclude such political goals from intervention is to risk doing more harm than good, or not enough good to really matter. In situations where the policies that need to be stopped are widely supported and sustained by local structures and culture, it is perhaps necessary to go a step beyond rescue and engage in nation-building.[24]

This, of course, raises the question of feasibility. If armed intervenors must have clearly defined political goals and must be prepared to see the process through to completion, then humanitarian intervention with the objective of nation-building is likely to be rare indeed. By its very nature, humanitarian intervention does not directly serve the national interests of the intervenors. Thus, the intervenors are sending their soldiers into harm's way, and expending talent and treasure for no direct national benefit. Nor will criminals quickly come to heel, nor chaos easily be corrected where havoc is being wreaked. Nation-building will not always be possible, and it will nearly always be difficult to gain popular support for it. Indeed, popular support for the United States of America interventions in Somalia, Haiti, and Bosnia has been lukewarm or non-existent. Perhaps, however, this is partly due to the lack of a clearly argued and consistent foreign policy on behalf of intervention.[25] Not to engage in nation-building in cases of political chaos or overwhelming poverty, however, would seem to risk doing less good than is required for an intervention to be truly humanitarian.

The just-war tradition also insisted that war must be declared by a *legitimate authority* based on the idea that only the state could be allowed to authorize the taking of life. Because of the danger of rationalization on the part of individual states, the decision to intervene should ordinarily be authorized by an international organization such as the United Nations and/or a regional security organization. The decision should be multilateral, not unilateral. Given the power differential among states, this does not guarantee probity in judgment, but it does enhance it through procedural restrictions.[26]

Finally, the just-war tradition requires that the *means* used be proportionate, and that the *conduct* of the intervention should also be just. The principles of noncombatant immunity and of proportionality have traditionally governed the conduct of warfare. Since the Vietnam debacle, U.S. military strategy has maintained that, in an intervention, massive military power should be brought to bear on an enemy for a short, defined period of time in the pursuit of a clearly defined and limited objective.[27] This strategy seemed to work in the Persian Gulf War, but even there, questions of proportionality persist. This hit-and-run strategy poses both moral and political concerns for nation-building forms of humanitarian intervention. Massive firepower suggests problems of indiscriminate and/or disproportionate attacks, and quickly withdrawing from the scene precludes the commitment necessary for nation-building activities.[28] Thus, a new military strategy fitting for humanitarian intervention and nation-building seems necessary, as well as troops who are trained and prepared for these sorts of missions, which are as much like social work as combat.[29]

Humanitarian intervention can be ethically justified, although it will need to be decided on a case-by-case basis. The argument in favor of humanitarian intervention and nation-building is certainly controversial, and critics raise important caveats. The just-war tradition does, however, provide a framework for the ethical analysis of situations where military intervention is being considered which can address the concerns of noninterventionists. A public articulation of this framework, and of the reasons that might justify intervention, could build public support for a foreign policy willing to take risks and pay the costs for a just world order.

Notes

1. National Conference of Catholic Bishops, *The Harvest of Justice Is Sown in Peace*, in *Peacemaking: Moral and Policy Challenges for a New World*, ed. Gerard F. Powers, et. al. (Washington, D.C.: United States Catholic Conference, 1994), 336.

2. Joel Dreyfuss, "Just Do It: Why We Should Intervene in Haiti," *Tikkun* 9 (September-October, 1994): 113. Michael Walzer is conscious that he is switching from the position against intervention that he took during the Cold War in now advocating some instances of humanitarian intervention in "The Politics of Rescue," in *Morality in Practice*, fifth edition, ed. James P. Sterba (New York: Wadsworth, 1997), 556 and passim [originally published in *Dissent* (Winter, 1995)].

3. J. Bryan Hehir, "Intervention: From Theories to Cases," *Ethics and International Affairs* 9 (1995): 3-6; Kenneth R. Himes, "The Morality of Humanitarian Intervention," *Theological Studies* 55 (1994): 84-85, 92-93.

4. Barbara Conry, "The Futility of U.S. Intervention in Regional Conflicts," in *Morality in Practice* (cited in note 2), 560 [abridged from *Cato Institute Policy Analysis* (May 9, 1994)]; Hehir, 8; Himes, 97.

5. Zachary Karabell, "Don't Do It," *Tikkun* 9 (September-October, 1994): 12; Larry Rohter, "Remembering the Past; Repeating It Anyway," *The New York Times*, September 24, 1994, E1, E3; J. Bryan Hehir, "Expanding Military Intervention: Promise or Peril?" *Social Research* 62 (Spring, 1995): 49; Hehir, "Intervention," 13.

6. Himes, 97; Conry, 560.

7. Conry, 560-561.

8. Gary L. Guertner, "Ethnic Conflict: The Perils of Military Intervention," *Viewpoints on War, Peace and Global Cooperation*, (1996-1997): 4,8; Conry, 559-560. Richard N. Haass does not absolutely insist that national interest be involved for an intervention to be justified, but still considers interests an important consideration. See Richard N. Haass, *Intervention: The Use of American Military Force in the Post-Cold War World* (Washington, D.C.: Carnegie Endowment for International Peace, 1994), 69-71.

9. Conry, 561; Guertner, 8-9; Crocker, "The Varieties of Intervention: Conditions for Success," in *Managing Global Chaos: Sources of and Responses to International Conflict*, eds. Chester A. Crocker and Fen Osler Hampson, with Pamela Aall (Washington, D.C.: United States Institute of Peace Press, 1996), 184.

10. Walzer, 556-557.

11. Conry, 562-563.

12. Karabell, 12; Hehir, "Expanding Military Intervention," 48-49.

13. Edward N. Luttwak, "If Bosnians Were Dolphins . . .," *Commentary* 96 (October, 1993): 28-29.

14. Luttwak, 27-28; Christopher Joyner, "When Human Suffering Warrants Military Action," *The Chronicle of Higher Education* 39 (January 27, 1993): 52; Walzer, 554, 558.

15. Kenneth R. Himes, "Catholic Social Thought and Humanitarian Intervention," in *Peacemaking: Moral and Policy Challenges for a New World*, ed. Gerard F. Powers, et. al., (Washington, D.C.: United States Catholic Conference, 1994), 218-220; National Conference of Catholic Bishops, *The Harvest of Justice Is Sown in Peace*, in *Peacemaking*, Ibid., 337; Walzer, 554.

16. National Conference of Catholic Bishops, *The Challenge of Peace*, in *Catholic Social Thought. The Documentary Heritage*, eds. David J. O'Brien and Thomas A. Shannon (Maryknoll, NY: Orbis Books, 1992), nn. 66-121.

17. See Richard B. Miller, "Casuistry, Pacifism, and the Just War Tradition in the Post-Cold War Era," in *Peacemaking: Moral and Policy*

Challenges for a New World (cited in note 15), 205-209; Himes, "Catholic Social Thought," 224-235; James P. Sterba, "Reconciling Pacifists and Just War Theorists," in *Morality in Practice* (cited in note 2), 545-552 [originally in *Social Theory and Practice* 18 (Spring, 1992)]; Robert Phillips and Duane L. Cady, *Humanitarian Intervention: Just War vs. Pacifism* (Lanham, MD: Rowman & Littlefield, 1996). Cady explicates the position of a philosophical pacifist.

18. Hehir, "Intervention," 7-8; Cady, *Humanitarian Intervention*, 61-62; National Conference of Catholic Bishops, *The Harvest of Justice Is Sown in Peace*, 337; Glen H. Stassen, *Just Peacemaking: Transforming Initiatives for Justice and Peace* (Louisville, KY: Westminster-John Knox Press, 1992); and Glen H. Stassen, "New Paradigms: Just Peacemaking Theory," *Bulletin of the Council of Societies for the Study of Religion* 25 (September-November, 1996): 27-31.

19. Hehir, "Intervention," 8. See also Walzer, 558 where he states: "I don't mean to abandon the principle of nonintervention—only to honor its exceptions."

20. See Hehir, "Intervention," 9, 11-13; Himes, "The Morality of Humanitarian Intervention," 100-101; Walzer, 356.

21. Walzer, 556.

22. This is the argument of Robert Phillips in *Humanitarian Intervention*.

23. Himes, "Catholic Social Thought," 227.

24. Walzer, 555.

25. Himes, "The Morality of Humanitarian Intervention," 101-104; Hehir, "Intervention," 13. Michael Mandelbaum, "Foreign Policy as Social Work," in *Foreign Affairs Agenda 1996: Critical Issues in Foreign Policy* (New York: Council on Foreign Relations, 1996), 79-81, passim [originally in *Foreign Affairs* (January-February, 1996)] argues that in its response to Bosnia, Somalia, and Haiti during its first year in office, the Clinton administration tried to turn U.S. foreign policy into social work, and failed. The focus was on U.S. values more than U.S. interests. While this might be a flawed enterprise, Mandelbaum suggests in part that the failure was because of an unwillingness to try to convince the U.S. people that this is a good idea and then inconstancy in the endeavor.

26. Hehir, "Intervention," 9; Himes, "The Morality of Humanitarian Intervention," 98-100; Kelly Kate Pease and David P. Forsythe, "Human Rights, Humanitarian Intervention, and World Politics," *Human Rights Quarterly* 15 (May, 1993): 297-308. This is a controversial point. Walzer, 557, says flatly: "Multilateralism is no guarantee of anything." Haass, does not require multilateral backing (or even popular

support) for intervention. Walzer also says, however, "Old and well-earned suspicions of American power must give way now to a wary recognition of its necessity." Multilateralism is a way of being wary of U.S. power.

27. See Luttwak, 29; Haass, 14-18.

28. Hehir, "Intervention," 10-11; Himes, "The Morality of Humanitarian Intervention," 101-102.

29. Mandelbaum, 79-81; Ernie Regehr, "Reply to Pursuing Human Justice in a Society of States," *The Conrad Grebel Review* 12 (Spring, 1994): 220-221; Chris Hedges, "Studying Bosnia's U.S. 'Prisoners of Peace'," *New York Times*, March 30, 1997, 11.